*Tennyson's Language*

# Tennyson's Language

DONALD S. HAIR

UNIVERSITY OF TORONTO PRESS
Toronto Buffalo London

© University of Toronto Press 1991
Toronto Buffalo London
Printed in Canada

ISBN 0-8020-5905-8

Printed on acid-free paper

**Canadian Cataloguing in Publication Data**

Hair, Donald S., 1937–
Tennyson's language

Includes bibliographical references.
ISBN 0-8020-5905-8

1. Tennyson, Alfred Tennyson, Baron, 1809–1892 –
Language. 2. Tennyson, Alfred Tennyson, Baron,
1809–1892 – Knowledge – Language and languages.
3. Languages – Philosophy – History. I. Title.

PR5594.H34 1991      821'.8      C91-093623-4

# Contents

# Acknowledgments

The late F.E.L. Priestley provided the context for the study of Tennyson's language, long ago, in his graduate seminar on Victorian poetry, and this book, I hope, honours his teaching. In the text and notes I refer to other scholars to whom I am indebted, but I must here name and thank two scholarly friends – Eleanor Cook and Dick Stingle – because they directed me to materials that were crucial to my thinking. I am grateful to Heather Jackson, who answered queries about Coleridge, and to the reference librarians at the Tennyson Research Centre in Lincoln – Sarah Medd, Susan Gates, and Eleanor Nannestad – who answered many questions about Tennyson's own library. Cécile Daoust-Mellamphy transferred the manuscript to disc with admirable skill, accuracy, and patience; Judy Williams did the copyediting with her customary care; and Prudence Tracy, Editor at University of Toronto Press, guided the book through the publishing process with her usual good judgment and efficiency.

Parts of chapter 5 first appeared in 'Tennyson's Faith: A Re-examination' (*University of Toronto Quarterly* 55 [1985–6] 185–203), and I am grateful to the editor, T.H. Adamowski, for permission to use the material here. In chapters 1 and 5, I draw upon another essay, ' "Matter-moulded forms of speech" ' (*Victorian Poetry* 27 [1989] 1–15), and I thank John Stasny, editor, for allowing me to use the article in an expanded form.

The University of Western Ontario awarded me a sabbatical to write this book and administered a SSHRCC Research Grant to support my investigations. I am grateful for both. This book has been published with the help of a grant from the Canadian Federation for the Humanities, using funds provided by the Social Sciences and Humanities Research Council of Canada.

*Tennyson's Language*

# Introduction

In his pioneering essay of 1980 – ' "Flowering in a Lonely Word": Tennyson and the Victorian Study of Language' – Patrick Greig Scott comments on 'how relatively silent the recent studies have been about Tennyson's own view of language, and about the kinds of linguistic awareness he might have expected of his readers.'[1] Etymology, Scott argues, is central to that awareness, which involves a shift in the understanding of the origin and derivation of words from the old philology, based mainly upon Locke, to the new philology, with its historical and comparative studies of world languages. Scott's subject is also mine. In this book I attempt to define Tennyson's own views of language, and to set those views in the context of both the old and new approaches to language study.

The subject seems inevitable in Tennyson criticism, not only because Tennyson is self-conscious about his medium in the poems themselves, but because both his education and his circle of friends made language study central to his thinking. The period of Tennyson's education and of his early publications was a time of intense interest in language, an exciting time, when the new philology from the continent, based on the pioneering work of an Englishman, Sir William Jones, but undeveloped in Britain because of the powerful influence of John Horne Tooke, at last became widely known and accepted. The late 1820s and early 1830s were a time of transition in philology in England, and Tennyson's thinking about language owed as much to the past as it did to the present.

Every artist has, of course, a technician's interest in his medium, and Tennyson's prosody was recognized, early on, as the work of a virtuoso. But my concern is more with theory than with practice: *his* theory, and the thinkers who enable us to understand it. I have focused on those thinkers Tennyson knew, in one way or another, or is likely to have known, and while such a focus might be limiting or narrow for other writers, for Tennyson it takes us to the centre of the language theories of his age.

To begin with, his education at Cambridge and his reaction against it gave him a knowledge of the principal aspects of the old philology, and particularly its philosophical foundation in Locke, for the curriculum at Cambridge during Tennyson's undergraduate years was largely empiricist in its orientation, and Locke and Paley were required reading. From an empiricist perspective, language is the arbitrary linking of word and thing or (to be more precise) of articulate sound and sensation (the datum provided to the mind by one of our five senses), so that all words can be traced back, ultimately, to the sensible world outside us. But Tennyson and his friends reacted against a curriculum which was, in their view, dry and matter-of-fact, and turned instead to the thinking that Mill was to label 'Germano-Coleridgian.' This thinking, derived in part from German criticism of the Bible, was a foundation of the new philology, and its chief voice in England was Coleridge's. The Apostles (that undergraduate Society at Cambridge which included most of Tennyson's friends, and Tennyson himself, officially for a short time only, unofficially for a lifetime) were Coleridgians, and John Sterling and Frederick Denison Maurice had established the character of the Society. In Coleridge's view, words were not the labels of dead things but rather living powers, ultimately participating in the Word, the 'verb substantive' which Coleridge identifies with the *Sum* or 'I AM' of God's mysterious answer to Moses out of the burning bush, the YHWH or ineffable name. From this perspective, words are symbols, and symbols in the radical sense that Trench was later to make clear: our contributions to a divine language imperfectly apprehended and understood. Language thus came to be linked with a providential view of history, which might seem to be only one damn thing after another, but was in fact progress toward 'one far-off divine event.' Words themselves, studied with care and reflected on attentively (and intensely), would gradually reveal a dynamic and divinely ordered world. Hence Coleridge's injunction, in his preface to *Aids to Reflection*, to 'accustom yourself to reflect on the words you use, hear, or read, their birth, derivation and history.'[2] Such attention (if not such faith) became more and more characteristic of Victorian reading and writing, so that when Ruskin, for instance, set out 'a few simple thoughts about reading' in his lecture 'Of Kings' Treasuries' at Manchester in 1864, he defined the reader as one who 'is learned in the *peerage* of words; knows the words of true descent and ancient blood, at a glance, from words of modern canaille; remembers all their ancestry – their intermarriages, distantest relationships, and the extent to which they were admitted, and offices they held, among the national noblesse of words at any time, and in any country.'[3]

Tennyson had a copy of *Sesame and Lilies* in his own library, and indeed had copies of many of the chief studies of language that make up the English contribution to the new philology. The central place that philology had for him was in large part the result of his friendship with the Apostles, whose subsequent careers confirmed their early interests. As Peter Allen writes in his history of the early years of the Society, 'The many Apostles who won high reputations as scholars in their lifetime – Kemble, Donne, Trench, Blakesley, Spedding, Alford, Thompson, Merivale and Edmund Lushington – were as innovative in their scholarship as was the Society as a whole in its social thought. It is a notable fact that their contributions to knowledge were all in the humanities, specifically in philology and the literary and historical studies related to it.'[4] And Hans Aarsleff, in his account of the Philological Society (formed in 1842) and its project for a New English Dictionary, comments on the 'community of outlook' of the original members, many of whom were closely connected with Cambridge, and especially with Trinity College.[5] At the centre of this group were John Mitchell Kemble and Richard Chenevix Trench, and both were friends of Tennyson. Trench sent to the poet a copy of the papers which set the program for the new dictionary – *On Some Deficiencies in our English Dictionaries* (London: Parker 1857) – and Kemble had earlier sent his translation of *Beowulf* (London: Pickering 1837). Both were added to other books of importance for the new philology: Sir William Jones' *Works* (the six volumes were in Tennyson's father's library at Somersby); Benjamin Thorpe's translation of Rask's *A Grammar of the Anglo-Saxon Tongue* (Copenhagen: Møller 1830); Charles Richardson's *A New Dictionary of the English Language* (2 vols. London: Pickering 1836–7); and Liddell and Scott's *A Greek-English Lexicon* (Oxford: Oxford UP 1845), with its use of 'a little Comparative Etymology, by quoting kindred Roots from Sanscrit, and other of the great family of Indo-European Tongues.'[6] Tennyson continued to add to these studies. He had William Barnes' *Poems of Rural Life in the Dorset Dialect* (London: Smith 1848), which included Barnes' 'A Dissertation on the Dorset

Dialect' with its passionate plea for purism in English, and he had Barnes' *Notes on Ancient Britain and The Britons* (London: Smith 1858), with its sections on the Welsh language and on place names derived from Welsh. He had Richard Garnett's *Philological Essays* (London: Williams 1859), some of which he may have known earlier in the *Quarterly Review*, Max Müller's *Lectures on the Science of Language* (London: Longman 1861), and Frederic William Farrar's *Language and Languages* (London: Longmans 1878), and these volumes, to which he would add the first parts of the *New English Dictionary* in the 1880s, indicate a lifelong interest in philology. In addition, his admiration for William Whewell and his friendship with Arthur Hallam and Frederick Denison Maurice have a bearing on Tennyson's views of language: Whewell's principles of scientific nomenclature were ultimately Kantian in their orientation, and Maurice, while not a philologist, was like his master Coleridge in making the study of words a central part of the moral and religious life. Hallam's thinking about metaphysics and poetry – his two favourite subjects – indicates the ideas with which Tennyson came into contact, and Hallam's 1831 review of *Poems, Chiefly Lyrical* emphasizes aspects of language that are vital for the poet, though perhaps they are of less concern to the philologist.

Those aspects are the image and the voice. Tennyson was not about to reject images as representations of things outside us, but he would loosen the image's appeal to the understanding, and strengthen its appeal to our emotions and passions. And he assumed, like his contemporaries, that voice is primary, and writing only a record of sounds. In *Les Mots et les choses* (1966) Michel Foucault has explored that assumption as it took shape in the work of Schlegel, Grimm, and Bopp, but it takes, I think, a peculiar Berkelean form in Tennyson: our articulate voice creates and sustains our world and, when it lapses into silence (as it must, inevitably), God's voice is still audible in nature, holding up creation and keeping it going.

Tennyson's understanding of language is not a philosophy, and Tennyson himself was not a systematic thinker, but he did read widely, and his allusions to language studies and theories of language, like his allusions to contemporary sciences, are precise and informed. One major allusion is 'matter-moulded forms of speech' in *In Memoriam*, and because this phrase suggests the epistemology that lies behind Tennyson's views of language, I begin with it.

# Chapter One

# 'Matter-moulded forms of speech'

Tennyson began his career at a time when, although the new philology from the continent, with its emphasis on the historical and comparative study of languages, was establishing itself in England, older notions about language were still very much about, particularly the notion that, in Hans Aarsleff's words, 'the chief end of language study is the knowledge of mind.'[1] The starting point for an examination of Tennyson's language must, then, be the epistemology which is suggested by it, and the eclectic nature of that epistemology is nowhere more apparent than in the phrase, 'matter-moulded forms of speech.'

The phrase comes from section xcv of *In Memoriam*. There Tennyson turns aside from the climactic experience of the poem and complains about the difficulty of expressing it:

> Vague words! but ah, how hard to frame
>    In matter-moulded forms of speech,
>    Or even for intellect to reach
> Through memory that which I became ...                    (45–8)

The usual paraphrase is a statement about the difficulty of conveying a spiritual experience in language that seems to be concerned primarily with the naming of material things. But the phrase is in fact much more complicated in its suggestiveness, and we can get at those complexities by focusing on the language theories of two seminal thinkers with whom Tennyson came in contact at Cambridge, Locke and Coleridge.

The facts of Tennyson's education are well known. When he was an undergraduate, theology had been replaced by 'moral philosophy,' and it was 'drawn almost entirely from the works of John Locke and William Paley.'[2] *An Essay Concerning Human Understanding* and Paley's three books (*Evidences of Christianity, Natural Theology,* and *Principles of Moral and Political Philosophy*) were required reading. Tennyson found the studies 'so uninteresting, so much matter of fact,'[3] he told his aunt in 1828, and his son wrote in his *Memoir* that 'the narrowness and dryness of the ordinary course of study at Cambridge, the lethargy there, and absence of any teaching that grappled with the ideas of the age and stimulated and guided thought on the subjects of deepest human interest, had stirred my father to wrath.'[4] Tennyson's reactions to Cambridge paralleled those of Arthur Hallam, who in the same year (1828) described Trinity College for Gladstone's benefit: 'The ascendant politics are *Utilitarian,* seasoned with a plentiful sprinkling of heterogeneous Metaphysics,'[5] including Transcendentalism. Hallam's father clearly approved of the curriculum. To another friend Hallam presents his father fulminating against Hare and Coleridge – 'they spin a spider's-web of language to catch foolish flies, who think that this mysticism is originality of thought!' – and recommending Paley and Locke: 'Read Paley; if he is not deep, which he often is not, he is always clear: his understanding is of the same kind with ours. Read Locke; read Bacon.' 'Meanwhile,' Hallam continues in his own voice, 'I cannot think my father right in his unqualified condemnation of Coleridge.'[6] And indeed it was the Coleridgians among the undergraduates who made up for the inadequacy of the official curriculum. They were the Apostles, and to this Society Hallam and Tennyson were elected in 1829. Peter Allen tells us that the group was 'described by one of its members as "Maurice and that gallant band of Platonico-Wordsworthian-Coleridgean-anti-Utilitarians,"'[7] and Edward FitzGerald bears witness to the reformation their studies brought about: 'The German School, with Coleridge, Julius Hare, etc. to expound, came to reform all our notions.'[8] They read widely: Hobbes, Locke, Berkeley, Butler, Hume, Bentham, Descartes, and Kant.[9] How carefully Tennyson read Locke or any of the others we do not know, and it may be that he learned of some of them in the same way that he was later to learn of Hegel, 'obiter, & obscurely through the talk of others.'[10] Hallam Tennyson does tell us that his father 'never much cared' for Coleridge's prose,[11] and, when William Allingham asked Tennyson in 1884 if he had ever met Coleridge, Tennyson replied, 'No, I was asked to visit him, but I wouldn't'[12] – this in contrast to his sought-after meeting with Wordsworth in 1842. Nonetheless, his son's statement does not suggest that Tennyson did not read the prose, and because *Aids to Reflection* was a central text for the Apostles, Tennyson could hardly have escaped the ideas. Hallam certainly cared for Coleridge's prose. He read both *Aids to Reflection* and the *Biographia Literaria* in 1828, and described the former to Gladstone as 'a theological, meta-physical, & therefore somewhat appalling volume at first sight, but amply rewarding a deeper search.'[13] He described his friend Tennant as a man 'who sat for months at the feet of Coleridge, and impowered his own mind with some of those tones, from the world of mystery, the only real world, of which to these latter days Coleridge has been almost the only interpreter.'[14] Tennyson was far less systematic in his thinking and in his study than Hallam was, but we know that he was quick to seize essential concepts and patterns – of evolution, for instance – and Ian Kennedy has explored the irregular but profound way in which Tennyson absorbed Carlyle's translations of Goethe and shared in the undergraduate enthusiasm for German thought and literature.[15] One can only conclude that there is no evidence that Tennyson read either Locke or Coleridge carefully, but there is plenty of evidence that these two thinkers, and the opposing philosophical traditions they represent, provided the context for the debates and discussions of Tennyson's undergraduate days, and for his own thinking. They also provide the context for the phrase with which we are at the moment concerned, and it, like so much else in Tennyson's thinking, suggests the working through of the problem that all serious university students face: making sense of their education.

'Forms of speech' are 'moulded' by 'matter' – this is one way of reading the phrase, and it is the empiricist way, which can be traced back to Locke. An essential idea in the empiricist view of language is that etymology means tracing words back to their source in sensations. Sensations, the data provided by our senses, crowd in upon our minds, where, in ways that Locke explains, they become ideas, those general-izations from experience that make up our knowledge. To these ideas, we attach sounds, and the arbitrary connection of spoken word and idea is the essence of Locke's language theory. This theory was elaborated, extended, and modified in the eighteenth century, the most important development of it, so far as the history of language study in England is concerned (Hans Aarsleff argues), being that of Horne Tooke, whose work was published between 1778 and 1805. James Mill, John Stuart Mill, and Coleridge all refer to Tooke and use him, and

Aarsleff's chapter 'Horne Tooke's Influence and Reputation' in his *The Study of Language in England, 1780–1860* is of great importance for an understanding of the dominant language theory in the first third of the nineteenth century. The chief point is this: because Tooke's reputation was so widespread and his influence so powerful, language theory in England remained firmly in the empiricist tradition, and was thus eagerly embraced by the Utilitarians. Tooke argues that all words can be traced to the names of ideas derived from sensation, his proof lying in his etymologies. The foundation of Tooke's work is in Locke, and the passage in the *Essay* is so seminal, as Aarsleff points out (31), that it is worth quoting. Locke writes, in the first chapter of his study of language:

It may also lead us a little towards the Original of all our Notions and Knowledge, if we remark, how great a dependance our *Words* have on common sensible *Ideas*; and how those, which are made use of to stand for Actions and Notions quite removed from sense, *have their rise from thence, and from obvious sensible* Ideas *are transferred to more abstruse significations*, and made to stand for *Ideas* that come not under the cognizance of our senses; *v.g.* to *Imagine, Apprehend, Comprehend, Adhere, Conceive, Instill, Disgust, Disturbance, Tranquillity*, etc. are all Words taken from the Operations of sensible Things, and applied to certain Modes of Thinking. *Spirit*, in its primary signification, is Breath; *Angel*, a Messenger: And I doubt not, but if we could trace them to their sources, we should find, in all Languages, the names, which stand for Things that fall not under our Senses, to have had their first rise from sensible *Ideas*. (3.1.5)[16]

This view of etymology as 'matter-moulded' would have been most immediately accessible to Tennyson in the dictionary which he owned and used, Charles Richardson's *A New Dictionary of the English Language* (2 vols. London: Pickering 1836–7). Both the arrangement of the entries and Richardson's 'Preliminary Essay' make very clear Richardson's central principle, 'so incontrovertibly demonstrated in the "Diversions of Purley;" namely, that a word has one meaning, and one only; that from it all usages must spring and be derived; and that in the Etymology of each word must be found this single intrinsic meaning, and the cause of the application in those usages.'[17] This 'one meaning' Richardson calls 'the literal meaning,' and it is the name of a sensation:

The lexicographer can never assure himself that he has attained the meaning of a word, until he has discovered the thing, the sensible object – *res, quae nostros sensus feriunt*; – the sensation caused by that thing or object (for language cannot sever them), of which that word is the name. To this, the term *meaning* should be strictly and exclusively appropriated; and this, too, may be called the literal meaning. (1:43)

In each of his entries, Richardson begins with 'the literal meaning,' then proceeds to its 'metaphorical application' – the transferring of 'the literal meaning' to 'supposed or assumed similar or correspondent objects or actions, or operations, in the human mind' (1:43) – and finally to the 'applications' of both literal and metaphorical meanings, a descent 'in wide and rapid course' through 'multitude and variety' (1:43).

Even those who reacted against the epistemology of Locke and recognized the weaknesses in the etymologies of Tooke did not reject the view that words are 'matter-moulded.' In *On the Study of Words*, that popular book first given as a series of lectures in 1851, and going through nineteen editions in its author's lifetime, Trench quotes Jean Paul ('All language is in some sort ... a collection of faded metaphors') and points out that 'words out of number, which are now employed only in a figurative sense, did yet originally rest on some fact of the outward world, vividly presenting itself to the imagination; which fact the word has incorporated and knit up with itself for ever.'[18] Carlyle has his Teufelsdröckh in *Sartor Resartus* describe language as 'the Flesh-Garment, the Body, of Thought': 'examine Language; what, if you except some few primitive elements (of natural sound), what is it all but Metaphors, recognised as such, or no longer recognised ... ?'[19] And Emerson in *Nature* argues for words as 'matter-moulded': 'Every word which is used to express a moral or intellectual fact, if traced to its root, is found to be borrowed from some material appearance. *Right*,' he says in an observation that sounds like Locke's, 'means *straight*; *wrong* means *twisted*.'[20] But though these thinkers might accept the view that words are the names of sensations, they rejected the materialism of Tooke and the atomism of Locke. Matter – or at least the appearance of matter – is, for Carlyle and Emerson, symbolic; it is itself a sign and all things are symbols. 'What metaphor does for Carlyle,' as G.B. Tennyson points out, 'is to *illuminate relationships*, to reveal connections between things not at first evident, and thus to suggest some vast and meaningful scheme in the universe.'[21] Nor can the 'literal meaning' of a word account fully for its significance. Trench would reject Richardson's 'only' ('that a word has one meaning, and one only') and insist that the subsequent history of a word and its cultural context are just as much a part of its meaning as its origin.

Tennyson's view parallels that of Trench and Carlyle. Like them, he accepts the fact that language is 'matter-moulded,' but refuses to limit its meaning to the sensations that gave rise to it. His use of the word 'spirit' is a good example, partly because Locke had used it as one of *his* examples: '*Spirit*, in its primary signification, is Breath...' (3.1.5). This etymology Tennyson places in the mouth of a personified Nature in *In Memoriam*: 'The spirit does but mean the breath: / I know no more' (lvi:7–8). But Nature in the poem presents a view of things based on the evidence of the senses alone, while the 'I' of the poem affirms that spirit is not only physical breathing: the breath of section xxxvi is the manifestation of 'the Word' or, as in both the Heath and Trinity manuscripts of the poem, 'Logos,' and the 'livelier breath' of section cxxii is, as the adjective indicates, a sign of a life not limited to the physical or material. The difference between the two major dictionaries Tennyson owned – Richardson's, and Liddell and Scott's *A Greek-English Lexicon* (Oxford: Oxford UP 1845) – is also the difference between Tennyson's view and that of Locke and Tooke. Richardson would limit meaning to the first linking of sound and sensation; Liddell and Scott, basing their work on that of Passow, make each entry the history of a word's usage, and their quotations let each word tell its story as it appears in particular times and contexts. In effect, *In Memoriam* tells the story of the word 'spirit,' from its 'matter-moulded' origin to its full meaning in Tennyson's actual experience.

But though Tennyson rejected the limitations placed on meaning by Richardson and Tooke, he was keenly conscious of the power of sensation in moulding words, and the phrase with which we are concerned appears in section xcv in the context of a complaint: the poet finds it hard to frame in speech derived from sensation an experience which is more than physical. The precise nature of his difficulty needs some explanation.

The difficulty is not, I think, that the experience is a spiritual one, and is thus incompatible with language that is 'matter-moulded.' The experience is indeed spiritual and involves revelation, but the poet's senses are not in abeyance at this moment, and verbs like 'touch,' 'flash,' 'wind,' 'whirl,' 'come,' and 'catch' – Tennyson uses all of them at the climax of section xcv – are at least metaphors for his sensory experience at the climactic moment. The difficulties of carrying across or translating experience (metaphor, we remember, has the literal meaning of transporting) are the same for sensation as they are for revelation, and perhaps Tennyson, in complaining about his hard task, is doing no more than referring to the basic problem of language when it is conceived of as metaphor (as it is in the empiricist tradition). The problem is compounded when the experience is complex, as this one certainly is, and it is primarily the complexity of the experience, and not the fact that it is spiritual, that creates Tennyson's difficulty. Locke's account of words that stand for complex ideas helps us explain the problem.

The name for a complex idea, Locke says, is like a knot which ties together a number of simple ideas (3.5.10). The mind 'puts such together, as may best serve its own Purposes' (3.5.6). Such words are often imperfect, and among the reasons for this imperfection is the fact that 'the *Ideas* they stand for, are very complex, and made up of a great number of *Ideas* put together' (3.9.5). That difficulty is surely Tennyson's problem here. He has, after all, witnessed Hallam's larger existence, where Hallam is paradoxically both himself and part of the universal spirit or 'Great Soul' (Tennyson's label in his comments to Knowles, but not used in the poem).[22] Tennyson abhorred the idea of being absorbed in (what a colleague of mine calls) the universal glue, but at the same time he believed the spirit to be free of the limitations that characterize earthly life. So the experience is complex, and also, we assume, utterly clear, like the experience Tennyson could induce by repeating his own name.[23]

Tennyson finds no single word for the experience, but instead fills eight-and-one-half lines with words which he immediately condemns as 'vague.' This criticism of his own language is itself in need of critical examination. We can take the word at face value, but we must also be aware that there is a sense in which the criticism is unjustified. Most readers of the poem are familiar with the fact that Tennyson changed 'His living soul' to 'The living soul' and 'mine in his was wound' to 'mine in this was wound.' Because the pronouns no longer refer to Hallam, the changes appear to be a move toward vagueness, but the definite article can be read as no less precise than 'his,' and the gesture implied in 'this' is more immediate than the reference in the possessive pronoun. In fact, one could argue that Tennyson was striving for greater precision ('The first reading … troubled me, as perhaps giving a wrong impression,' he wrote in his notes in the Eversley edition) while at the same time retaining the strong sense of pointing at something real but not nameable. This sense depends upon the pronouns, and a pronoun (as all freshman teachers tell their students) stands for a noun and so needs a clear and unambiguous antecedent. 'This' clearly refers to 'The living soul,' with the definite article indicating something both unique and universal, and because 'this' is put for 'The living soul,' its relation to its antecedent is metonymic. This sense of a close relationship affects our reading of the crucial words, 'that which is,' because 'that' does not have an antecedent, and yet we have a strong sense of reference, simply because we know that pronouns work in that way. 'Which is' has the effect of a restrictive clause – it makes its antecedent precise and particular – and it points to reality itself. Tennyson thus exploits the essential nature of the pronoun. Nonetheless, he condemns his words as 'vague,' a charge against both the periphrasis ('that which is') and the metaphors that elaborate it. Locke helps us to understand their inadequacy.

Periphrasis and metaphor are both, in Locke's view, abuses of language, one defeating the speed of communication, the other its truth. 'He that hath complex *Ideas* without Names for them, wants Liberty and Dispatch in his Expressions, and is necessitated to use Periphrases' (3.10.31), and periphrasis, Locke insists, works against one of the ends of language, the 'ease and *quickness*' (3.10.23) with which it conveys one person's thoughts to another. So Tennyson does not say 'God' or 'Great Soul'; instead he says, simply, 'that which is.' He thus avoids the associations of the nouns but must replace them with several words. Metaphor, in Locke's view, is an abuse of language that, by joining together ideas which 'have no certain connexion in Nature' (3.9.5) and by insisting on the identity of unlike things, falls under the 'Art of Rhetorick,' 'that powerful instrument of Error and Deceit' (3.10.34). Tennyson does use metaphors – 'the deep pulsations of the world,' 'Aeonian music,' 'the steps of Time,' 'the shocks of Chance,' 'the blows of Death' – and immediately rejects them as 'vague.' His adjective draws attention to the distance across which idea is carried to idea. Metaphor ordinarily attempts to collapse that distance, but Tennyson here increases it. The fact that the metaphors are a bit worn adds to our sense of their inadequacy. Timothy Peltason goes even further. 'The language of the trance' is in his view 'the least exciting in the poem, dragged down by the knowledge of its own inevitable failure to capture the uncapturable experience.'[24]

Locke helps us to understand another way in which words are 'vague.' While Tennyson does indeed link Time, Chance, and Death with sensory experience, and thus, one would think, makes them precise and clear, Locke tells us that words have no power in themselves and cannot evoke an experience in someone who has not already had it. Just as Locke begins *An Essay Concerning Human Understanding* by rejecting innate ideas, so, too, in book 3 he rejects the view that words in any way participate in the being of those things they name. A word may be a metaphor, but it is not synecdoche, and no word can produce in us the idea of anything unless we have first had the experience of that thing, the experience consisting of sensations that build themselves in our minds into the idea to which the word is attached. 'For Words being Sounds,' says Locke, 'can produce in us no other simple *Ideas*, than of those very Sounds. ... He that thinks otherwise, let him try if any Words can give him the taste of a Pine-Apple, and make him have the true *Idea* of the Relish of that celebrated delicious Fruit' (3.4.11). Tennyson's experience in section xcv is unique, but words not shared with anyone else would fail to convey the nature of the moment, and he has to fall back on words that appeal to common experience. They, too, fail, and can work only by inference. No wonder Tennyson calls his language 'vague.'

Tennyson is also hampered by the fact that, in Locke's view, language is conventional and (except for proper names) abstract, and these two adjectives help us further define the range of meanings in his 'vague.' 'God having designed Man for a sociable Creature,' Locke begins book 3, 'made him not only with an inclination, and under a necessity to have fellowship with those of his own kind; but furnished him also with Language, which was to be the great Instrument, and common Tye of Society' (3.1.1). Language can fulfil this function only if there is general agreement on the signification of words and if language provides a quick and concise means of communication. So language is conventional 'when by Use or Consent, the Sound I make by the Organs of Speech, excites in another Man's Mind, who hears it, the *Idea* I apply it to in mine, when I speak it' (3.3.3). And language is abstract, 'for quickness and dispatch sake' (3.3.10), because 'it is beyond the Power of humane Capacity to frame and retain distinct *Ideas* of all the particular Things we meet with' (3.3.2), and a distinct name for each particular thing would frustrate the ends of language (3.1.3). So 'one word was made to mark a multitude of particular existences' (3.1.3), to stand for ideas that have become general through a separation of them from particular 'circumstances of Time, and Place, and any other *Ideas*' (3.3.6), in short, through a process of abstraction. '*General and Universal,'* Locke keeps insisting, 'belong not to the real existence of Things; but *are the Inventions and Creatures of the Understanding,* made by it for its own use, *and concern only Signs,* whether Words, or *Ideas'* (3.3.11). Hence his distinction, which he returns to again and again, between the real essence of things and their nominal essence. The real essence we cannot know. The nominal essence, though it is entirely 'the Workmanship of the Understanding' (3.3.12), is necessary for the purposes of human life. It is the sense that we make of our experience.

This last point – the need for words and their ordering of our experience – brings us to a second and quite different reading of 'matter-moulded forms of speech.' We note that two of the words in this phrase refer to shaping; 'forms' is usually associated with the Ideas of Plato, and 'moulds' is Coleridge's word; he insisted that Plato's Ideas 'should be translated *"Moulds"* and not *"Forms."'*[25] (Locke had already used both words to refer to one 'Opinion' 'Concerning the real Essences of corporeal Substances,' and this is the opinion 'which supposes these *Essences,* as a certain number of Forms or Molds, wherein all natural Things, that exist, are cast, and do equally partake' (3.3.17). In the light of these words, the 'forms of speech' are not 'moulded' by 'matter' but created by the shaping power of the mind; their antecedent, however, is our experience of 'matter,' an experience also shaped by the mind. Isobel Armstrong's adjective is 'mind-moulded'[26] in contrast to 'matter-moulded,' but her words suggest a sharp opposition between mind and matter, subject and object, while Coleridge insisted on redefining the relations between the two in ways that Tennyson shared. The hyphen in 'matter-moulded' gives equal emphasis to sensations and to our ordering of them, and this interplay of world and mind gives language its nature and form. This interplay needs to be defined carefully, and for such a definition Coleridge's criticism of Locke is useful, but before turning to it we might consider the authority that Locke himself gives to the shaping power of the mind, an authority obscured by Locke's reputation in the nineteenth century (explored in Hans Aarsleff's excellent essay).[27]

Language, in Locke's view, is not only conventional and abstract but also arbitrary. A word is a sign of an idea, and an idea is that generalization arrived at from one of two sources: sensation (the data that our senses provide of the world around us) and reflection ('that notice which the Mind takes of its own Operations,' 2.1.4). We attach words to ideas, 'not by any natural connexion,' says Locke, 'but by a voluntary Imposition, whereby such a Word is made arbitrarily the

Mark of such an *Idea*' (3.2.1). 'Arbitrarily' is the key word here. Its Latin antecedent means 'to think' in the sense of 'to be of the opinion that,' and opinion is a crucial matter for Locke, since the whole purpose of the *Essay* is to distinguish knowledge from 'Belief, Opinion, and Assent' (1.1.2). About knowledge we can be certain, because it is based on the evidence of our senses, but 'Belief, Opinion, and Assent' belong on a scale of diminishing probability, which takes us down through 'Belief, Conjecture, Guess, Doubt, Wavering, Distrust, Disbelief, etc.' (4.16.9). Opinion, it seems, ought to be dismissed because it involves the mind's relating of ideas without being able to prove that such relations actually exist in the world outside us. But Locke does not dismiss opinion. On the contrary, he insists that it is necessary for the purposes of human life. Why is it necessary? Because knowledge is limited:

The Understanding Faculties being given to Man, not barely for Speculation, but also for the Conduct of his Life, Man would be at a great loss, if he had nothing to direct him, but what has the Certainty of true *Knowledge*. For that being very short and scanty, as we have seen, he would be often utterly in the dark, and in most of the Actions of his Life, perfectly at a stand, had he nothing to guide him in the absence of clear and certain Knowledge. He that will not eat, till he has Demonstration that it will nourish him; he that will not stir, till he infallibly knows the Business he goes about will succeed, will have little else to do, but sit still and perish. (4.14.1)

But we do not, in fact, 'sit still and perish'; we go about our daily business without the aid of proof, and on the basis of assumptions which are obviously necessary. Locke calls such assumptions 'belief' or 'opinion'; Tennyson calls them 'faith.'

Locke's emphasis on the needful activity of the mind in compensating for the limitations of knowledge is the basis of his language theory. For all that he has to say in book 3 about the difficulties and inadequacies of language, he keeps reminding us that language is the expression of human concerns and the result of human needs. We do not provide names for everything, but only for those things that have a bearing on our physical, moral, and religious life. Language is arbitrary, not because we are capricious in our response to our experience, but because we are selective; every word is 'the free choice of the Mind, pursuing its own ends' (3.5.6), and hence the word 'arbitrary' itself must be understood (as its root indicates) as referring to a judgment made by the mind. We cannot prove that there is anything in the world around us which corresponds to our needs and concerns as expressed in language, but we act as if we could, and our language is the expression of that faith. We are not far from Coleridge's statement in *Aids to Reflection*, that book so important for the Apostles: 'For if words are not THINGS, they are LIVING POWERS, by which the things of most importance to mankind are actuated, combined, and humanized.'[28] Trench extends Coleridge's statement even further, to argue that there are no 'merely *arbitrary* words, standing in connexion with nothing but the mere lawless caprice of some inventor.' From the perspective of the new philology he insists that 'there is no word which is not, as the Spanish gentleman loves to call himself, an "hidalgo," or son of something. ... All are embodiments, more or less successful, of a sensation, a thought, or a fact; or if of more fortuitous birth, still they attach themselves somewhere to the already subsisting world of words and things, and have their point of contact with it and departure from it, not always discoverable, as we see, but yet always existing.'[29]

In his criticism of Locke, Coleridge emphasizes the degree to which Locke's epistemology involves the shaping power of the mind. If we ignore Coleridge's prejudice ('As usual he spoke with contempt of *Locke's* Essay,' Henry Crabb Robinson recorded)[30] and his efforts to prove, in his 1801 letters to Josiah Wedgwood, that 'Mr. Locke's whole System ... pre-existed in Des Cartes,'[31] and focus instead on his criticism of Locke's use of the word 'Idea,' we can see that he was arguing for a view of mind and of language which was of great importance for Tennyson's circle at Cambridge. Coleridge was well aware of Locke's reputation at the turn of the century, for he mentions 'the union, now proverbial, of the two names – Newton & Locke' (2:702), and he says, 'Ask what Locke did, & you will be told if I mistake not, that he overthrew the Notion, generally held before his time, of innate Ideas, and deduced all our knowledge from experience' (2:686); but, Coleridge argues, Locke was defining 'innate' in his own way, and 'these Innate Ideas were Men of Straw' (2:686): 'Mr. Locke would have never disgraced his Essay with the first Book, if he had not mistaken innasci for synonimous [sic] with connasci, whereas to be "born in," and to be "born *at the same time with*," are phrases of very different import' (2:691). The first defines ideas as the content of the mind, the second as the shaping powers of the mind itself. Coleridge is interested primarily in the second definition. He finds in Des Cartes' 'communes notiones' and in Locke's 'intuitive knowledge' 'those Laws in the conformation of the mind by which all men *necessarily* perceive ideas in certain *Relations* to each other,' and he relates them to Aristotle's account of 'a power inherent in all living Beings determining the manner in which external objects must act upon them' (2:692), and to Plato's Ideas. 'By *Ideas* Plato, notwithstanding his fantastic expressions respecting them, meant what Mr Locke calls the original Faculties & Tendencies of the mind, the internal Organs, as it were, and *Laws* of human Thinking: and the word should be translated *"Moulds"* and not *"Forms"* ' (2:682). Then, 'by the usual Process of language Ideas came to signify not only these original *moulds* of the mind, but likewise all that was cast in these moulds' (2:682). But Coleridge wants to restore the word Idea to the shaping powers, rather than the content, of the mind. In his *Philosophical Lectures* he is reported as saying:

if you only substitute for the phrase the ideas being *derived from* the senses, or *imprest upon* the mind, or in any way supposed to be brought in – for nothing can be more mechanical or pagan-like than the phrases used in the *Essay on the Human Understanding* [sic] – if for this you only substitute the word *elicit [ed]*, namely that there are no conceptions of our mind relatively to external objects but what are *elicited* by their circumstances and by what are supposed to be correspondent to them, there would be nothing found in Locke but what is perfectly just.[32]

Among the Apostles this understanding of innate ideas was the basis of a view of language as God-given, and what God gave was not a vocabulary but the power to shape and relate. Adam's naming of every living creature in Genesis is the story on which such a theory is focused – that story has always been central to language theory – and it turns up in both Donaldson and Trench. John William Donaldson was an undergraduate at Trinity in 1831–4, an Apostle, and afterwards a philologist of some importance, and in his *The New Cratylus* (1839) he argues that language is 'the necessary and spontaneous result of man's constitution.' The words in Genesis, he says, 'imply that the power of speaking merely and not language was given to man, and therefore there are no grounds for the inference which a modern writer would draw from the passage, that the language of Adam was an immediate revelation from the divinity. Adam was so constituted that he had the power of speech and this power he exercised first of all in giving names to the different species of animals.'[33] Trench's theory of the origin of language is better known, because of the immense popularity of *On the Study of Words*. In his 'Introductory Lecture' Trench acknowledges his indebtedness to Tooke and Coleridge, and repeats Coleridge's statement that words are living powers. He rejects the view that would make language 'an *accident* of human nature,' gradually developed by us from the 'inarticulate cries' by which we first expressed our emotions and desires, and from the sounds we made to imitate the sounds in nature. Language is God's gift:

> Yet this must not be taken to affirm that man started at the first furnished with a full-formed vocabulary of words, and as it were with his first dictionary and first grammar ready-made to his hands. He did not thus begin the world *with names*, but *with the power of naming*: for man is not a mere speaking machine; God did not teach him words, as one of us teaches a parrot, from without; but gave him a capacity, and then evoked the capacity which He gave. (14)

That which evokes this power is the created world. Here is Trench's account of that relationship:

> I believe that we should conceive the actual case most truly, if we conceived this power of naming things and expressing their relations, as one laid up in the depths of man's being, one of the divine capabilities with which he was created: but one (and in this differing from those which have produced in various people various arts of life) which could not remain dormant in him, for man could be only man through its exercise; which therefore did rapidly bud and blossom out from within him at every solicitation from the world without and from his fellow-man; as each object to be named appeared before his eyes, each relation of things to one another arose before his mind. It was not merely the possible, but the necessary, emanation of the spirit with which he had been endowed. Man makes his own language, but he makes it as the bee makes its cells, as the bird its nest; he cannot do otherwise. (15)

Language is thus natural because it is the expression of a God-given capacity, and it is to this capacity, I think, that Tennyson is referring when he uses the words 'mould' and 'forms.' (In his 1830 poem, 'A Dirge,' he uses the phrase 'God's great gift of speech,' but there is nothing to indicate the exact nature of that gift.)

In a full examination of Coleridge's philosophy of language, James McKusick argues that Coleridge undertook a lifelong 'quest for a criterion of linguistic "naturalness,"' a quest culminating in his *Logic* where, McKusick argues, 'Coleridge seeks to revise Kant's *Critique of Pure Reason* by demonstrating that the categories of the understanding are grounded in prior linguistic structures. Cognitive universals, in Coleridge's view, merely reflect linguistic universals.'[34] These ideas are already apparent when Coleridge is discussing the words 'understanding' and 'substance' in his *Aids to Reflection*, that book so important for the Apostles. In making the distinction that Coleridge (following Kant) insisted was crucial to his thought, the difference between the reason and the understanding, Coleridge identifies the name of a thing with our understanding of it:

The Name of a thing, in the original sense of the word Name, (*nomen*, νούμενον, τὸ, *intelligible, id quod intelligitur*) expresses that which is *understood* in an appearance, that which we place (or make to *stand*) *under* it, as the condition of its real existence, and in proof that it is not an accident of the senses, or affection of the individual, not a phantom or *apparition*, that is, an appearance that is *only* an appearance. (152–3)

The understanding generalizes 'the notices received from the senses in order to the construction of *names*' (153), and 'the act of comparing supposes in the comparing faculty, certain inherent forms, that is, modes of reflecting not referable to the objects reflected on, but predetermined by the constitution and (as it were) mechanism of the Understanding itself' (149). These 'certain inherent forms,' fused with the materials supplied by our senses, together make up our knowledge. Coleridge takes delight in pointing out that the very word 'substance,' which in our ordinary existence we so firmly use to denote that which is independent of us and not to be changed by us in any essential way, is in fact parallel in meaning to the word 'understanding.' '*Quod stat subtus*, that which stands *beneath*, and (as it were) supports, the appearance' (5), he says in a note on the word 'substance' in one of his introductory aphorisms, and he returns to the word in his conclusion. '*Subject* and *substance* are words of kindred roots, nay, little less than equivalent terms' (264–5), he says. He rejects the assumptions about reality that lie behind the empiricist view of language, 'the habit ... of applying all the words and phrases expressing reality, to the objects of the senses: more accurately speaking, to the images and sensations by which their presence is made known to us' (272). The 'certain inherent forms' that the mind brings to experience are just as essential as sensations themselves, and an idea is the fusion of the two. Coleridge identifies these ideas with language, and I quote again that important sentence from the 'Author's Preface' to *Aids to Reflection*: 'For if words are not THINGS, they are LIVING POWERS, by which the things of most importance to mankind are actuated, combined, and humanized' (xix).

Coleridge uses the word 'things' twice in this sentence, first to point to objects that are separate from us, and hence fixed and dead, and then to point to the same objects fused with 'certain inherent forms' in the mind, so that they become the powers by which we actually live. In a well-known passage in an 1800 letter to William Godwin, Coleridge writes that he 'would endeavor to destroy the old antithesis of *Words & Things*, elevating, as it were, words into Things, & living Things too.'[35] 'Things' is a particularly useful word for Coleridge in this context also, and again he uses it in two senses. In the dominant empiricist philosophy of his time, 'things' referred to objects and events in the world outside the mind, facts not to be changed by the human perception of them. But Coleridge insists that we cannot know any 'thing' without an act of the mind, and each word, a 'living thing,' is in fact a power within the mind itself, one of those by which we select, shape, and make sense of, sensations. McKusick points out that Coleridge, like Tooke, links through etymology the words 'thing' and 'think,' but 'Coleridge derives the noun, "thing," from the verb, "to think," whereas Tooke derives the verb from the noun. Coleridge is clearly attempting to rework Tooke's materialist position in order to make it compatible with his own' (48). Tennyson's position is closer to Coleridge's than it is to Tooke's, and we can see it not only in his use of the words 'moulded' and 'forms' but also in his description of his task as poet: 'fitting aptest words to things.'

The phrase comes from section lxxv of *In Memoriam*, and an empiricist context immediately suggests itself. 'Things,' we usually assume, are cold hard facts, objects in the world around us. To these 'things,' in the vulgar empiricist view of language, we arbitrarily attach words (arbitrarily because there is no natural or inevitable connection between the word and the thing); the 'things' are primary and true, and the words are only a fiction. Swift, we remember, satirizes this vulgar view of the relation of words and things in book 3 of *Gulliver's Travels*. In the School of Languages of the Academy of Lagado, Gulliver learns of a scheme to abolish words entirely, since 'Words are only Names for *Things*,' and he observes men with great bundles on their backs, full of objects which they take out and show to each other by way of carrying on a conversation.

In *In Memoriam*, 'things' rarely refers simply to physical objects. It does have that sense in section xlv, where the baby learns the difference between himself and 'the things I touch,' but more usually 'things' are living creatures. Sometimes the 'thing' is the 'I' of the poem, the 'guilty thing' who creeps to Hallam's door in section vii; sometimes, as in 'the thing beloved' in section lii, the 'thing' is Hallam himself. In xxxv, 'so sweet a thing' is man in his physical existence, and in cxi 'the thing' is man in his social and moral being. 'Things' may also mean 'events' or 'happenings.' 'These things' of xiii refers to the poet's life with his dead friend, and to his experience of his death; in xiv, the returning Hallam might 'ask a thousand things of home,' and these are close to the 'new things' of xl, the events of a loved daughter's life after marriage, or, more broadly, 'the course of human things' in cxxviii. There are 'things divine' (xxxvii) and 'earthly things' (xliv), 'things above' and 'these things' on earth that will 'pass' (both in lxxxv). In all these instances where 'things' means 'events,' one senses the human mind distinguishing and recognizing events, and in that very act becoming aware of their significance. 'The glory of the sum of things' (lxxxviii) may be momentarily grasped by the poet, but he is more often aware of the process of arriving at that sum. Tennyson sometimes uses the phrase 'all things' to refer to the whole of creation (as in lxxviii, the second Christmas poem, or in cxxi, where the evening star 'watchest all things ever dim / And dimmer'), but the word often involves a sense of human agency shaping creation and moving it toward its appointed end. 'I was *born* to other things,' the poet asserts in cxx when he is rejecting materialism, and, in the allegorical cxiv, Knowledge, with her limited power, submits 'all things to desire,' and thus is guided by Wisdom. The very first lyric, with its belief 'That men may rise on stepping-stones / Of their dead selves to higher things,' suggests this same fusion of the poet's mind and the creation in which he finds himself. 'Such things to be' is the confident phrase of lxxiii, though that confidence is undermined by Hallam's early death. 'Things' thus comes to be synonymous with human concerns, and the epistemology suggested in the word parallels that which I have been exploring in Coleridge. We find ourselves in a creation which is not of our own making, but we also discover that we are an essential part of that creation. Questions about the extent of our knowledge and the conduct of our lives depend upon this interaction of our minds and creation. There is a phrase at the end of section cxxiii that sums up the epistemology with which I am concerned. In that section, the speaker speeds up geological time, so that 'The hills are shadows, and they flow / From form to form, and nothing stands.' Here is the speaker's reaction to Lyell's picture of earth's physical changes:

> But in my spirit will I dwell,
>   And dream my dream, and hold it true;
>   For though my lips may breathe adieu,
> I cannot think the thing farewell.

Thinking the thing. The words are ordinary and colloquial but, as so often in Tennyson, ordinary words carry a great weight of meaning, and the thing and the thought are both necessary to human knowledge and to human conduct.

They are also necessary to God's purposes. For if language is a gift of God, its operations are providential, and words are symbolic in the radical sense given by Trench in his *On Some Deficiencies in our English Dictionaries*, that pamphlet of 1857 that Tennyson had in his library. Trench gives examples of the limitations of the entries in Johnson's dictionary, and one of his examples is the word 'symbol.' Jeremy Taylor, he points out, 'employs "symbol" in the sense which the Greek σύμβολον sometimes had, namely, the contribution which each person at a pic-nic throws into the common stock.'[36] In a footnote, Trench quotes from Taylor's *The Faith and Patience of the Saints*, a sermon from Taylor's *Works* – also in Tennyson's library: 'Christ hath finished his own sufferings for expiation of the world, yet there are portions that are behind of the sufferings of Christ, which must be filled up by his body, the Church, and happy are they that put in the greatest *symbol*; for in the same measure you are partakers of the sufferings of Christ, in the same shall ye be also of the consolation.' Trench himself uses the word 'symbol' in its original Greek sense on the penultimate page of his *On Some Deficiencies*, when he is talking about the need for volunteer readers in compiling a dictionary and throwing their 'symbols' into the common stock (56). Tennyson too uses the word in this sense in section lxxxv of *In Memoriam*, where speech comes of 'My old affection of the tomb' (77): 'So shall grief with symbols play' (95), the 'symbols' being the 'dear words of human speech' (83) with which he would communicate with Hallam. The emphasis is on participation. Language may be limited and inadequate, but it is also our contribution to something larger than ourselves; words may fail, but speech itself is the assurance that we are not alone in the universe.

Tennyson's fellow students, with their indebtedness to Coleridge, were not the only members of the university who provided him with an alternative to the dominant empiricist philosophy. Though the *Essay Concerning Human Understanding* was a set text, and though students were expected to demonstrate a knowledge of it on examinations (Kemble, Hallam told his father, got into trouble because 'he was not content with answering the questions from Locke, & Paley, but took the trouble of commenting upon them!!'),[37] members of the faculty too were reacting against Locke, the two most prominent critics being Trinity College men, Adam Sedgwick and William Whewell. They 'delivered some of the strongest and most widely read attacks on Locke during the entire century,'[38] and Whewell dedicated his *Philosophy of the Inductive Sciences* (1840) to Sedgwick because he knew him as a 'fellow-labourer' in the work of criticizing 'the fallacies of the ultra-Lockian school.' For Whewell Tennyson had 'a great respect' and, when undergraduates harassed 'Billy Whistle' (this was Whewell's nickname) in the street, Tennyson and his friends cheered him.[39] There was a copy of the first edition (1837) of Whewell's *History of the Inductive Sciences* in Tennyson's library; Tennyson 'carefully studied' Whewell's *Of the Plurality of Worlds* within a year after its publication in 1853,[40] and his early contacts with Whewell – Whewell was his tutor – must have made Tennyson aware of Whewell's central ideas. These Whewell sets out in book 1, chapter 2 of his *Philosophy*, a chapter called 'Of the Fundamental Antithesis of Philosophy,' but it is clear that these ideas, Kantian in their origin, had long been part of his thinking, and he summarizes them in the introduction to his *History*. For the literary critic, his quotation from Wordsworth is a good introduction to his 'fundamental antithesis'; for the critic of Tennyson in particular the lines are suggestive, since Tennyson was thoroughly familiar with Wordsworth's poems, and said to Locker-Lampson in 1869, 'I have a profound admiration for "Tintern Abbey!"'[41] Here is Whewell:

A philosophical poet has spoken of

> All the world
> Of eye and ear, both what they half create,
> And what perceive.

But it is clear, that though they *half* create, they do not wholly create: there must be an external world of colour and sound to give impressions to the eye and ear, as well as internal powers by which we perceive what is offered to our organs. The mind is in some way passive as well as active: there are objects without as well as faculties within; – Sensations, as well as acts of Thought.[42]

In every statement summarizing his thought, Whewell returns again and again to this position. 'The antithesis of *Sense* and *Ideas*,' he says in one of his aphorisms in the 1847 edition of his *Philosophy*, 'is the foundation of the Philosophy of Science. No knowledge can exist without the union, no philosophy without the separation, of these two elements' (2:443). In the introduction to his *History*, he calls these two elements 'Facts and Ideas; observation of Things without, and an inward effort of Thought.'[43] In the second chapter of his *Philosophy*, he calls the same elements 'THINGS and THOUGHTS': 'In every part of my knowledge there must be some *thing* about which I know, and an internal act of *me* who know' (1:17). 'Without Thoughts, there could be no connexion; without Things, there could be no reality' (1:18). Whewell lists 'Reflexion and Sensation' as one of the ways of expressing his 'Fundamental Antithesis,' but he is careful to note that there is 'a great difference between Locke's account of Sensation and Reflexion, and our view of Sensation and Ideas':

He is speaking of the origin of our knowledge; – we, of its nature and composition. He is content to say that all the knowledge which we do not receive directly by Sensation, we obtain by Reflex Acts of the mind, which make up his Reflexion. But we hold that there is no Sensation without an act of the mind, and that the mind's activity is not only reflexly exerted upon itself, but directly upon objects, so as to perceive in them connexions and relations which are not Sensations. (1: 28)

Elsewhere Whewell calls these 'connexions and relations' 'Fundamental Ideas' – they are Cause, Likeness, Substance, and others – and they are his version of Kant's categories. Unlike Kant, Whewell explicitly identifies these 'connexions and relations' with language.

The 'Fundamental Ideas' make up 'the *Alphabet*, by means of which we interpret Phenomena' (2: 443):

Man is the Interpreter of Nature, and Science is the right Interpretation. And this image … is, in many respects, instructive. It exhibits to us the necessity of both elements; – the marks which man has to look at, and the knowledge of the alphabet and language which he must possess and apply before he can find any meaning in what he sees. (1: 37)

*Signs* and *Meaning* are Ideas, supplied by the mind, and added to all that sensation can disclose in any collection of visible marks. (1:38)

An example of one such idea is likeness, which, Whewell argues, is fundamental to all language, and which in particular governs the use of common names. The act of naming begins with our ability to apprehend each thing we perceive as a unit: we see that 'to single out special objects requires a mental operation as well as a sensation' (1:467). His example is a tree. How can we see one tree, when 'we have, spread before us, a collection of colours and forms, green and brown, dark and light, irregular and straight: this is all that sensation gives or can give'? The answer lies in the ability of the mind to perceive a unit: 'We see the green and the brown, but we must *make* the tree before we can see it' (1:467). Berkeley and Kant both lie behind this statement, and Berkeley, as we shall see, is one of the philosophers who helps us to understand the poetry of sensation. Whewell goes on immediately to link the mind's making with language. Our 'power of perceiving in the appearances around us, likeness and unlikeness' (1:469) enables us to classify the object, and to indicate its kind by naming it a 'tree,' for 'all language necessarily implies recognition of resemblances' (1:470). On this basis, Whewell argues against the Lockeian position that language is purely arbitrary and conventional:

Thus amid the countless combinations of properties and divisions of classes which the structure of language implies, scarcely any are arbitrary or capricious. A word which expressed a mere wanton collection of unconnected attributes could hardly be called a *word*; for such a collection of properties no truth could be asserted, and the word would disappear, for want of some occasion on which it could be used. Though much of the fabric of language appears, not unnaturally, fantastical and purely conventional, it is in fact otherwise. (1:473)

Such is Whewell's position in the debate that originated in Plato's *Cratylus*, and his was an influential voice, for he made 'scientific terminology and nomenclature ... a field ... particularly his own,' and was recognized as 'the leading expert on the coinage of new terms.'[44] Much of Whewell's explicit commentary on language is indeed devoted to technical terms ('Aphorisms concerning the Language of

Science' is the last major section in his *Philosophy* 2:479–569) and to their place in the philosophy of the 'Classificatory Sciences' (1:466–512). His concern with the language of science parallels Tennyson's concern with fitting 'aptest words to things,' for, like Tennyson, he begins with common language and adapts it to his purposes; indeed, in his third aphorism he says that, *'In framing scientific terms, the appropriation of old words is preferable to the invention of new ones'* (2:502). But Whewell's aim is different:

when our knowledge becomes perfectly exact and purely intellectual, we require a language which shall also be exact and intellectual; – which shall exclude alike vagueness and fancy, imperfection and superfluity; – in which each term shall convey a meaning steadily fixed and rigorously limited. (2:479)

But common language has 'a certain degree of looseness and ambiguity,' 'something of vagueness and indistinctness,' and 'contains, in every sentence, a tinge of emotion or of imagination' (2:479). The things with which Tennyson is concerned are just as much emotional and imaginative as they are scientific, and hence his task of finding 'aptest words' is a more difficult one.

With Coleridge and Whewell – and behind them both, Kant – in mind, we can understand in yet another way why 'matter-moulded forms of speech' are inadequate to 'frame' the experience of section xcv of *In Memoriam*. This explanation rests upon the distinction Coleridge always insisted upon, between the understanding and the reason, and he devotes one whole part of *Aids to Reflection* to the 'difference in kind' between the two faculties. Reason is 'the Source and Substance of Truths above Sense, and having their evidence in themselves' (143); the Understanding, by contrast, 'is truly and accurately defined in the words of Leighton and Kant, a "faculty judging according to sense"' (153). Tennyson's phrase suggests that language is the workmanship of the understanding, and hard to use for an act of pure reason, 'a direct aspect of Truth, an inward Beholding' (the words are Hooker's, quoted by Coleridge when he is defining Reason [148]). The 'forms of speech' are the expression of 'certain inherent forms' Coleridge finds in the Understanding, 'modes of reflecting not referable to the objects reflected on, but pre-determined by the constitution and (as it were) mechanism of the Understanding itself' (149). While Reason is an *'imm*ediate Beholding' of universal truths, the Understanding is a *'mediate* Apprehension' of these truths (155), and its forms, and those of language, are our reflection or turning back of these truths in an active response to them. But the response is not the truths themselves, but only our experience of them.

The limitations of the understanding are clearer in Kant himself than they are in Coleridge, particularly in his *Prolegomena to every future Metaphysic, which can appear as a science*. The *Prolegomena* Kant published in 1783, two years after the *Critique of Pure Reason*, in an attempt to make the *Critique* more accessible, and to draw attention to its principal points and their significance, easily lost sight of in the systematic treatment necessary in such a work. John Richardson, the first English translator of Kant, published his translation of the *Prolegomena* in 1818, and there was a copy of it in Tennyson's library. Tennyson likely did not know the *Critique of Pure Reason* itself before he wrote *In Memoriam*, and the copy of it in his library is Max Müller's translation of 1881. Nonetheless, we know from the *Memoir* that the Apostles read and discussed Kant, and Hallam undertook to learn German in 1829 with the hope that he would 'walk with Kant, and the author of Faust in another year.'[45] Tennyson himself, many years later (in 1874), professed to have 'but a gleam of Kant,' and said that 'I have never delivered myself to dialectics,'[46] but the gleam *was* a gleam and not total darkness. Richardson's translation, however inadequate – and René Wellek has given some indication of how 'very inaccurate and clumsy' it is[47] – made Kant available to English readers, and Richardson, like Coleridge, uses the word 'forms' for the shapes that the mind brings to experience; 'the form of sensitivity' is a phrase that recurs, with variations, in the translation. I use Richardson's translation, awkward though it is, in the quotations that follow.

The senses, Kant says, give us 'a representation by no means of things in themselves, but of the way in which they appear to us.'[48] Experience 'can never teach the nature of things in themselves (noumena)' (63), nor is that nature Kant's primary concern. He deals, rather, with our judgment of experience, and with 'the pure conceptions of the understanding' (75) that, as he keeps saying, make experience possible. These conceptions, he also keeps saying, have 'their undoubted objective rightness, but indeed with regard to experience only' (89); with reference to things in themselves they 'have no signification whatever' (92).

In fact, when we, as is reasonable, consider objects of sense as mere phenomena, we hereby allow at the same time, that they bottom upon a thing in itself, though we know it not as to its internal nature or essence, but as to its phenomenon, that is, the way, in which our senses are affected by this unknown something. The understanding therefore, just by its assuming phenomena, grants the existence of things in themselves also, and so far we can say, that the representation of such beings as form the substrata of phenomena, consequently of mere beings of the understanding, is not only admissible, but unavoidable.

And our critical deduction by no means excludes beings of that sort (noumena), but rather limits the principles of the esthetic to this, that they shall not extend to all things, by which extension every thing would be turned to mere phenomenon, but that they shall only hold of objects of a possible experience. Hereby then creatures of the understanding are only granted with the inculcation of this rule which admits of no exception, and which is, 'that we know nothing at all determinate of these pure creatures of intellect, nor is it possible for us to know any thing of them, because our pure conceptions of the understanding as well as our pure intuitions extend to nothing but objects of possible experience, consequently to mere creatures of sense, and, the moment we quit these, not the least signification remains to those conceptions.' (95–6)

Hence the importance, Kant insists, of 'the distinguishing of ideas, that is, of pure conceptions of reason, from categories, or pure conceptions of the understanding, as cognitions of a quite distinct species, origin and use' (118). The former cannot be confirmed or refuted by experience; they 'extend to the completeness, that is, the collective unity of all possible experience and thereby beyond every given experience, and become transcendent' (117). One such transcendent idea is that of a Supreme Being.

William Knight came away from an 1870 conversation with Tennyson thinking 'He was an idealist at heart.' 'Faith in the great Kantian triad (God, Duty, Immortality) dominated his life.'[49] And John Addington Symonds gives an account (dating from 1865) of Tennyson as an idealist, unable to comprehend things in themselves, but sure of 'ideas.' Here is part of Symonds' transcription of Tennyson's conversation: 'Then, about matter. Its incognisability puzzled him. "I cannot form the least notion of a brick. I don't know what it is. It's no use talking about atoms, extension, colour, weight. I cannot penetrate the brick. But I have far more distinct ideas of God, of love, and such emotions."'[50] When we put Tennyson's 'matter-moulded forms of speech' in this Kantian context, we can see that he is attempting to use language that is based on the categories of the understanding to give an account of a direct and immediate experience of 'the living soul.' In Kant's view, the categories, in reference to things in themselves, 'have no signification whatever' (92). Tennyson does not empty his words of significance, but he does affirm how 'hard' it is to use language in this way.

We have been focusing on 'forms' or 'moulds' in relation to individual words (and have thus been exploring theories of naming or of designation), but there is a complementary meaning of these terms that points to sentences or propositions. This reading involves the view that truth lies, not in discrete words, but in the structures or 'forms of speech,' the context in which words have a place. 'Both Words & Ideas,' Coleridge tells Wedgwood in one of his 1801 letters, 'derive their whole significancy from their coherence. The simple *Idea* Red dissevered from all, with which it had ever been conjoined would be as unintelligible as the word *Red*; the one would be a *sight*, the other a Sound, meaning only themselves, that is in common language, meaning nothing.'[51] Hence any theory of language must concern itself with syntax and grammar as much as with the origin and formation of words, and these areas of study are the two major divisions of philology.

The formation of sentences – that is, the theory of syntax – had, in European thought, usually been traced back to Aristotle, to his *Categories* and to a few brief but influential sections in his *On Interpretation*. The assumptions on which this theory rests are, first, that all objects in the world outside us have an individual and independent existence and, secondly, that those objects have qualities or attributes or characteristics – colour, odour, relations, and the like – that allow us to distinguish them, classify them, and relate them. Syntax pictures this order of things outside us – matter and its accidents – by naming the object and saying things about it; by starting with the noun, that is, and proceeding to predication. The categories indicate the things that can be predicated of any substance, and hence are the principles underlying adjectives, adverbs, and verbs. The noun-substantive and the predicate together make up the basic structure of the proposition, which is true when the things predicated or asserted about the object correspond with our actual observation. This picture theory of the truth of propositions reappears in Locke's account of language, when the question, what is truth, leads him away from a theory of words to 'forms of speech.' That question he asks in book 4 of the *Essay*, and he answers by saying that it is '*the joining or separating of Signs, as the*

*Things signified by them, do agree or disagree one with another'* (4.5.2), such statements being propositions. In book 3, Locke devotes only one brief chapter to propositions and the words that make them possible. These words Locke calls 'particles,' whereby the mind signifies 'the *connexion* that [it] gives to *Ideas, or Propositions, one with another'* (3.7.1), to create, first, 'whole Sentences' and then 'a coherent Discourse' (3.7.1), 'one continued Reasoning or Narration' (3.7.2). These words are all marks of actions of the mind, and one uses them 'to *shew* what *Connexion, Restriction, Distinction, Opposition, Emphasis,* etc. he gives to each respective *part of his Discourse'* (3.7.2). It is possible to read Tennyson's phrase 'forms of speech' as *'the joining or separating of Signs'* and to see that these 'forms' are 'matter-moulded' in so far as the proposition, to be true, must picture the world of objects and their qualities. And since these objects seem to be essentially different from 'the living soul' Tennyson experiences in this passage, the attempt to use such a proposition must inevitably be 'hard.' But just as we could not stay with a Lockeian understanding of words as a full account of Tennyson's phrase, so we cannot stay with a Lockeian understanding of propositions. Two matters are of some importance in our moving forward from Locke: the history of language study in the eighteenth century, and the new understanding of the parts of speech and their relations that the comparative and historical study of language made possible.

Language theory following Locke placed greater emphasis on 'forms of speech,' and this development has been studied in some detail, particularly by Stephen Land and Murray Cohen. Land calls his study *From Signs to Propositions,* and he traces the shift from a concept of language as a collection of words to a concept of language as a sign system, from (to use his terms) 'atomism' to 'formalism.' Land takes Locke as one of his chief examples of the view that language is 'an *aggregate* of signs.' But, as the eighteenth century moved on, 'semantic theory came to place less emphasis upon individual words and more upon matters of syntactic, metaphorical, and morphological structures. The word or sign was slowly replaced as the unit of significance by the sentence or expression.'[52] Cohen, in *Sensible Words,* traces essentially the same shift, but he demonstrates that the development was by no means so clear and steady in direction as Land seems to imply, and he gives the reader a more complex sense of the period by dealing with 'the changing forms of basic texts,' especially 'school texts and projectors' pamphlets.'[53] Coleridge was the heir of this shift from words as discrete units to words as form and, as James McKusick has shown, saw grammar as 'the most distinctive feature of human language.'[54] The pattern he arrived at – an elaboration of the 'tri-fold or tri-une demonstration' that he learned from the seventeenth-century theologian Richard Baxter – Coleridge calls a 'Noetic Pentad,' and it appears in both *Aids to Reflection* and *Table Talk*. 'There are seven parts of speech,' says Coleridge in his *Table Talk* for 18 March 1827, 'and they agree with the five grand and universal divisions into which all things finite ... will be found to fall.'[55] In his diagram, the truth of language depends upon relationships, actions, and reactions within an embracing whole that Coleridge identifies with God himself.

But it was the new philology that gave fresh interest to old questions about the parts of speech: what are they? how many are there? how are they related to each other? Since Plato and Aristotle, the noun and the verb seemed to be the basic parts of speech – McKusick gives us a useful summary of the noun-verb controversy up to the end of the eighteenth century[56] – and now one, now the other was presented as the part of speech from which all the remaining parts were derived. But with the gradual acceptance and the widening knowledge of the new philology in England after 1830, there was a revolution in the understanding of the relations of the kinds of words. Among Tennyson's books was Richard Garnett's *Philological Essays*, first published in the *Quarterly Review* and the *Proceedings of the Philological Society* between 1835 and 1848, and Garnett was one of the scholars responsible for making known in England the work of Franz Bopp on Sanskrit and of August Friedrich Pott on Greek. From their work the pronoun emerged as a crucial part of speech.

Garnett's review of 'Prichard on the Celtic Languages,' which had first appeared in the *Quarterly Review* (57 [1836] 80–110), is his major essay, and to its ideas he was to return again and again. For though Prichard deals with only one group of languages, he has, Garnett shows, thrown light on the formation of language in general. That light is a theory of grammar, of the parts of speech and their relations. Garnett reviews earlier theories, beginning with the noun. 'The common definition of a noun is that it is the name of a *thing*,'[57] but in fact, Garnett argues, it is the name of a conception – a quality or attribute – founded on perception. Names of things 'are attributive nouns, used by a sort of synecdoche, to express a substance by one or more of its distinctive *qualities*' (88), and words denote 'the *attributes* and *categories*, or *relations* of things' (90). He criticizes Tooke for identifying words and things, and then tackles the verb. 'Tooke's dictum that a verb is *a noun and something more*, is true as far as it goes; but he has not informed us *what* this something more is' (91). But the new philology, with its comparative study of languages, suggested that undefined element: 'Some progress was made in ascertaining the nature of verbs, when it was shown that the personal terminations are in reality personal pronouns' (92).

Every verb includes in it a subject and predicate, or makes an assertion respecting some given person or thing. It must therefore *have a subject*, that is to say, it must be in some *person*. Take away this subject, and the verb becomes a *noun*, as the supines are in Latin, and the infinitives in all languages. The root of the verb is therefore a noun or attribute; and the personal terminations, as we have seen, are to be resolved into pronouns. (92)

Prichard, says Garnett, 'has shown that the personal terminations in Welsh are pronouns' (92), but Prichard seems unaware of the significance of his findings. 'Most grammarians have regarded the personal pronouns as a kind of *substantives, intrinsically* denoting the person speaking, the person spoken to, and the person spoken of' (97), but 'we consider this theory to involve an utter impossibility' (97). 'What we call personal pronouns are, at least originally were, nothing more than *demonstratives*' (97–8), and since all words express some characteristic attribute or relation, the relation expressed by pronouns is that of place: here I or there you perceive and name this particular attribute or category. The pronoun points to the perceiving mind as the location in which that attribute or category is apprehended. Garnett goes on to discuss the identity of pronouns and particles, the establishment of this identity being, he says, 'perhaps, the most important discovery in modern philology' (101), and he refers the reader to Bopp for 'a full exposition of the manner in which pronouns enter into the composition of words – the terminations and cases of nouns and participles – the formation of abstract substantives – and the suffixes of adverbs' (106). A.W. Schlegel had thought such terminations meaningless in themselves, but they are in fact among the oldest and most important parts of language. The result of Bopp's work, Garnett argues, is the emergence of two kinds of words: 'He appears to have established his leading positions – that pronouns and particles are closely related, and that they form a totally distinct class from nouns and verbs – on a firm basis' (103). Frederic William Farrar, quoting Garnett, would later label these 'two great divisions' 'Matter-words' and 'Form-words': 'To the former class belong Nouns and Verbs, which supply the main materials of Thought and Speech, and signify perceptible objects or distinct actions; to the latter belong pronouns, particles, &c., which express our perceptions as modified by numerous relations of Space and Time.'[58] This sentence comes from Farrar's *Chapters on Language* (1865), which was in Tennyson's library together with the same author's *Families of Speech* (1870), the two of them in a volume called *Language and Languages* (1878), a copy of which Farrar had presented to Tennyson. For Farrar in fact sometimes uses Tennyson's poems as illustrations, and in *Chapters on Language* in particular he quotes section xlv of *In Memoriam*, where 'The baby new to earth and sky' learns the use of the personal pronouns, and 'So rounds he to a separate mind' (9). Farrar comments: 'The first conception which man must learn is the conception of his own separate independent existence, and without this conscious distinction between the Ego and the Non-ego ... he cannot advance a single step' (52) in the gradual development of language. In his own language theory, Farrar argues that all matter-words are onomatopoetic in origin, and develop out of imitative sounds, while form-words have their origin in interjections. Our concern at the moment, however, is with the 'two great divisions' of words and the implications of those classes. The chief implication is a Kantian one: the form-words frame our experience of the world outside us, and make that experience possible.

John William Donaldson, acknowledging his indebtedness to Garnett and, beyond him, to Grimm, Bopp, and Pott, links the 'two great divisions' of words explicitly with Kant in his *The New Cratylus* (1839), so named because of his opposition to Tooke and his conviction that Tooke simply continued to reproduce the etymological sophistries Plato had long ago exposed in *his Cratylus*. Donaldson's starting point, as I have already indicated, is the story of Adam's naming of the beasts, and of that story Donaldson says: 'The ultimate results of human consciousness are that the thinking subject *is*, and that there *is* something without him; that there is, in the language of the German philosophers, a *me* and a *not-me*, or, if you will, he *knows* that he himself exists, and *believes* that there is something which is not himself' (46). Donaldson links this account of consciousness to Kant's distinction between human faculties, and to Kant's categories: man 'has perception, conception, association, which constitute his Understanding. He compares, generalizes, knows, and discourses; these are the operations of his Reason. And all his thoughts are modified by and subordinated to his primary intuitions of space and time' (58). If language is really the product of Reason, 'we should expect to find traces of all these conformations of the mind in the structure of our speech. And so it is' (58). Like Garnett, Donaldson argues that there are 'two primary elements of speech,' the pronoun and 'all significant terms which are not pronouns' (58), including nouns and verbs. These two elements are the expression of the 'me' and its relation to the 'not-me.' The pronoun Donaldson defines as 'an organizing element which enters into all words' and which 'in its different forms is an expression of the first great fact of consciousness, that we are and that there is something without us' (58–9). The other element he calls 'a material element,' and it 'includes the names of all the objects, which present themselves to us in the outward world' (59) and the names of actions as well, so that nouns and verbs are not essentially different. In Donaldson's account of the organizing and material elements in language we can discern the philologist's equivalent of Wordsworth's half creating and half perceiving, for Donaldson argues that the pronoun is also the expression of our presuppositions of space and time. Hence the pronoun is not only a separate word but also enters into other words 'by way of prefix, suffix, or both' (60). Words containing roots – the material elements of language – become nouns or verbs through the pronominal element, and inflections and conjugations are the expression of space and time, 'the cases of the nouns expressing the position of some object with regard to other objects, the persons of the verb the point from which the action begins, or at which it ends' (64).

This Kantian approach to the parts of speech adds an element missing from Locke's picture theory of syntax: it draws attention to the perceiving consciousness. David Shaw's metaphor for such self-consciousness is the framing of a picture, and he identifies this metaphor with the idealist's revolt against the account of the mind as a mirror and of the sense of sight as a window. Among other idealists, J.F. Ferrier, whose *Institutes of Metaphysics* Tennyson read in 1854, 'revives a form of synthetic *a priori* judgement to refute the naïve empirical assumption that it is ever possible to mirror an unmediated world of primary facts, plain, exposed, and naked to the eye,' and this epistemology is the foundation of the many Victorian experiments with framed narration.[59]

'Frame' is a key word in Tennyson's complaint in section xcv of *In Memoriam*: 'how hard to frame ... that which I became.' In Donaldson's terms, 'matter-moulded forms of speech' are the 'material element' of Tennyson's language, while the poet's consciousness, expressed in the infinitive, is the 'organizing element.' In this context, the difficulty lies not so much in the 'material element' as it does in the 'organizing element,' and there is a sense that the categories of the poet's consciousness are only partially suited to comprehending the experience. Not wholly unsuited, I should add, for then the experience would not have been, at all. (When Donaldson in the fourth edition of *The New Cratylus* mentions revelation in a footnote in his chapter on the philosophy of language, he points out that revelation 'must be within the limits of our intellectual capacity, and must be capable of approving itself to our reason and conscience. Whatever is unintelligible is simply not revealed.')[60] Nonetheless, human consciousness is capable of only limited expression of the experience. Tennyson is very close to complaining about God's Economy, that concept so central to Tractarian thinking, where, in G.B. Tennyson's words, God's truth 'is hidden and given to us only in a manner suited to our capacities for apprehending it.'[61] But the poet's concern is not with God's handling of revelation but with our receiving of it. The stanza in which the complaint appears is intensely self-conscious, and the task may be 'hard,' but in fact Tennyson does 'frame' his experience, however inadequately. His stanzaic form is a frame, and so are his periphrases, 'that which is' and 'that which I became,' periphrasis being a figure which, by words, circles round or frames an idea, but the pronouns, from a philologist's point of view, are the crucial organizing element.

The word 'frame' also appears in section xlv of *In Memoriam*, the one Farrar was later to quote to illustrate the development of the pronominal element in language:

The baby new to earth and sky,
  What time his tender palm is prest
  Against the circle of the breast,
Has never thought that 'this is I:'

But as he grows he gathers much,
  And learns the use of 'I', and 'me',
  And finds 'I am not what I see,
And other than the things I touch.'

In this account of the development of human consciousness, Tennyson focuses on the 'use' of the pronouns. It is possible to read the line 'And learns the use of "I", and "me"' as a factual description of the child learning, through imitation, to say the personal pronouns, but the last two stanzas of the lyric indicate a different view of this learning. The pronouns are the expression of the child's individuality, 'As through the frame that binds him in / His isolation grows defined' (11–12). This 'frame' makes possible both 'clear memory' (10) and the consciousness of self, and 'to learn himself' (15) is, paradoxically, to transcend 'the frame that binds him in.' Thus self-consciousness is inescapably double: he is bound in his 'frame,' and at the same time the 'frame,' recognized as such, releases him from the prison of the self.

Emily Tennyson once said to Jowett that 'Whole philosophies might be contained in a line of verse,'[62] and 'matter-moulded forms of speech' is certainly one such line. From a Lockeian perspective, the phrase suggests that all words, however general or abstract, may be traced back to sense-data; that language is the arbitrary attaching of a sound to a sensation; that words picture the world outside us. From a Coleridgian perspective, the phrase also suggests the shaping power of the mind and the patterns or forms by which it makes experience intelligible. Tennyson holds together both perspectives, and the new philology with its historical and comparative study of conjugations and declensions, and its division of all words into pronominal or organizing elements and sensational or material elements, made this double view seem almost inevitable.

As a coda to this discussion, we might look at a lecture that Frederick Denison Maurice gave 'about 1838.' It is called 'On Words,' and it was printed in his *The Friendship of Books and Other Lectures.* Tennyson had a copy of the second edition of this volume in his library (London: Macmillan 1874), and his son recalls his 'reading with admiration' a passage from it.[63] Maurice was a long-time friend of Tennyson, and the poet may have been aware of the lecture or of the ideas in it much earlier. Like Tennyson, Maurice was not a philologist, but he was aware of the advances in philology, and he linked them with his own views, which owed much to Coleridge and, through him, to German thinkers. In the lecture, Maurice recommends the study of words, and attacks the usual view that words as the signs of ideas are arbitrary and conventional. 'In life and practice words are most real, substantial things. They exercise a power which we may deny if we choose, but which we feel even while we are denying it. They go forth spreading good or mischief through society. Surely there must be something solemn and deep in their nature.'[64] And indeed there is. Men 'only create their words as they create the breath, which goes forth from the lungs with which God has provided them, by help of the air with which He has surrounded them' (36). This sentence suggests that language is an innate and natural capacity in us, while the next sentence suggests that the study of words is the key to a providential view of history. Man 'begins to feel that in words are stored up facts which may enable him better to understand the history of mankind, and to interpret and admire the purposes of their Creator concerning them' (36). Maurice criticizes both Dr Johnson and Horne Tooke; the former is 'mighty in collecting, piling up, accumulating' (39) passages illustrating meanings, but 'Is there no common meaning, not even a bead-string to hang the different meanings upon?' (44); the latter 'takes us at once to the root, or what he believes to be the root' (47), but 'the hard and material character of his mind led him to stop there' (48). Maurice's own position is a mediating one. He acknowledges that words are the signs of sensations but also insists, like Coleridge, that words are living powers, and that these powers are revealed by their history. The passage in which he sets out this position could be read as his gloss on 'matter-moulded forms of speech':

I think it is very important they should understand, that words do indeed bear witness to man's connection with that which is earthly and material, because he *is* so connected, and because everything which he does and utters must proclaim this truth: but that if you look them fairly in the face, they are also found to testify, and that not weakly or obscurely, of man as a spiritual being; nay, that it is impossible steadily to meditate upon the history of any single word without carrying away a conviction that he is so, which all the materialism in the world cannot set aside. (51)

There is a 'vital principle' (53) in words, Maurice insists, and so words are inextricably linked with our social, moral, and political lives:

for it is almost impossible to conjecture how much light would be thrown upon our national history, upon the history of our wars, arts, and manufactures, above all upon the history of our mental and spiritual progress, by an examination of the senses which words have borne at different times; of the impressions they have received from different persons; of the new applications which they have gained from different discoveries; of the changes they have undergone from different revolutions. To know through what difficulties and under what influences our language attained strength and maturity, and how any symptoms of declension or decay, which it may now exhibit, are connected with a similar declension in our moral feelings, in our reverence for institutions, or in the vigour of our search after truth, must be very useful and important for any Englishman, especially for those who are to be in any way the guides and teachers of their brethren. (54–5)

In *Idylls of the King*, Tennyson would link words and society in this same way, and that poem, as we shall see, is his fullest working out of the implications of the new philology. But in his earlier works there is a greater emphasis on words in relation to sensations and on the affective power of language, and it is to these matters that we must now turn.

*Chapter Two*

# 'A landscape-painter in words, a colourist'

Poetry has always been thought of as affecting the eye and the ear more than the other senses, its effects being explored in the conventional analogies between poetry and painting, and between poetry and music. In his 1831 review of the *Poems, Chiefly Lyrical*, Hallam deals with Tennyson's work almost entirely in terms of sight and hearing, these two senses, he told Tennyson in a letter, being 'those employed in the processes of imagination.' This letter was written at about the same time as the review (it is dated 26 July 1831), and in it Hallam contrasts his own senses, 'less vivacious by nature,' with Tennyson's, 'universal and all powerful, absorbing your whole existence, communicating to you that energy which is so glorious.'[1] In a parallel passage in the review, Hallam focuses on both the eye and the ear of poets of sensation:

Susceptible of the slightest impulse from external nature, their fine organs trembled into emotion at colors, and sounds, and movements, unperceived or unregarded by duller temperaments. Rich and clear were their perceptions of visible forms; full and deep their feelings of music. So vivid was the delight attending the simple exertions of eye and ear, that it became mingled more and more with their trains of active thought, and tended to absorb their whole being into the energy of sense.[2]

Sensitivity of eye and ear results in 'word-painting' and 'word-music' in poetry, and these are the labels that Dr Robert Mann uses to defend Tennyson's most sophisticated development of the techniques of the poetry of sensation, *Maud*, the poet's favourite among his own works.[3]

'Word-painting' and 'word-music' ('sound-symbolizing' is Mann's parallel for the second label) are bound up with the theory of expression, and I will later deal with them in that context. My concern at the moment, however, is to distinguish the activities of the two senses: the appeal of language to the eye is sharply different from the appeal of language to the ear. Word-painting as a technique of the poetry of sensation rests upon a theory of vision that can be traced back to Berkeley, for whom 'suggestion' (his version of the principle of association) is a key word. Word-music as a technique of the poetry of sensation is sometimes imitative (as it is in onomatopoetic words and lines) but is more usually expressive, the tones and cadences of the human voice being considered the natural uttering of emotion. The figure linked with word-music is prosopopoeia, while it is the image which is the primary element of word-painting.

My chapter title is from William Allingham's diary for 1884. 'Other gifts he has,' Allingham writes after a conversation with Tennyson about dream landscapes, 'but T. is especially and pre-eminently a landscape-painter in words, a colourist, rich, full and subtle.'⁴ For the time being I want to set aside the appeal to the ear of the poetry of sensation – that is the subject of the next chapter – and focus instead on the relation between language and the sensations provided to the mind by the sense of sight. For any investigation of word-painting, Hallam's review of Tennyson's volume of 1830 is a good starting point. This review has already been well used by those who see the poetry of sensation as anticipating the theories and techniques of twentieth-century poetry; Hallam's reputation, re-established by Yeats and kept alive by McLuhan in his essays on Tennyson and in his 1956 selections from the poetry, remains strong in the work of a contemporary critic like Carol Christ, who has given Hallam a major place in her *Victorian and Modern Poetics* (1984). However much we can see Hallam as looking forward, we need to be aware, too, of the extent to which he looks back, and if we gaze into the essay not as a crystal ball but as a rearview mirror, there appear some language theories which enable us to understand Tennyson's diction in fresh ways.

The review is eclectic, and Lawrence Poston is right to say that 'any discussion of Hallam's poetics should begin by emphasizing the catholicity of his appropriation of the Romantics.' Poston is himself concerned with linking Hallam and Coleridge, the issue being 'how to achieve a "pure" poetry which was not detached from moral considerations,'⁵ but the mirror reveals other and earlier predecessors as well.

For Hallam's two passions in life were metaphysics and poetry – his linking of the two is a constant theme in his letters – and he told a correspondent that reflecting on 'the e[ssent]ial forms of the Mind's operation' 'is meat & drink to me.'[6] His central terms, sensation and reflection, are echoes of Locke's, and we can hear Hartley in the phrases 'a regular law of association,' 'the forces of association,' 'the elements of those complex emotions,' and 'the process of their combination.'[7] Hallam had in fact been taking 'occasional plunges into David Hartley,' he told Tennyson in October, 1830[8] (he would write the review the following summer), but in his thinking about the psychology of association he owes perhaps more to Berkeley, to whom he refers in a familiar way in a letter of 1828: 'with regard to the Extent of Human Knowledge, no real advance has been made beyond Hume & Berkeley.'[9] Locke, Hartley, Hume, Berkeley – these are the thinkers upon whom Hallam draws to construct a theory of poetic language. Our starting point in exploring this theory must be Hallam's central terms, sensation and reflection.

The terms themselves are Locke's and come from book 2 of *An Essay Concerning Human Understanding*. The *Essay* was, as I have already indicated, a required text at Cambridge in the period when Hallam and Tennyson were students there, and the epistemology of book 2 – that our knowledge consists of generalizations from experience – was the part of the *Essay* that was most widely known. (Hardly anyone read the whole *Essay* or understood its purpose, as Hans Aarsleff has shown.)[10] Locke uses the terms to label the two sources of all our ideas, Sensation being the 'several distinct *Perceptions* of things' which our senses convey into our minds (2.1.3), and Reflection being 'that notice which the Mind takes of its own Operations' (2.1.4).[11] Locke assumes that sensation is prior to any activity of the mind, it being the role of the understanding to compare, abstract, and generalize, and thus to arrive at the ideas and propositions which make up our knowledge.

We soon notice that Hallam does not use the terms precisely as Locke does. In Locke they are associated (though different) sources of our ideas; in Hallam they are opposites. The poetry of reflection is a poetry of ideas, and its central concern is with truth expressed in statements or propositions; the poetry of sensation juxtaposes images, and its central concern is the vividness and subtlety of its appeal to our senses. Hallam's use of the terms perhaps owes something to Hume's contrasting of impressions and ideas, Hume's distinction lying in 'their different degrees of force and vivacity': 'The most lively thought is still inferior to the dullest sensation.'[12] For Hallam, the threat to liveliness and freshness of sensation is in the 'logical relations' of ideas, and his ideal lies in the kind of truth he calls 'beauty,' that unity of thought and feeling which is apprehended by the sympathetic imagination.[13]

It is Berkeley, more than any other thinker, who enables us to understand the precise nature of this freshness of sensation. Berkeley's theory of vision is the foundation of his philosophy, and although in the nineteenth century the philosophy was often disregarded because of its immaterialism (based on the notorious view that things exist only when perceived), his theory of vision remained, as John Stuart Mill pointed out in an 1842 article in the *Westminster Review*, 'one of the least disputed doctrines in the most disputed and most disputable of all sciences, the Science of Man.'[14] Adam Smith, Reid, Stewart, Whewell, Hartley, Brown, and James Mill all, writes Mill, made Berkeley's teaching their own. This 'received doctrine of modern metaphysicians' Berkeley first set out in his earliest published work, *An Essay towards a New Theory of Vision* (1709). There he distinguishes sensation from 'an act of judgment grounded on experience.'[15] 'To perceive is one thing; to judge is another' (1:265), writes Berkeley in his 1733 vindication and explanation of his theory. Moreover, the sensations of one sense are sharply different from those of another sense, however much our judgment obscures the differences. We do not, for instance, see distance. The eye sees only 'lights and colours in sundry situations and shades and degrees of faintness and clearness, confusion and distinctness' (1:202), while the idea of distance, like the idea of solidity and certain ideas of figure, depends upon the sense of touch. There is no necessary connection between the ideas perceived by the two senses, nor are there any ideas common to both: 'That which is seen is one thing, and that which is felt is another' (1:189).

This insistence on the distinctness of our sensations prior to our inferences and acts of judgment is a crucial matter for the artist who would render, not the fruits of experience, but experience itself. The value of Berkeley's theory of vision is perhaps clearest for the painter, who must place colours, lights, and shades on a canvas. It was Ruskin who, in spite of his implicit rejection of Berkeley's immaterialism in his chapter on the pathetic fallacy in book 3 of *Modern Painters*, recognized the link between Berkeley's theory and the painter's practice. In his *The Elements of Drawing* (1857), he tells his students that the world 'presents itself to your eyes only as an arrangement of patches of different colours variously shaded,' and then says, in a note: 'The whole technical power of painting depends on our recovery of what may be called the *innocence of the eye*; that is to say, of a sort of childish perception of these flat stains of colour, merely as such, without consciousness of what they signify, – as a blind man would see them if suddenly gifted with sight.'[16] Ruskin does not name Berkeley at this point, but the blind man suddenly gifted with sight is a recurring figure in Berkeley's works, so Ruskin's allusion is unmistakable. Monet's comment that 'ninety per cent of the theory of Impressionist painting is in ... Ruskin's *Elements of Drawing*' allows us to draw a line from the great French painters of the late nineteenth century back through Ruskin to Berkeley.

Tennyson has a place in this line. The conventional analogy between poetry and painting (*ut pictura poesis*) is redefined by Tennyson in ways that Berkeley's theory of vision illuminates. 'What we immediately and properly perceive by sight,' Berkeley had written in *The Theory of Vision ... Vindicated*, 'is its primary object, light and colours' (1:265), and 'light and colours' are prior to judgment. In the early 1870s, in response to interpretations of *Idylls of the King*, Tennyson said, 'Poetry is like shot-silk with many glancing colours. Every reader must find his own interpretation according to his ability, and according to his sympathy with the poet.'[17] The statement, with its clear distinction between seeing and judging, between 'many glancing colours' and 'interpretation,' has a Berkelean ring to it, and certainly William Knight came away from an 1870 conversation with Tennyson with the impression that the poet could be described as a Berkelean. 'He was an idealist at heart,' Knight recorded by way of conclusion to the interview; 'Underneath the realism of his nature, this other feature rose above it. He was not so much of a Platonist as a Berkelean.'[18] But when we remember 'matter-moulded forms of speech' and Tennyson's emphasis on the shaping power of the mind, it seems unlikely that he would accept Ruskin's argument about the innocence of the eye. He would be more likely to agree with E.H. Gombrich's assertion, in our own time, that the innocent eye is a myth: 'the postulate of an unbiassed eye demands the impossible,' Gombrich argues in *Art and Illusion* (1960), because perception itself involves organizing and judging, and our hopes and fears, guesses and expectations 'sort and model the incoming messages.'[19] Words too are the organizing and judging of our experience, as Berkeley himself recognizes.

Far from being 'flat stains' of colour, words are, in Berkeley's account of them, the result of inference and experience, and can never be as innocent to the eye as 'different colours variously shaded.' Even words which name objects of the senses are in fact 'collections of ideas,' as the philosopher points out at the beginning of his *The Principles of Human Knowledge* (1710):

> By sight I have the ideas of light and colours with their several degrees and variations. By touch I perceive, for example, hard and soft, heat and cold, motion and resistance, and of all these more and less either as to quantity or degree. Smelling furnishes me with odours; the palate with tastes, and hearing conveys sounds to the mind in all their variety of tone and composition. And as several of these are observed to accompany each other, they come to be marked by one name, and so to be reputed as one thing. Thus, for example, a certain colour, taste, smell, figure and consistence having been observed to go together, are accounted one distinct thing, signified by the name *apple*. Other collections of ideas constitute a stone, a tree, a book, and the like sensible things. (2:41)

This passage, like so much else in Berkeley's work, is an elaboration of a passage in *A New Theory of Vision*: 'The ideas intromitted by each sense are widely different and distinct from each other; but having been observed constantly to go together, they are spoken of as one and the same thing' (1:188; see also his definition of a unit, 1:214–15).

The principle that is responsible for the formation of the unit to which a word is arbitrarily attached is association. In one of the notes out of the nearly nine hundred that Berkeley jotted down in preparation for the writing of his major works (it is #225 in what is now called his *Philosophical Commentaries*), he asks, of the 'sensations of sight' and the 'sensations of touch,' 'is it onely the constant & long association of ideas entirely different that makes me judge them the same?' (1:29). Berkeley's affirmative answer to that question appears again and again in his work, though the word 'association' itself rarely occurs. Instead, he uses phrases like 'an habitual connexion' or 'the customary and close connexion' whereby distinct ideas of different senses 'are so blended and confounded together as to be mistaken for one and the same thing' (1:204). But Berkeley would free us from such habitual connections, and make us aware of 'distinct ideas' and their multiple possible relationships. His theory of vision makes possible two things of great importance for the poet of sensation: the association of ideas in a configuration held together by emotion, and the downplaying of a conventional (ie Aristotelian) grammar, with its pattern of predication and subordination, as the chief guide to the reader's response and as the chief determinant of meaning.[20]

These matters are crucial for a full understanding of Hallam's assertion that the poets of sensation live in 'a world of images.' He may have had in mind Tennyson's opinion that 'an artist ... ought to be lord of the five senses,' an opinion Hallam quotes in a letter of 1831 as something that 'Alfred is wont to say,'[21] but Hallam is aware of the dangers, moral and intellectual, of being 'lord of the five senses' (Tennyson was too, as his use of the phrase in 'The Palace of Art' indicates); nevertheless in this same letter he goes on to insist that 'poetry cannot be too pictorial, for it cannot represent too truly, and when the object of the poetic power happens to be an object of sensuous perception it is the business of the poetic language to paint.' In such painting, the chief element is the image.

The primary meaning of the word 'image' is picture, imitation, or copy (either material or mental), and the word contains the same root as the Latin verb *imitari*. Images may refer to the figures and tropes of rhetoric, but as the word was used in the seventeenth century, it was distinct from them. Ray Frazer traces the origin of the term to seventeenth-century empiricism, with its suspicion of language and distrust of figures.[22] Locke's attack on rhetoric as 'that powerful instrument of Error and Deceit' (3.10.34) in book 3 of his *An Essay Concerning Human Understanding* is typical. Metaphors and other tropes are fictions produced by the mind; images, by way of contrast, are the mind's true pictures of the world outside us. Frazer argues that it was Hobbes who established this sense of the word 'image' and brought it into common use. In the first two chapters of *Leviathan*, for instance, Hobbes sums up his epistemology by tracing all our knowledge to sense, the 'cause of Sense' being 'the Externall Body, or Object, which presseth the organ proper to each Sense.' This pressing leaves a representation or appearance that Hobbes calls an 'image,'[23] and he assumes that the image is a true picture of the object that gave rise to it. Locke's parallel term is 'idea,' and an 'idea' is a true sign of things outside the mind: 'For since the Things, the Mind contemplates, are none of them, besides it self, present to the Understanding, 'tis necessary that something else, as a Sign or Representation of the thing it considers, should be present to it: And these are *Ideas*' (4.21.4). To these 'ideas' one attaches names, articulate sound being (in the central proposition in Locke's language theory) 'marks for the *Ideas* within his own Mind' (3.1.2). Stephen Land neatly sums up the relationships: 'whereas the relation between word and idea is for Locke necessarily arbitrary, the relation between idea and thing is necessarily natural.'[24] Hobbes' distinction between natural and arbitrary signs involves similar relationships.[25]

But though in Locke the relation between idea and thing is 'natural' (that is, the idea is a true picture of the thing), and the relations among ideas are true if they correspond to the relations we actually observe in the world around us, Berkeley frees things from any necessary relationship, and draws them all into our ideas. One idea may become the sign of another, not because there is a necessary connection between them, but because 'they have been observed to go together' (1:176). Philonous, Berkeley's spokesman in his *Three Dialogues* of 1713, says that 'from a frequently perceived connexion, the immediate perception of ideas by one sense suggests to the mind others perhaps belonging to another sense, which are wont to be connected with them,' and these others are 'only suggested to the mind by experience grounded on former perceptions' (2:204). One sensation or 'idea' becomes the sign of another sensation or 'idea' by regular association, and by 'sign' Berkeley means no more than this close and customary linking. As a result, our sensations or 'ideas' suggest others but do not indicate a necessary relationship, and it was for this reason, James McKusick argues, that Coleridge finally rejected Berkeley.[26] Moreover, though Berkeley is well aware of the empiricist and materialist view of sensations or 'ideas,' where the mind is in effect a mirror and sensations are a picture of the world outside us, he rejects such a view – if 'ideas' 'are looked on as notes or images, referred to *things* or *archetypes* existing without the mind, then are we involved all in *scepticism*' (2:78) – but he has Hylas, the materialist in the *Three Dialogues*, voice it. 'There are two kinds of objects,' Hylas tells Philonous, 'the one perceived immediately, which are likewise called *ideas*; the other are real things or external objects perceived by the mediation of ideas, which are their images and representations' (2:203). In Stephen Land's words, Berkeley's ideas 'strictly speaking ... are not "of" anything'[27] because in his ontology nothing outside the mind exists for them to represent. An 'idea' is not a representation of anything, and it 'can be like nothing but an idea,' he says in *The Principles of Human Knowledge* (2:80). Instead, 'light and colours, tastes, sounds, &c. are ... all equally passions or sensations in the soul' (2:197).

Berkeley's freeing of ideas from any necessary relationship, and his internalizing of them as 'passions or sensations in the soul,' provide a suggestive context for Hallam's phrase, 'a world of images.' This phrase he uses to describe the poets of sensation: 'Other poets *seek* for images to illustrate their conceptions; these men had no need to seek; they lived in a world of images.'[28] Hallam seems not particularly concerned with deciding whether the sign is a true picture of a world outside the mind (as is suggested by the word 'image'), or whether it is, as in Berkeley, a passion or sensation in the soul. Both philosophical positions are useful to him, and indeed, Hallam suggests both in his description of the poet of sensation, who lives 'a life of immediate sympathy with the external universe' as a result of his soul's seeking beauty.[29] His chief concern is the suggestiveness of the image, a web of relations made possible by the detaching of the image from a one-to-one relation with its object, and by the placing of it in a configuration whereby it becomes the sign of other images and of the emotions with which they are associated.

'The most important and extensive portion' of the lives of the poets of sensation, Hallam writes, 'consisted in those emotions which are immediately conversant with the sensation.'[30] Hallam's diction – 'conversant' – suggests a language and, indeed, sensations make up a natural language when they, by association, become the signs of emotions. Berkeley's example, in *A New Theory of Vision*, is 'the passions which are in the mind of another.' Though they are 'of themselves to me invisible,' 'I may nevertheless perceive them by sight, though not immediately, yet by means of the colours they produce in the countenance. We often see shame or fear in the looks of a man, by perceiving the changes of his countenance to red or pale' (1:173). The colours 'signify' the passions 'for no other reason than barely because they have been observed to accompany them' (1:195). Verbal language may approximate this natural language, and may, in fact, come so close to it that the sensation or 'idea' of which the word is the sign all but disappears.

I entreat the reader to reflect with himself, and see if it doth not often happen either in hearing or reading a discourse, that the passions of fear, love, hatred, admiration, disdain, and the like arise, immediately in his mind upon the perception of certain words, without any ideas coming between. At first, indeed, the words might have occasioned ideas that were fit to produce those emotions; but, if I mistake not, it will be found that when language is once grown familiar, the hearing of the sounds or sight of the characters is oft immediately attended with those passions, which at first were wont to be produced by the intervention of ideas, that are now quite omitted. (2:37)

Berkeley's examples are the words 'a *good thing*,' 'danger' (which arouses a feeling of dread), and 'Aristotle' (which arouses a feeling of reverence). Hallam's comment on Tennyson's title, 'Recollections of the Arabian Nights,' suggests a similar direct linking of word and feeling. 'What a delightful, endearing title!' he exclaims. 'How we pity those to whom it calls up no reminiscence of early enjoyment, no sentiment of kindliness as towards one who sings a song they have loved, or mentions with affection a departed friend!'[31]

This immediate association of word and emotion is anticipated by Locke's direct linking of name and idea, a linking which depends upon association: '*there comes by constant use*, to be such *a Connexion between certain Sounds, and the* Ideas *they stand for*, that the Names heard, almost as readily excite certain *Ideas*, as if the Objects themselves, which are apt to produce them, did actually affect the Senses' (3.2.6). This bypassing of actual objects by language is central to Edmund Burke's discussion of words in his *A Philosophical Enquiry into the Origin of our Ideas of the Sublime and Beautiful.* (The eight volumes of the 1801 edition of *The Works of ... Edmund Burke* were in Tennyson's library.) Words are superior to images because words are more affecting: 'Indeed so little does poetry depend for its effect on the power of raising sensible images, that I am convinced it would lose a very considerable part of its energy, if this were the necessary result of all description.'[32] Words do not call up precise images. Abstractions – 'virtue, liberty, or honour' (164) – clearly do not, nor do '*simple abstract* words' like 'red, blue, round, square, and the like' (164). Even (what he calls) '*aggregate words*' – they are 'man, horse, tree, castle, &c.' (164) – do not raise in the mind a precise picture or image. The business of poetry, as of rhetoric, is 'to affect rather by sympathy than imitation; to display rather the effect of things on the mind of the speaker, or of others, than to present a clear idea of the things themselves' (172).

The 'effect of things on the mind of the speaker' is displayed primarily in the relations among sensations. Association establishes a configuration or multi-dimensional pattern – 'multi-sensible' would be a more accurate adjective – all parts of which are apprehended simultaneously, and each part of which is capable of evoking the whole instantaneously, of bringing before us, in Locke's memorable phrase, 'the whole gang': for where the association of ideas is 'wholly owing to Chance or Custom,' Locke says, 'the one [idea] no sooner at any time comes into the Understanding but its Associate appears with it; and if they are more than two which are thus united, the whole gang always inseparable shew themselves together' (2.33.5). Hartley's central proposition makes Locke's statement a general rule: '*Any Sensations A, B, C, &c. by being associated with one another a sufficient Number of Times, get such a Power over the corresponding Ideas, a, b, c, &c. that any one of the Sensations A, when impressed alone, shall be able to excite in the Mind b, c, &c. the Ideas of the rest.*'[33] Words, too, may suggest a configuration or multi-sensible pattern. Hartley's example, in his section 'Of Words,' is 'Nurse.' For the child, that word becomes not only more and more particular but also increasingly rich. Not only does the child learn to distinguish the essential meaning of that word from 'Particularities, Circumstances, and Adjuncts' such as 'Dress' and 'Fire,' but he also experiences sensations 'besides those of Sight, such as grateful or ungrateful Tastes, Smells, Warmth or Coldness,' and 'these Sensations must leave Traces, or Ideas, which will be associated with the Names of the Objects, so as to depend upon them' (1:272).

I have been indicating how association accounts for the suggestive and affective power of words, and thus undermines the Lockeian ideal of naming (attaching a sound to a clear and distinct idea), but association (particularly Berkeley's version of it) also gives us a theory of grammar which counteracts the linear and consecutive character of a language like English, where meaning depends primarily upon word order and its patterns of predication and subordination. 'Light and colours, tastes, sounds, &c. are ... all equally passions or sensations in the soul' (2:197), Berkeley says in his *Three Dialogues*, and it is the adverb 'equally' that indicates a radical reordering of grammar. The theory of the syntactical unit or sentence is usually traced back to Aristotle and his comments on language, a few brief paragraphs in his early work, *Peri hermeneias*, Englished as *On Interpretation*. Though brief, these sections had a pervasive influence on grammatical theory in Western Europe. Hans Arens has reproduced some of the many commentaries in his *Aristotle's Theory of Language and Its Tradition: Texts from 500 to 1750* (1984),[34] while G.A. Padley has investigated the place of Aristotle in Renaissance grammatical theory and in the search for a universal grammar.[35] That the theory involves so much classifying and subdividing depends upon the fact that it appears in the context of a work on propositions, and that it follows the *Categories*, where Aristotle sets out the ten things that can be predicated of any subject. Aristotle's world-view is, in Padley's words, one 'which sees objects as consisting of matter (*substance*) and whatever it is that gives each object its particular form (*accident*)' (243). The parallel in language theory is the view that the noun is primary, and predication consists of things that can be said about the noun. Even the verb seems to be, in Aristotle's view (as James McKusick argues, 35) a special class of noun. Thus language, with its predications and parts (all of them depending on the noun), is a reflection of the world outside us, a world made up of things that have classifiable qualities. Berkeley undermines all this categorizing and, as Stephen Land remarks, had he constructed a full language theory, 'he would unquestionably have produced the first significantly non-Aristotelian grammar in the Western world.'[36] Neither Hallam nor Tennyson develops the full syntactic implications of Berkeley's epistemology, but we can see that both are moving away from the Aristotelian ordering of experience – measuring ideas 'by their logical relations'[37] is Hallam's way of putting it – and allowing for relations that are non-logical, emotional, and experiential. Though the poet of sensation must necessarily use English syntax, where words are arranged sequentially, and where one's experience of them – one's initial experience, at least – is linear, his aim is to juxtapose sensations in such a way that they evoke in us a configuration or multi-dimensional pattern held together by association or (to use one of Berkeley's favourite words) suggestion. Tennyson does not simply juxtapose words, but he does juxtapose syntactical units – think of the opening lines of 'Mariana,' for instance – and does not provide any logical or necessary links between them. It is the reader who must bridge the gaps.

In his review, which is in effect a lesson in how to read a grammar that is more Berkelean than Aristotelian, Hallam deals with the question of how the reader, whose initial experience of the poem must be linear and sequential, can recreate in himself the configuration of sensations, especially when the senses of the poets of sensation 'told them a richer and ampler tale than most men could understand, and who constantly expressed, because they constantly felt, sentiments of exquisite pleasure or pain, which most men were not permitted to experience.' Association, however, is common to all: 'Every bosom contains the elements of those complex emotions which the artist feels, and every head can, to a certain extent, go over in itself the process of their combination, so as to understand his expressions and sympathize with his state.' 'Elements,' 'process of their combination' – the diction is Hartley's, and Hallam is describing an experience that is sequential or (to use Hartley's adjective) 'successive.' His next sentence but one, however, indicates that the 'process of their combination' takes place within a context. The reader must begin with that context – Hallam calls it a 'leading sentiment' – if he would recreate the configuration:

For since the emotions of the poet, during composition, follow a regular law of association, it follows that to accompany their progress up to the harmonious prospect of the whole, and to perceive the proper dependence of every step on that which preceded, it is absolutely necessary *to start from the same point*, i.e. clearly to apprehend that leading sentiment of the poet's mind, by their conformity to which the host of suggestions are arranged.[38]

'Suggestions' is Berkeley's word, and one notices how Hallam combines sequence ('the proper dependence of every step on that which preceded') and configuration ('host of suggestions') in this single sentence. The technique by which the 'leading sentiment' is established is repetition.

Repetition guides the reader in recognizing those relations in the poem that shape all aspects of it into a complex pattern. One of the oldest techniques in poetry, repetition also plays a crucial role in the psychology of association. If sensations are to '*get such a Power*' of evoking a particular configuration in us, they must, as Hartley says in his central proposition – I have already quoted it in its entirety – be associated with one another '*a sufficient Number of Times.*' Berkeley refers obliquely to repetition in his recurring adjectives 'familiar' and 'habitual.' The poet of sensation, whose aim is to avoid a logical ordering, also provides the repetitions which characterize our sensory experience. We note that the three poems Hallam considers in some detail in his review – 'Recollections of the Arabian Nights,' 'The Ballad of Oriana,' and 'Adeline' – all make use of repetition, and that the repeated words and units are so obvious that Tennyson's use of the technique sometimes seems heavy-handed. Nonetheless, in Hallam's account of the movement of 'Recollections of the Arabian Nights' we can begin to see a paradigm for the reader's initial (and sequential) experience of the poem of sensation.

'The first stanza,' he writes, 'places us at once in the position of feeling, which the poem requires.' This feeling is the 'happy ductility of childhood,' and to this feeling all the images are related: 'The scene is before us, around us; we cannot mistake its localities, or blind ourselves to its colours.' The images in each stanza have no necessary or logical connection with each other. In associationist terms, they are related by contiguity in space, with the 'I' (the speaker) noting each sensation as he moves downstream and then enters 'the great / Pavilion of the Caliphat.' Hallam praises Tennyson's images for their 'exquisite accuracy and elaborate splendour,' but points out that we are never allowed to forget the shape of the whole, the refrain being the chief reminder. 'Amidst all the varied luxuriance of the sensations described, we are never permitted to lose sight of the idea which gives unity to this variety, and by the recurrence of which, as a sort of mysterious influence, at the close of every stanza, the mind is wrought up, with consummate art, to the final disclosure.'[39] This 'final disclosure' is the words, 'the golden prime / Of good Haroun Alraschid,' and the diction of romance confirms the poem's dominant feeling, the 'happy ductility of childhood.'

The same techniques are apparent in 'Mariana.' The epigraph from *Measure for Measure* establishes the context and the leading sentiments the reader expects to find. The reader knows immediately Mariana's type – the abandoned woman – and guesses her sorrow, disappointment, and frustration. 'Alfred's Mariana grew up,' Hallam told the poet's sister, Emily, 'by assimilative force, out of the plaintive hint left two centuries ago by Shakespeare,'[40] and this hint is the first guide to the reader. The images – 'blackest moss,' 'rusted nails,' 'broken sheds' – have only a contiguous relationship, and their effectiveness depends upon a use of language that approximates Berkeley's theory of vision – approximates it because these nouns are already, in Berkeley's view, 'collections of ideas,' and represent judgments the mind makes about the sensations of the eye. It would be possible for the poet to provide only colours, lights, and shades, and leave the reader to collect these 'ideas' into a single substantive – the result would be a riddle poem like Emily Dickinson's 'A Route of Evanescence,' where the 'ideas' of 'Emerald,' 'Cochineal,' and 'a revolving Wheel' give us the visual experience of a hummingbird – but the technique involves too much periphrasis for Tennyson's purposes in 'Mariana.' Instead, he provides the effect of an innocent eye by using common nouns which seem, in our ordinary experience, to be as neutral and suggestive as Berkeley's lights and colours. We are not aware that we are judging our visual experience when we respond to it with nouns like 'moss' and 'nails'; we think only that, through long use and custom, those words are linked with those objects. The propositions about these objects are juxtaposed, and fall into a configuration around Mariana's repeated statement, 'He cometh not.' The refrain is the chief guide to the response of the reader, who gradually recognizes that the images are presences that are a substitute for 'his' absence, and that they are held together by the emotions evoked by that absence. Like the Ancient Mariner, Mariana seems condemned to tell again and again the experience that has trapped her in a state between life and death, and her compulsive use of 'dreary' and 'aweary' in association with 'He cometh not' is the sign of her obsession. These repeated words gain their full force only through the images. 'Dreary' and 'aweary' may evoke some feeling in us, but they are not nearly so effective as (what Hartley calls) 'the usual associated Circumstances.' 'Words denoting the Passions do not,' Hartley points out, 'for the most part, raise up in us any Degree of the Passions themselves, but only the Ideas of the associated Circumstances.' The child may learn words like 'Love, Hatred, Hope, Fear, Anger, &c.,' Hartley says, and these words may indeed have some power of 'raising the Miniatures or Ideas of these Passions,' but 'the Power of associated Circumstances to raise the Passions' is of greater importance (1:275–6).

Repetition makes possible the effect of the final stanza where, after so much compulsive reiteration, the changes in the refrain are striking:

> Then, said she, 'I am very dreary,
>   He will not come,' she said;
> She wept, 'I am aweary, aweary,
>   Oh God, that I were dead!'

The shift in adverbs from 'only' to 'then' suggests progression rather than hopeless repetition, and even the reversal of 'she said' to 'said she' perhaps indicates a change. More important is the shift in the two central statements. 'He cometh not' is now 'He will not come,' and the shift in tenses indicates a shift from repeated disappointment to the recognition of a permanent state. Mariana's response also changes, from 'My life is dreary' to 'I am very dreary,' and we begin to feel that she is now locating her feelings, not in something vaguely external ('My life') but in herself. She is, perhaps, taking control of all the associations which, up to this point, have seemed to render her helpless. Her weeping may be only a repetition of the tears that 'fell with the dews at even' and again 'ere the dews were dried,' but they may also be a release, the first stage in her recovery.

The effectiveness of the language of 'Mariana' thus depends upon two assumptions the reader must share with the poet: first, that our sensations or 'ideas' (Berkeley's word) are real and true, whether we define their truth as a picture of a world outside us – an image – or as movements and passions within the soul; secondly, that these sensations or 'ideas' are a natural language, a language established by association, which makes sensations signs of other sensations and of emotions. Of this natural but non-verbal language our ordinary language can be a representation if the poet arranges his images, not in terms of their logical relations, but in terms of our actual sensuous experience, which is characterized by juxtaposition and by the repetitions that gradually establish links and form our sensations into configurations. Hallam reported in a letter that Fanny Kemble, the actress whom he admired, had said of Tennyson, 'he is the greatest painter in poetry that I know,'[41] and perhaps she said this because she recognized that Tennyson had so thoroughly mastered the techniques of rendering in language the experience of the eye.

# Chapter Three

# 'I hear a voice'

The poetry of sensation appeals to the ear as strongly as it does to the eye, and the source of this appeal is in the experience and nature of the poets themselves: 'their fine organs trembled into emotion' at sounds as well as colours and movements, their feelings of music were 'full and deep,' and they themselves were 'full of deep and varied melodies.'[1] Hallam's words suggest the conventional analogy between poetry and music, poetry being articulate sound, while music expresses what words cannot. The analogy narrows this difference, and we must define the ways in which Hallam is drawing together the two arts. Our starting point is language as articulate sound.

In Locke's language theory, articulate sounds serve a purely utilitarian purpose. They are *'Signs of internal Conceptions,'* of ideas within the mind, 'whereby they might be made known to others, and the Thoughts of Men's Minds be conveyed from one to another' (3.1.2). Articulate sounds are attached to ideas, 'not by any natural connexion ... but by a voluntary Imposition, whereby such a Word is made arbitrarily the Mark of such an *Idea*' (3.2.1). Association – which A.S.P. Woodhouse long ago called the 'master principle' of empiricism[2] – strengthens the link between sound and idea: *'there comes by constant use, to be such a Connexion between certain Sounds, and the* Ideas *they stand for, that the Names heard, almost as readily excite certain Ideas, as if the Objects themselves, which are apt to produce them, did actually affect the Senses'* (3.2.6). Locke does not use the word 'association' in this passage, nor does he approve of the substitution of sounds for objects, but he does recognize the power of articulate sounds, the power arising from repeated use and experience of them. Nonetheless, there is no natural connection between sound and idea.

The object that we call a tree may just as readily be called *arbre* or *Baum*, the connection resting upon custom, use, and (to appropriate Locke's words from a different context) 'tacit Consent' (3.2.8).

The aesthetics of the eighteenth century qualify in major ways Locke's insistence on the arbitrary connection of sound and idea. The effect of these theories is to make the connection less arbitrary and more natural, the foundation of this shift being the argument, advanced in various ways and in various contexts, that sound in language, especially in poetic language, is expressive rather than imitative. Expression and imitation are the two poles of eighteenth-century aesthetics, and the gradual emergence of expression as the dominant Romantic theory, in poetry as well as music, is James Anderson Winn's subject in that part of his history of the relations between the two arts, *Unsuspected Eloquence* (1981), that deals with the late eighteenth and early nineteenth centuries. English writers, more conservative than their continental counterparts, clung to imitative theories (however understood), but were more and more interested in the affective power of music, and thought that poetry ought to be more like music, looser, more fluid, 'more sensuous, more affective, more "organic" in its form' (although, as Winn shows, these adjectives embody myths about music, 'not the developments actually taking place in the work of Haydn and Mozart').[3]

A typical treatment of this shift from the imitative to the affective is in James Beattie's 'On Poetry and Music, as they affect the Mind' (written in 1762 but not published until 1776). He poses the question 'Is Music an Imitative Art?' and argues that it is not: 'Sounds in themselves can imitate nothing directly but sounds, nor in their motions any thing but motions.'[4] And while it is possible to echo the sounds in nature, 'the natural sounds and motions that music is allowed to imitate, are but few' (443). The merit of such music is 'inconsiderable' (448), since 'Pathos, or Expression, is the chief excellence of music' (461). Beattie had earlier in the essay argued that 'all true poetry' is 'addressed to the heart, and intended to give pleasure by raising or soothing the passions' (384); the affective power of poetry depends upon the poet's sensibility – it must 'engage him warmly in his subject' (388) – and on the strength and sincerity of his own feelings. Like many other critics, Beattie quotes with approval the Horatian dictum, 'If you would have me weep, you must first weep yourself' (388), and this dictum is the basis for his theory of expression. 'The foundation of all true music,' he argues, 'and the most perfect of all musical instruments, is the human voice' (443). 'The end of all genuine music is, to introduce into the human mind certain affections, or susceptibilities of affection' (443), and for this purpose the human voice is especially suited. 'Different passions and sentiments ... give different tones and accents' to it (450), and these tones and accents, like looks and gestures, are a natural language, the sounds being the audible signs of the feelings, and as true as the image is in the language of sight: 'so strict is the union between the passion and its outward sign,' Beattie argues, 'that, where the former is not in some degree felt, the latter can never be perfectly natural' (476). 'The *language of Poetry* must be an imitation of the *language of Nature*,' which is usually understood as 'those tones of the human voice, attitudes of the body, and configurations of the features, which, being *naturally* expressive of certain emotions of the soul, are universal among mankind, and every where understood' (499), but which Beattie (anticipating the Victorian fondness for a persona separate from the poet) redefines as 'that use of speech, or of *artificial language,* which is suitable to the speaker and to the occasion' (500) – suitable, that is, not only to the 'outward circumstances,' but also to 'the internal temperature of the *understanding* and *passions*' (505):

Certain vocal tones accompany certain mental emotions. The voice of sorrow is feeble and broken, that of despair boisterous and incoherent; joy assumes a sweet and sprightly note, fear a weak and tremulous cadence; the tones of love and benevolence are musical and uniform, those of rage loud and dissonant; the voice of the sedate reasoner is equable and grave, but not unpleasant; and he who declaims with energy employs many varieties of modulation suited to the various emotions that predominate in his discourse. (568–9)

Though such tones are ways of saying the unsayable, Beattie argues for the value of combining the sign of a feeling – the tone or sound itself – with the sign of an idea – the articulated word. 'The expression of music without poetry is vague and ambiguous' (463), he says:

Without this auxiliary, a piece of the best music, heard for the first time, might be said to mean something, but we should not be able to say what. It might incline the heart to sensibility: but poetry, or language, would be necessary to improve that sensibility into a real emotion, by fixing the fancy upon some definite and affecting ideas. (465)

Words as signs of ideas are an artificial language; words as signs of feelings are a natural language, and the appeal of sound, rhythm, and cadence is not to the understanding but to the passions, the origin and (through sympathy) the end of these aural sensations.

Sir William Jones' 'Essay on The Arts, Commonly Called Imitative' parallels Beattie's essay in its concerns, and is perhaps closer to Tennyson. The six-volume edition of Jones' *Works*, published in 1799, was in Tennyson's father's library and, according to Hallam Tennyson, Jones was 'amongst the authors most read' by the Tennyson boys at home,[5] though they were likely more attracted to Jones' translations of Oriental love poetry than they were to his critical essays. (Arthur Hallam's easy reference to 'Ferdusi or Calidas' in his 1831 review indicates a widely shared interest in Oriental poetry.) Jones' purpose, in the essay with which we are concerned, is to take the common view of poetry and music as imitative arts and turn it around: 'their greatest effect is not produced by *imitation*, but by a very different principle; which must be sought for in the deepest recesses of the human mind.'[6] This principle is expression, and the origins of poetry give us the clue to it:

> It seems probable then that *poetry* was originally no more than a strong, and animated expression of the human passions, of *joy* and *grief*, *love* and *hate*, *admiration* and *anger*, sometimes pure and unmixed, sometimes variously modified and combined: for, if we observe the *voice* and *accents* of a person affected by any of the violent passions, we shall perceive something in them very nearly approaching to *cadence* and *measure*. (4:550)

From this beginning, Jones develops his definitions: 'we may define *original and native poetry* to be *the language of the violent passions, expressed in exact measure, with strong accents and significant words*; and *true musick* to be no more than *poetry, delivered in a succession of harmonious sounds, so disposed as to please the ear*' (4:555–6). 'Thus will each artist gain his end, not by *imitating* the words of nature, but by assuming her power, and causing the same effect upon the imagination, which her charms produce to the senses' (4:560). There is much of interest in Jones' essay (including his comments on sympathy and his assimilating of Burke), but for our purposes we must focus on the fact that Jones, like Beattie, hears in sounds, cadences, and measures the expression of the passions. Prosody may be an art, with its terms and techniques, but its origin is, as Jones says, 'in the deepest recesses of the human mind,' and our feelings and emotions are its life and energy.

Tennyson was, from the beginning, a skilful technician. When he was twelve, he was already instructing his aunt in the 'unusual' metre of the Chorus in *Samson Agonistes* ('the difficulty will vanish when I inform [the reader], that it is taken from the Greek'),[7] and later Hallam, projecting a translation of Dante's *Vita Nuova*, turned to Tennyson as an expert ('I expect to glean a good deal of knowledge from you concerning metres'),[8] since Tennyson was already known among his contemporaries for having 'uncommon power over varied metres and rare harmonies of sound and sense.'[9] Nonetheless, Hallam praised Tennyson in his 1831 review not primarily as a technician, but for his expressive power. Among Tennyson's 'five distinctive excellencies' he includes 'the variety of his lyrical measures, and exquisite modulation of harmonious words and cadences to the swell and fall of the feelings expressed.'[10] He makes the link between prosody and feelings more explicit later in the review, when he is discussing 'The Ballad of Oriana.' Its effect he compares to that of the songs of Dante and Petrarch, 'mighty masters' who

produce two-thirds of their effect by *sound*. Not that they sacrifice sense to sound, but that sound conveys their meaning where words would not. There are innumerable shades of fine emotion in the human heart, especially when the senses are keen and vigilant, which are too subtle and too rapid to admit of corresponding phrases. The understanding takes no definite note of them; how then can they leave signatures in language? Yet they exist; in plenitude of being and beauty they exist; and in music they find a medium through which they pass from heart to heart. The tone becomes the sign of the feeling; and they reciprocally suggest each other.[11]

Tones in poetry are like colours in painting, Hallam continues; both have a 'suggestive power.' Farrar would later, in *Language and Languages* (1878), reiterate the analogy between tones in music and colours in painting, and would indicate why tones make up a natural language: they are produced by the instinctive tightening or relaxing of the muscles of our vocal chords. The word 'tone,' he points out, is derived from the Greek τείνω 'because it depends on the greater or lesser tension by which it is produced.' [12] The etymology Farrar uses had been given in greater detail in Liddell and Scott's *A Greek-English Lexicon*. They identify the root as 'tan' or 'ten' (the former is the root in Sanskrit), and the words derived from it involve the action of stretching out or extending. ('Is not your very *Attention* a *Stretching-to*?' asks Carlyle's Teufelsdröckh when he is discussing words as matter-moulded.) Tones are thus the signs of feelings, not because the connection is an arbitrary and conventional one, but because our physical makeup produces sounds whose link with our feelings is natural and inevitable.

Hallam does not provide a technical analysis to expand upon his theory, but he does comment on the repetition of Oriana's name, and defends Tennyson from the charge that it 'occurs once too often in every stanza.' He argues that 'the proportion of the melodious cadences to the pathetic parts of the narration could not be diminished without materially affecting the rich lyrical impression of the ballad.'[13] The narrative – the story of a mistress accidentally killed by her lover's arrow, gone astray in battle – certainly has its pathos, but Hallam is more interested in the 'lyrical' aspects of the ballad, 'lyrical' meaning primarily the tones and cadences as expressive of human feelings. 'Melodious cadences' are his immediate concern, and cadences are the fall of the voice from the point of highest emphasis in a syntactical unit. The word is derived from the Latin verb *cadere*, to fall, and refers, strictly speaking, only to the dropping of the voice, but in practice the word refers to the whole rhythmical unit, with its swelling and falling, tensing and relaxing. Tennyson handles these units in the ballad with great skill and subtle variation. Each line with its refrain, 'Oriana,' makes up one unit, the pattern being lengthened in the fifth and sixth lines of each stanza, where two lines and the name make up the unit. The rhythm in the longer lines is (to use Hopkins' adjective) a rising rhythm, the dominant feet being iambs and anapests, while the name 'Oriana' is a double trochee, its falling rhythm simply repeated throughout the poem. The long lines with their rising rhythms suggest the keying up of the lover's emotions in all their complexity: the tense (and intense) loneliness of his restless and aimless wandering, his psychological entrapment in his present situation, his compulsive retelling of the story, and his fear of the future ('I dare not die and come to thee,' 96). In contrast to the long lines with their stressed 'not,' the falling rhythm of 'Oriana' suggests a letting go, a sudden release of pent-up emotion, if only for a moment, until the lover's will pushes him to go on again. The classical cadence with which Tennyson's cadence here has most in common is the *cursus velox*, the quick run which is marked by the rapid double trochee at the end, with its characteristically swift resolution of a more slowly paced unit.[14]

But the cadence is not the only 'signature in language' of the lover's emotions. The vowel sounds in the name 'Oriana' itself are also signs of feeling, and their suggestive power is perhaps most clearly described in the *Guesses at Truth* of Augustus and Julius Hare, read by Hallam in 1828, and recommended by him to Gladstone as 'well worth a perusal.'[15] Here is Julius Hare on the expressive nature of vowels and consonants:

But not only in the sense and spirit of words, are types to be detected; their outward form and sound are significant. To revisit the point whence we started, even the proportion between the vowels and consonants in a language will shew the relative influence of the feelings and of the understanding over the people who speak it. German grammarians have called consonants the objective, vowels the subjective element of language. As the end of human speech is two-fold, to utter feelings and to communicate thoughts, we may reasonably look to find the organs of speech adapted to this double purpose. And we do so find them. The vowels express what is felt: they come more immediately from that part of the body which is less under the dominion of the will: they make the whole melody of speech: the interjections in which our bursting emotions find vent, consist chiefly of vowels, repeated sometimes over and over again, and occasionally kept from running and melting into each other by some recurring consonant. Thus they resemble the notes of beasts and birds, which are mainly vocalic, with the admixture of a consonant or two ... In consonants on the other hand, fashioned as they are by those organs about the mouth over which we have a fuller and readier controul [sic], one beholds something like the operation of the formative principle on the raw material of language, the shaping and modifying and combining or syllabling action of the intellect.[16]

Vowels as the expression of the emotions, consonants as related to the will and understanding: this distinction became a commonplace – Farrar, for instance, repeats it in *Language and Languages* (74) – and it accounts for the different effects of the long lines and the refrain in Tennyson's ballad. The speaker's strongest emotions find expression in Oriana's name, its 'o's' and 'a's' contrasting with the often plosive consonants in the long lines. The ballad could be taken as a good example of the 'practical maxim' at which Hare arrives:

Inasmuch as vowels, like feelings, may be indefinitely prolonged, while consonants are yet more fleeting and momentary than thoughts; English poets who write for song, should study to introduce as many syllables as they can with full distinct sonorous vowels, especially in those places where the voice is meant to dwell. (2:214)

A parallel example is the refrain of 'Mariana.' Her emotions are most fully apparent in the long and sustained 'e' sounds in the repeated adjective 'aweary' and in its rhyme word 'dreary.' This vowel Tennyson plays off against the consonants of the statement, 'He cometh not,' and particularly of the wish, 'I would that I were dead!', the plosive 'd' ending the line with the same swift finality as that of the end Mariana longs for.

The affective power of Tennyson's own voice can be understood as depending upon this same playing off of vowels and consonants. Since Tennyson was in the habit of reading his poems aloud to his friends, there are plenty of ear-witness accounts of the experience; all of them give evidence of the voice's expressive power, and many of them suggest that that power depended upon the sustained sounds that came from the poet's inmost recesses, 'deep' being the favoured adjective to suggest this source. Edmund Lushington's description of 'the deep melodious thunder of his voice with all its overwhelming pathos'[17] is typical, not only because of the adjective, but also because of the analogy with a sound in nature (such sounds being popularly thought of as expressive and hence 'musical'). Also typical is Henry Taylor's phrase, 'deep-mouthed music,' in his 1864 poem, 'The Hero, the Poet, and the Girl,' the poet of the title being Tennyson.[18] William Allingham gives in his *Diary* several accounts of Tennyson's reading, and of Tennyson's criticizing others (and Allingham himself) for voicing lines inadequately – for not giving full length and weight, that is, to the vowel sounds. On an 1867 walk beyond Lyme Regis, Allingham, in a burst of enthusiasm at the beauty of the August landscape, quoted the line, 'Bowery hollows crowned with summer sea.' 'T. (as usual), "You don't say it properly" – and repeats it in his own sonorous manner, lingering with solemn sweetness on every vowel sound.'[19] Edward FitzGerald has left us the best-known description of Tennyson's reading aloud; he draws upon Tennyson's own account, in 'The Epic,' of the reciting of the 'Morte d'Arthur' by its fictional creator, Everard Hall: 'Mouthing out his hollow oes and aes, deep-chested music, this is something as A.T. reads ... His voice, very deep and deep-chested, but rather murmuring than mouthing, like the sound of a far sea or of a pine-wood.'[20] H.D. Rawnsley heard Tennyson read 'Ode on the Death of the Duke of Wellington' in 1884, and he, like FitzGerald, was struck by Tennyson's rendering of the vowel sounds. Rawnsley describes 'how he lengthened out the vowel *a* in the words "great" and "lamentation" till the words seemed as if they had been spelt "greaat" and "lamentaation," and how he rolled out and lengthened the open oes in the words "To the nooise of the moourning of a mighty naation.'"[21] Both FitzGerald and Rawnsley make the 'o' and the 'a' the prime examples of expressive sound, the effect of Tennyson's reading aloud depending on the playing off of these and other vowel sounds against the consonants. The vowels make a kind of drone sound – FitzGerald calls it 'murmuring' – which Tennyson interrupts with the consonants, produced in part by 'mouthing.' This combination made Tennyson's reading aloud seem more like a chant than like ordinary speech, the effect depending upon the sostenuto. Wilfrid Ward, Blanche Warre-Cornish, Sir Charles Stanford, and Arthur Coleridge all describe the poet's reading as a 'chant,' and Emily Ritchie uses the word 'incantation.'[22] 'Intoned' was a favourite word, too, among those who heard Tennyson read, and Aubrey de Vere's use of it is particularly interesting. When he first heard the 'Fragments of an Elegy' that were soon to be published as *In Memoriam*, he reported that 'the pathos and grandeur of these poems were to me greatly increased by the voice which rather intoned than recited them,'[23] and this playing off of intoning and reciting is another way of talking about 'murmuring' and 'mouthing.'

We can now begin to understand all that Edward FitzGerald means when he says, of 'The Ballad of Oriana,' that 'Tennyson used to repeat [it] in a way not to be forgotten at Cambridge tables.'[24] The lover chants his mistress' name, with its sustained 'o's' and 'a's,' and the chant is the expression of the strong feelings of grief, love, regret, and despair, feelings 'too subtle and too rapid,' as Hallam says, 'to admit of corresponding phrases.' Instead, the whole range of feelings is focused on the single word, and the tones with which that word may be pronounced are also many and varied, Tennyson's rendering of these tones accounting, I think, for the impression his reading made on his friends at Cambridge. On the printed page the word is unchanging; only in the voice do its varying affective powers become apparent. In his study of *The Printed Voice of Victorian Poetry* (1989), Eric Griffiths makes the point that print is potentiality, a 'permanent possibility' of various and often conflicting feelings which are realized in the voice. At any moment of saying, however, only one tone is possible, and while we may see in the writing that a word or line may be spoken in two ways, 'you cannot have them, vocally, both ways at once.'[25] For reading, like a musical performance, is a moving art – moving our feelings *and* moving through time – and so the repetitions of Oriana's name in the ballad are designed for a virtuoso reader, like Tennyson himself, a reader who knows how to use his voice to render the exact tone suggested by the longer lines and the varying contexts they provide for the name.

Hallam says, after quoting the entire ballad, that 'the last line' – it is the line 'I hear the roaring of the sea, / Oriana' – 'the last line, with its dreamy wildness, reveals the design of the whole.' He then goes on to analyse the 'abrupt application' of this line, borrowed from an old ballad, 'to the leading sentiment, so as to flash upon us in a few little words a world of meaning.'[26] His analysis is largely devoted to a theme ('the accordance of inanimate Nature' with the lover's passion), but the meaning is more than this idea. The lover's expression of powerful emotions through the repetition of Oriana's name is in fact evidence of the power of nature in him, and the 'roaring of the sea' is an exact parallel to the uttering of his emotions. The sound is the sign of nature's power, and the 'roaring' is a natural language no different, ultimately, from the vowel sounds which spring from the depths of the lover's heart. Moreover, the analogy with the sea had a special significance for Tennyson. ' "Somehow," he would say, "water is the element I love best of all the four." ' From his boyhood, he 'had a passion for the sea, and especially for the North Sea in wild weather – "The hollow ocean-ridges roaring into cataracts," '[27] and it was the sound of the sea as much as its appearance which stirred Tennyson's imagination. FitzGerald uses two similes to describe Tennyson's voice: 'like the sound of a far sea or of a pine-wood.'[28] The latter originated with Carlyle, to whom FitzGerald gave credit for it when recounting a discussion with him about whether or not Tennyson had an ear for music;[29] the former is apparently FitzGerald's own, but it must have originated in his knowing Tennyson's 'passion for the sea,' and his sense that, for Tennyson, the sound of the sea corresponded to his own expressive power. Oriana's lover, hearing 'the roaring of the sea,' also finds an analogy for the entire range of his emotions, and the 'world of meaning' that Hallam finds in these 'few little words' is the world of the passions, suggestively linked to the power of nature itself.

Sir William Jones, we remember, had said that an artist will gain his end, 'not by *imitating* the works of nature, but by assuming her power,' and we remember, too, that the correspondence between a power in man and a power in nature is Wordsworth's central theme. For Tennyson, that power is primarily an oral one. While Dwight Culler is surely right in his richly suggestive comment that 'it is not too much to say that language and poetry played for Tennyson the same role that nature played for Wordsworth,'[30] it is also clear that Tennyson apprehended nature aurally, and that he heard in nature a voice. Not articulate speech, at least initially, but expressive sounds which seemed like the raw material, or the basis, of language. The voices of wind, water, and birds turn up in the poetry and in the *Memoir* more frequently than any others, and the voice of the sea oftenest of all. The sea has an astonishing range of tones: it whispers, murmurs, moans, thunders, and roars. That the voices of nature were for Tennyson primarily expressive is clearest in his response to seeing and hearing a nightingale in moonlight: 'her voice vibrated with such passion that he wrote of "The leaves / That tremble round the nightingale" in "The Gardener's Daughter." '[31]

To affirm, as Tennyson does, that sea, wind, and birds all have a voice is to personify them, and the figure was thought of as being particularly suitable to the expression of passion. It was called 'personification,' but it was also called 'prosopopoeia,' and this sense of the term adds another dimension to Dwight Culler's treatment of it in his important essay, 'Monodrama and the Dramatic Monologue' (1975). Culler defines prosopopoeia 'or impersonation' as 'an ancient rhetorical form in which a person, historical or imaginary, is represented as actually speaking'; the making of such speeches was a standard schoolboy exercise 'well up into the nineteenth century.'[32] But to such 'impersonation' we must add the account of the figure given by Hugh Blair in his *Lectures on Rhetoric and Belles Lettres* (1783: a copy of the eighth edition of 1801 was in Tennyson's father's library at Somersby). Blair was one of the group of critics from 1750 through the 1780s that James Engell has called the 'New Rhetoricians' because they focused less on formal definitions and divisions of figures and more on the power of language, particularly its affective power and its place in human psychology. In this context, Engell says, 'Art ceases simply to imitate or describe nature and begins instead to imitate our experience of nature.'[33] Blair focuses on the animating of inanimate objects, the first degree being 'when some of the properties or qualities of living creatures are ascribed to inanimate objects; the second, when those inanimate objects are introduced as acting like such as have life; and the third, when they are represented, either as speaking to us, or as listening to what we say to them.'[34] Blair's account of prosopopoeia is close to Tennyson's practice of attributing to nature a voice and, moreover, prosopopoeia was considered one of the most passionate of the rhetorical figures. Beattie makes this point in his essay 'On Poetry and Music, as they affect the Mind,' and Blair makes it too in his lecture on the 'Origin and Nature of Figurative Language.' Such language 'always imports some colouring of the imagination, or some emotion of passion' (1:347), and prosopopoeia is an especially forceful figure. Its foundation lies 'deep in human nature' (1:407), and 'on innumerable occasions, it is the very language of imagination and passion, and, therefore, deserves to be attended to, and examined with peculiar care' (1:410). Hence Blair (who can be seen as moving toward the view of Paul de Man, in our own time, that prosopopoeia is the master trope of poetic discourse) devotes a large part of one lecture to this figure. Its three 'degrees,' which he describes, are all to be found in that unusually passionate lyric, 'Come into the garden, Maud,' where Tennyson exploits the full range of prosopopoeia, and in particular its third 'degree.' Early on in this version of a pastoral invitation, the flowers are represented as listening while the lover speaks; in one of the two climactic stanzas, the flowers themselves speak. The conjunction of figure and voice is the strongest possible expression of passion, and to this conjunction Tennyson added his own reading voice. Of all his poems, *Maud* was his favourite for reading aloud, and no one who has heard the Steytler recording can doubt either the power or the pathos of Tennyson's performance. [35]

But to insist upon prosopopoeia as a figure particularly suited to the expression of passion is not to account fully for Tennyson's response to nature. After all, the figure involves the attributing to nature of feelings not its own, and for this reason Ruskin attacked the figure (whether one calls it prosopopoeia or personification or animism) as a distortion or delusion caused by the emotions of the viewer, a pathetic fallacy. The attack is in the third volume (1856) of *Modern Painters*, and Ruskin quotes the second-last stanza of 'Come into the garden, Maud' (where the flowers speak) as one of his examples. Tennyson was aware of this chapter and discussed it with Locker-Lampson in 1869, defending a line from Wordsworth, but saying that a line from Alexander Smith 'went too far.' 'He said the same of Kingsley,' Locker-Lampson writes, 'that "the cruel, crawling wave" was too much like a live creature.' [36] The line – it is 'The cruel, crawling foam' (not 'wave') from *Alton Locke* – is one Ruskin comments on, but Tennyson's agreement with Ruskin's assessment indicates only the need for judgment on the part of the poet when he is using this figure since, as J. Hillis Miller has shown, Ruskin hides 'the fact that ordinary language is full of unavoidable catachreses and prosopopoeias which are facts of nomenclature, not the result of false perception or uncontrolled feeling.'[37] Unspoken by Tennyson is another aspect of the figure entirely, and that is that, in his view, the voice is not attributed to nature by an act of displacement on the part of a human being, but is actually to be heard in nature. Attribution suggests that there is an absence or gap in nature that may be filled by human consciousness; if nature truly has a voice, the human listener must still make sense of what he hears, but nonetheless the articulated words are not entirely the invention of the poet. Nature really does have a voice, and the listening poet responds to it by making it intelligible, or at least by suggesting that its power may ultimately be intelligible.

Looking back on his childhood from 1890, Tennyson recalled that 'before I could read, I was in the habit on a stormy day of spreading my arms to the wind, and crying out "I hear a voice that's speaking in the wind."'[38] His memory coincides with the earliest stanza of his poetry that we have, written when he was about eight. In it, nature 'whispers' rather than 'speaks':

> Whateer I see, whereer I move
> These whispers rise & fall away;
> Something of pain, of loss, of love,
> But what, twere hard to say.[39]

This stanza Tennyson incorporated in a poem called 'Whispers,' dated 1833 but not published until his son included it in the *Memoir*. Here is the whole poem, including the last four lines as printed by Ricks from two manuscript sources:

> 'Tis not alone the warbling woods,
>> The starred abysses of the sky,
> The silent hills, the stormy floods,
>> The green that fills the eye –
> These only do not move the breast;
>> Like some wise artist, Nature gives,
>> Through all her works, to each that lives
> A hint of somewhat unexprest.
>
> Whate'er I see, where'er I move,
>> These whispers rise, and fall away,

Something of pain – of bliss – of Love,
  But what, were hard to say.
I could not tell it: if I could
  Yet every form of mind is made
  To vary in some light or shade
So were my tale misunderstood.

One notes that the whispers of nature are, Tennyson assumes, expressions of feelings that are also human feelings; that these whispers are
a natural language; that it is the task of the poet to make articulate
these primal sounds, to 'say' what it is he hears in nature. Lying
behind these assumptions is the commonplace that nature is, like the
Bible, the book of God, or that nature is the language of God which
one has to learn to read or speak. The idea that nature is the language
of God was an important one for Coleridge. In *Coleridge's Philosophy of
Language*, James McKusick has shown how the divine language topos
underwent changes in Coleridge's thinking as he responded to Plato,
Hartley, and Berkeley, but the topos remained, and McKusick defines,
on the basis of passages from the poetry, the relation between human
language and the divine language: 'Coleridge does not, like Berkeley,
regard human language as a paradigm to which divine language must
conform; instead, he regards divine language as an ideal toward which
human language should aspire.'[40] With Tennyson, the pattern is more
like that of a partnership. The primal sounds of nature (of which we
are a part) and the articulate sounds of human speech – one heard, the
other said – combine to make the speech that shapes the ongoing
experience of our lives.

The poet's 'saying' of these inarticulate natural sounds is, one notes,
full of difficulties. In the earliest four-line stanza, the task is 'hard,'
perhaps impossible. In the 1833 'Whispers,' the task is still impossible
('I could not tell it'), but the conditional clause that follows suggests
otherwise ('if I could') and presents a new difficulty: 'every form of
mind is made / To vary in some light or shade.' The differences in
individual minds mean an inevitable failure to understand the poet's
'saying,' and so the poet is engaged in a double struggle: to make
articulate the sounds of nature, and to persuade others of the truth
(both intellectual and emotional) of his 'tale.' The poet's voice (and
'voice' is a key word in Tennyson's poetry) is thus typically agonistic.
Tennyson nearly always locates it in the context of an ongoing struggle

and, as he begins to articulate the sounds of nature, the conflict begins to take shape.

The conflict may take the form of a debate, as it does in two poems that are dated 1822, 'Youth' (not published until it appeared in the *Memoir*) and 'The Two Voices' (published in 1842 but at least partly written before Hallam's death). In the former, the debate is suggested in the poet's articulating the sounds of nature. At first, nature, though speaking with various voices, is univocal. The lines are conventional (and for this reason, likely, Tennyson was reluctant to publish them):

> I heard Spring laugh in hidden rills,
>     Summer through all her sleepy leaves
> Murmured: a voice ran round the hills
>     When corny Lammas browned the sheaves ...          (13–16)

'When I was somewhat older grown,' the speaker affirms, 'These voices did not cease to cry' (21–2), but they eventually become voices of a past that is irretrievable:

> So lived I without aim or choice,
>     Still humming snatches of old song,
> Till suddenly a sharper voice
>     Cried in the future 'Come along.'          (37–40)

With the voice of the future crying 'Come along' and the voices of the past mourning 'Come back, come back,' we sense the beginning of a struggle for the speaker himself, and perhaps the beginning, as well, of a debate between the voices, now equivocal in character. The speaker has a sense of ultimate truth lying behind these conflicting voices, but that truth is unknowable, and he can only continue to struggle to make sense of his actual aural experience. The immensely complex character of nature's language is summed up in a remarkable stanza, incomplete syntactically, and consisting of five nouns that are all, apparently, in apposition to 'voice':

> A rumour of a mystery,
>     A noise of winds that meet and blend,
> An energy, an agony,
>     A labour working to an end.          (57–60)

The nouns sum up the character of an oral existence: the 'voice' presents not final truth but hearsay, final truth remaining a 'mystery' that one can approach inadequately through common talk or opinion; the 'voice' is a 'noise' – Tennyson must have been aware of the Latin *rumor*, and in these two lines is presenting a little lesson in etymology – but the noise is linked with a conventional image for spirit; the 'voice' is a moving force or 'energy' that results in conflict, suffering, and struggle, but the rhyme words ('blend' and 'end') indicate a single purpose or pattern behind all this diversity. Tennyson incorporated line 60 in 'The Two Voices' – it is line 297 there – and in that poem the debate, so brief and conventional in 'Youth,' is developed at length. The voices are no longer explicitly of nature, but they are certainly about nature. Though each claims that the other cannot know or prove the truth of its statements, neither can prove its own arguments, and so there is no discovery of a final truth, and no resolution except in the situation, inevitably open-ended, in which the speaker actually is: the dawn, and the church-going scene. Voices that are associated with struggle, that locate the hearer (and debater) in a situation for which there is no final resolution, that seem to be the defining characteristic of our actual experience of life (as opposed to any abstracting or systematizing of our experience) – these are some of the things Walter Ong in our own age calls the 'psychodynamics of orality.'[41]

The more one examines not only the poetry but the biography, the more it becomes arguable that the oral seemed more natural for Tennyson than the written. His usual method of composition grew out of his boyhood practice, recounted to Locker-Lampson, who in turn repeated it to Hallam Tennyson: 'He would rove through the fields composing hundreds of couplets, and shouting them to the skies.'[42] Tennyson continued to compose on his walks or in his study, repeating the lines to himself, while the actual recording of them in writing was a secondary matter. 'My father was always careless about his manuscripts,'[43] his son says in retelling the story of Tennyson's leaving in lodgings the 'butcher-ledger-like book' that contained *In Memoriam*, and the carelessness stemmed in part from the oral nature of his poetry. 'He would murmur his new passages or new lines as they came to him, a habit which had always been his since boyhood, and which caused the Somersby cook to say "What is master Awlfred always a praying for."'[44] Friends and acquaintances bear witness to Tennyson's facility in oral composition, and the repetitions and the volubility are characteristics Ong associates with an oral culture.[45] The repetitions included alliteration: 'when I spout my lines first,' Tennyson told his son, 'they come out so alliteratively that I have sometimes no end of trouble to get rid of the alliteration.'[46] The volubility was a lifelong characteristic. At Cambridge 'he would improvise verses by the score full of lyrical passion.' He made 'To the Vicar of Shiplake' while he was driving away from the village where he was married, and in Scotland in 1853, he went out walking and, his hostess recalled, 'All the way going home he was making the most absurd nonsense-ballad-verses, generally in Scotch.'[47] James Knowles has left us the most detailed account of Tennyson's oral methods of composition: the saying aloud of passages he had made with 'the characteristic profuseness of genius,' the repeating of them 'but seldom twice in the same words,' the refining of the passages, and finally 'the mechanical toil of writing them down' – though thousands never were written down, and disappeared 'up the chimney.'[48] In 'Will Waterproof's Lyrical Monologue' (1842), the speaker, a thin disguise for the poet himself, asks his Muse

> To make me write my random rhymes,
>     Ere they be half-forgotten;
> Nor add and alter, many times,
>     Till all be ripe and rotten.          (13–16)

In spite of Tennyson's care with the printed word – his liking for trial editions of his poems (because 'poetry looks better, more convincing, in print') and his dislike of variant readings ('the chips of the work-shop')[49] – the oral nature of poetry was for him primary, and shaped his work far more than the letters on the page. Sound, in his view, evoked a sympathetic response, while print distanced his audience. In an 1839 letter to his future wife, Tennyson complained that 'In *letters*, words too often prove a bar of hindrance instead of a bond of union.'[50] He was in the habit of reading texts aloud, not only his own poems and the poems of others, but an astonishing range of works of fiction, science, and history. The *Memoir* is full of statements that 'he read aloud,' 'he read to us,' 'he read poetry to us,' 'A. read me some Lucretius,' 'he read aloud *Tom Brown's Schooldays* to my mother,' he 'translated aloud three Idylls of Theocritus,' 'my father would translate the *Odyssey* aloud into Biblical prose,' he 'repeated ballads to us,' and so on.[51] Instinctively he seemed to feel that the text came alive only when it was spoken.

Voice, then, is central to Tennyson's understanding of language. The varied tones of the human voice are the expression of passions and emotions, which are natural to us, and which link us with nature, which also has a voice. The task of the poet is to take the power he shares with nature and articulate it. Onomatopoeia (like 'the sparrow's chirrup' and 'the wooing wind' in 'Mariana') is a small and inconsiderable part of this task, since it involves only imitation: an echoing that is parallel to mirroring for the eye. Much more difficult is the shaping involved in articulating or 'saying' the meaning of the sounds of nature, a mysterious and ultimately divine language imperfectly apprehended by us. ('We have five senses,' Tennyson told Locker-Lampson in 1869, 'but ... if we had been born with only one of these, our ideas of Nature would have been very different, much more limited' – and if we had been born with five hundred, we would be creatures 'in advance of anything we could conceive of!')[52] The 'saying' involves the participating of our minds with nature, but human speaking will never fully manifest the 'something' that its sounds signify. Hence, all 'saying' is partial, inconsistent, and fragmentary. It involves a struggle toward ultimate truth and a struggle with limited and conflicting truths, and both struggles, in our actual experience, are open-ended and unresolvable. The important thing, as we shall see with In Memoriam and Idylls of the King, is to keep speaking.

# Chapter Four

# 'At the sound of my name'

'There are two different conceptions of language to be found in Tennyson's work and indeed throughout the nineteenth century,' Dwight Culler writes in the first chapter of his book on Tennyson's poetry:

> On the one hand, there was the view that words were the poor husks of reality, abstract denotative counters which were the product of the understanding generalizing upon sense experience. Such words corresponded to classes of objects in the phenomenal world but to nothing more. On the other hand, there was still alive something of the older conception of language as a magical instrument, a means of incantation or ritual, which gave one power over reality or revealed its true nature. By this view words were proper names, containing the ontological secret of a thing.[1]

This second view of language is my concern in this chapter, and it is a concern that is never entirely absent from Tennyson's work. The dominant view in his thinking is the Germano-Coleridgian one that Tennyson learned through the Apostles, and through the reaction against Locke by Whewell, Maurice, and others, and this view differs from both the empiricist concept of language as conventional and arbitrary and the older concept of language as magic. In the empiricist view, language is essentially metaphor, since this figure best defines the relation between words and things: it is the identifying of unlike things, a fiction made by the mind but without any foundation in things themselves. The opposite view is language as synecdoche. This figure presents us with words that participate in the essential being of the things they name, so that to know the name of something is to possess it or to have power over it.

These two concepts of language are as old as Plato's *Cratylus*. In that dialogue, Socrates presides over a discussion with Hermogenes, who argues that names are conventional and arbitrary, and Cratylus, who argues that names are natural and inevitable. Neither position is finally tenable. As Coleridge was fond of saying, 'Extremes meet,' and both Hermogenes and Cratylus ultimately make impossible the distinction between truth and falsehood; for both, words are true, and cannot be false – a result to which Jowett draws attention in the introduction to his translation of the dialogue.[2] Nonetheless, Cratylus' view has continued to have its attraction, especially for poets who have some sense of being in the line of Orpheus and Amphion.

When the Devil appears at Magus' bidding in *The Devil and the Lady*, that extraordinary play Tennyson wrote when he was fourteen, 'I come oh I come,' he says to Magus, 'at the sound of my name' (1.1.41 – speak of the Devil!). While other nouns may be generalizations or abstractions and represent classes of things, proper names for Tennyson are at least potentially different, and may participate in the essential being of the persons they name. This sense of the ontological oneness of name and person is bound up, in Tennyson's thinking, with the mystery of individual identity, which he calls in 'De Profundis' 'this main-miracle' (55) – 'that thou art thou,' he says, addressing his newborn son, 'With power on thine own act and on the world' (55–6). But his metaphysical speculations were not nearly so convincing as his own experience, and the kind of experience he could induce by repeating his own name was a particularly powerful one. There are two descriptions of it in the *Memoir*, one written for his son, Hallam, the other recounted by John Tyndall. Here is the first:

'A kind of waking trance I have frequently had, quite up from boyhood, when I have been all alone. This has generally come upon me thro' repeating my own name two or three times to myself silently, till all at once, as it were out of the intensity of the consciousness of individuality, the individuality itself seemed to dissolve and fade away into boundless being, and this not a confused state, but the clearest of the clearest, the surest of the surest, the weirdest of the weirdest, utterly beyond words, where death was an almost laughable impossibility, the loss of personality (if so it were) seeming no extinction but the only true life.' 'This might,' he said, 'be the state which St.

Paul describes, "Whether in the body I cannot tell, or whether out of the body I cannot tell." '3

It is clear from this account that Tennyson's own name is, in his experience, more than just a sound that refers, by use and convention, to him as an individual. It is, rather, the symbol of his uniqueness. Tennyson has in effect done what Coleridge recommends in the preface to *Aids to Reflection* ('accustom yourself to reflect on the words you use, hear, or read, their birth, derivation and history') and this approach to his own name is the art of reflection, the method that Coleridge is teaching. (The method is evident in Tennyson's simile in 'Lancelot and Elaine': 'As when we dwell upon a word we know, / Repeating, till the word we know so well / Becomes a wonder, and we know not why,' 1020-2.) The end of this art is knowledge of the self, 'and by reflection alone can it be obtained,' says Coleridge. 'It is every man's interest and duty to acquire' self-knowledge, 'or to what end was man alone, of all animals, endued by the Creator with the faculty of *self-consciousness*?'4 Self-consciousness is closely related to reflection (we remember that Locke defines reflection as 'that notice which the Mind takes of its own Operations,' 2.1.4), for reflection is literally a turning back or bending back again, a second time (the first turning back or bending back is the act of the mind in shaping sensations), and hence is the mind's awareness of its own acts. Such self-reflexiveness is the mark of the transcendental man; he not only lives by the powers of his mind, but watches himself so living; he is both in this life and above it, and his transcendence allows him to see that the shapes he brings to phenomena must have existed prior to his experience, to make his experience possible – 'just as (to use a frequent illustration of Coleridge's) we see, before we know that we have eyes; but when once this is known to us, we perceive that eyes must have pre-existed to enable us to see.'5 Tennyson's reflection on his name thus reveals to him his own essential being, and the name is (to use Coleridge's terms) not a 'thing' but a 'living power.' But Tennyson goes beyond epistemology to ontology, and affirms that the name participates in the essence of his being, which is one with 'boundless being.' What that essence is he 'cannot tell': is it in the body? Is it out of the body? Is it some mysterious fusion? 'I cannot tell,' for that being is 'utterly beyond words,' and can be suggested only by antithesis and paradox.

St Paul's statement which Tennyson quotes is antithetical. Tennyson's own words are not obviously paradoxical, but they become so on closer examination. 'Utterly beyond words,' for instance. The ordinary meaning of 'utter' is 'to speak' or 'to give expression to,' and it is the verb most appropriate to the expressive theory of language, since it is related etymologically to 'outer' – a relationship Mill uses in his 1833 essay, 'What is Poetry?', read by Hallam in the *Monthly Repository* and noted by him as 'a good essay on the nature of poetry.'[6] Yet paradoxically this 'outering' leads 'beyond' itself; words only manifest the inadequacy of words, and undermine or destroy themselves. Words perplex, and yet, Tennyson insists, this is 'not a confused state.' Also paradoxical is the way in which Tennyson induces this state. He speaks his name, and the speaking is evidence of his sense of the power of (to use Ong's noun) orality. We note, however, the precise way in which Tennyson defines this speaking: 'repeating ... silently.' Sound and silence are fused in a paradox like that of the 'silent-speaking words' of section xcv of *In Memoriam*: successful speech annihilates itself in silence. The silence, we should add, is not an absence but rather a presence that cannot be expressed, because it can be (as an essence) nothing other than itself. 'Speech is of Time, Silence is of Eternity,' says Carlyle's Teufelsdröckh, but he immediately proceeds to close the gap between the two with his doctrine of symbols: 'In a Symbol there is concealment and yet revelation: here therefore, by Silence and by Speech acting together, comes a double significance. And if both the Speech be itself high, and the Silence fit and noble, how expressive will their union be!'[7] Here is a new way of looking at the paradox: it is not just the yoking together of contraries, but an expressive union. Tennyson's name is a symbol in this sense. It includes (again to use Teufelsdröckh's words) 'some embodiment and revelation' of Tennyson's essential being; it participates in that essence, and yet is not that essence itself. It is a living power, and that power manifests itself in speech.

When Tennyson recounts this experience in 'The Ancient Sage' (1885), he (using the sage as his dramatic mask) explicitly calls the name a symbol:

> for more than once when I
> Sat all alone, revolving in myself
> The word that is the symbol of myself,
> The mortal limit of the Self was loosed,
> And past into the Nameless, as a cloud
> Melts into Heaven. I touched my limbs, the limbs

Were strange not mine – and yet no shade of doubt,
But utter clearness, and through loss of Self
The gain of such large life as matched with ours
Were Sun to spark – unshadowable in words,
Themselves but shadows of a shadow-world.          (229–39)

Name as symbol is different in essence from words, 'shadows of a shadow-world,' and this latter phrase parallels 'matter-moulded forms of speech.' The word 'shadow' suggests the theory of language which is based upon the image, the mind's mirroring of the appearances of the world outside it, to which sounds are arbitrarily attached. The state he experiences is 'unshadowable' because it is imageless (like Shelley's 'deep truth'), and only a symbol which shares its essence can give him access to it. Such áccess involves crossing boundaries that are marked by ordinary language. 'Night' and 'day,' 'ill' and 'good' the sage calls 'counter-terms,' and they are, he says, 'border-races, holding, each its own / By endless war' (250–2). Such terms belong to the finite world (the Latin *finis* being a boundary or border), and borders make our experience intelligible to us. They also conceal the essence of our being, and hence crossing the border must finally be our goal. I almost said 'crossing the bar,' and indeed the phrase would not be inappropriate. The image – a sandbank across a harbour-mouth – is a metaphor for the boundaries drawn by our senses, and by the words we attach to our sensations. 'The pilot has been on board all the while,' Tennyson explained in his notes in the Eversley edition, 'but in the dark I have not seen him.'

The border-races image for words appears in the poem after another passage in which the sage affirms that opposites in language are in fact manifestations of unity. The subject in this passage is time, and Tennyson usually treats time in a Carlylean (and Kantian) fashion, as a mode of perception (in an 1839 letter to his future bride, he told her to 'Annihilate within yourself these two dreams of Space and Time').[8] In this passage he links such perception with language:

But with the Nameless is nor Day nor Hour;
Though we, thin minds, who creep from thought to thought
Break into 'Thens' and 'Whens' the Eternal Now:
This double seeming of the single world!          (102–5)

The language theory by which we can best understand this passage is

Coleridge's, and it too presents us with a pattern of opposites that are in fact expressions of unity or (in terms of the Neoplatonism that lies behind so much of Coleridge's thought) of the One. The theory is in a diagram which he calls 'the Noetic Pentad,' and it appears not only in *Aids to Reflection* but also in his *Table Talk* and *Logic*. This last text Tennyson could not have known, but the diagram is central to Coleridge's thinking about language, and the Ancient Sage is giving us a parallel pattern. 'There are seven parts of speech,' Coleridge says, 'and they agree with the five grand and universal divisions into which all things finite, by which I mean to exclude the idea of God, will be found to fall.'[9] The primary part of speech is neither a noun nor a verb, but a fusion of both (Coleridge thus presents a solution to the noun-verb controversy),[10] a fusion Coleridge calls the 'verb substantive,' 'the *identity* or co-inherence of Act and Being.'[11] Coleridge identifies the 'verb substantive' with the name of God, 'the INEFFABLE NAME, to which no Image can be attached,' and of this name all language is the expression. The name is the answer God gives to Moses out of the burning bush ('I am that I am'), and while it is easy to think of the name as indicating a changeless and eternal being, the Hebrew verb, as Bernard Anderson points out in *Understanding the Old Testament*, differs from the English 'to be' in suggesting ongoing activity, creativity, the divine guidance of earthly events, and the future accomplishment of divine purpose.[12] Coleridge suggests some of this activity by giving the name as '*I am in that I will to be*' in the *Logic*.[13] Out of this 'verb substantive' come noun and verb, which Coleridge presents as opposites (he labels them 'thesis' and 'antithesis'), and adjective and adverb, modifiers of these opposites, while the infinitive and the participle unite these opposites when they act as gerunds (he labels the participle a 'synthesis,' the infinitive a 'mesothesis'). This Noetic Pentad shows the parts of speech in a dynamic relationship, each depending upon its opposite, and all depending from the name that gives them their power and meaning.

Through his experience with his own name, Tennyson affirms that he participates in this divine being. 'The human soul seems to me always in some way – how, we do not know – identical with God,' he said in an 1865 conversation.[14] 'You never, never can convince me that the *I* is not an eternal Reality, and that the Spiritual is not the only true and real part of me,' he told his son in 1869.[15] Language, in this context, is not simply the arbitrary linking of sound and idea, nor is it 'matter-moulded.' Rather, it comes 'out of' – these are the prepositions in Tennyson's account of repeating his own name – 'out of' his essential being. The prepositions suggest expression, and expression is the uttering or (literally) outering of something within. That something is not just emotion but the essential self, which is (in some indefinable way) part of God or the One. The Ancient Sage advises the young man, his antagonist in this dialogue, how to discover 'the Nameless':

If thou would'st hear the Nameless, and wilt dive
Into the Temple-cave of thine own self,
There, brooding by the central altar, thou
Mayst haply learn the Nameless hath a voice ...       (31–4)

The young man's voice must be the outering of the voice he discovers within, and expression is thus the manifestation of one's essential being. Tennyson's language, viewed as the expression of his 'I' or essential being, is related to 'Alfred Tennyson' in the same way that human language as presented by Coleridge is related to the ineffable name. If language is magic, it is so not because one possesses someone else's name and so has power over that other, but because one grasps the true nature of one's own name and in the expression of it shapes one's world. *The Devil and the Lady* anticipates this shift by exploring the link between language and magic.

The Magus is a conventional figure in the Romantic period, at a time when magic, as Anya Taylor has argued, in decline as a system of belief, 'reemerges as a way of thinking about art and the psychology of creativity.'[16] The protagonist of *The Devil and the Lady* is called Magus, and the play itself is, Dwight Culler says, about 'the magical power of the word,'[17] but in fact Magus' powers are limited and his words often ineffective, so that the play seems to be exploring the limitations of language as magic rather than celebrating its powers. There is in fact only one instance in the play where a word participates in the essence of the being it names, and this is when the Devil says that he comes 'at the sound of my name.' Even this instance is not a very satisfactory one. Magus calls up the Devil by describing him, but does not in fact name him. Elsewhere in the play there is talk about charms, in which words are magic not because they share in the being of the things they name, but because their sounds have the power to move. When words are used as charms, the moving is usually physical motion, as when Amoret, confronted by the Devil, wishes 'that I could speak Latin whose magic sounds / And Elfin syllables might drive thee far / To thy remotest Hell' (1.5.56–8). The meaning is a secondary consideration; the 'magic sounds' are everything, and if they overwhelm the sense, so much the better. The Devil fears this magic, but his reaction is largely a conventional one to (what he calls) 'a woman's art':

> What deprecations, amulets and charms,
> What exorcisms, crossings and bead countings,
> What Ave-Maries will be played against me!
> I value not your amulets and charms
> The twentieth part of half a rotten murphy
> Or a split pea, albeit I do confess me
> I'm apt to turn tail on an Ave-Mary,
> And quail a little at a Pater-Noster,
> Except when it's said backwards.          (1.2.12–20)

This conventional physical response to charms is only to be expected. Far more difficult for the Devil is language in its social and moral context. His metonymy for 'a woman's art' is her tongue, 'the most dangerous member of the Body' (1.5.28), he says:

> Unto the wise a blessing and a benefit,
> A healing balm of mild Persuasion,
> A sewer up of rents, sweet Pity's oracle,
> A curber of dissension's contumely –
> But in the mouth of the improvident
> Worse than an Adder's fang.
> It prompts the brain to hatch, the hand to execute,
> The heart to shake off conscience, the back
> To throw away the burden of restraint,
> The saucy foot to spurn authority.          (1.5.29–38)

The tongue is thus a revolutionary instrument, and the Devil fears the words that come straight from it. But even more difficult to cope with is the deceiving tongue.

The tongue in relation to the heart, and both in relation to the will – this is the central concern of the play. It is significant that Magus, for all his magic powers with words, has no control over Amoret's heart and will. His magic, like Prospero's, is a 'rough magic,' with power over physical nature but not over a human being's inner nature. When

Amoret is insisting that she will miss Magus when he is absent, Magus says, 'Sweet Amoret I would / Thy tongue were not at variance with thy heart' (1.4.9–10), and this 'variance' is the cause that propels this comedy and winds up its plot. She insists on her truth and sincerity, and her similes are of measure and harmony:

> True as the handle of the horologe
> As ever movèd by the works within,
> So move my lips responsive to my heart:
> True as the many-chorded Harp returns
> Harmonious answers to a master's touch –
> So speaks this tongue congenial to my Soul.           (1.4.11–16)

Such a fabrication about words is the very danger from which Magus is trying to protect her: 'the easy lapse / Of honeyed words from amatory lips' (1.4.106–7). Moreover, this expressiveness, far from being an artless outpouring of emotion, is a calculating one designed to deceive, and Magus' magic powers, unable to control the mind and will of another, cannot even discover another's thoughts and desires. 'I cannot trace the windings of a heart, / The searchless windings of a woman's mind' (1.4.27–8), he says, and he goes on to develop the labyrinth image, both here and a little later:

> Who shall know Man, or freely explicate
> The many folds of character, or who
> Shall bear the lamp of subtle scrutiny
> Into the deep recesses of the heart?
> Each Being is a world within himself ...           (1.4.58–62)

and for each, one might add, language is the shaping of his or her world.

In the central action of the play, each of the suitors faces a veiled figure whom he sees according to his own world, which here is that of his profession and the language associated with it. Each world view is in collision with every other world view. Hence the flyting of the lawyer and the apothecary in 2.4, the clash of them with the sailor in 2.5, and the rivalry of all six suitors in 2.6 – 'noisy and contentious brawls,' the Devil says, brawls characterized by a 'dissonance of tongues' (2.6.70–1). He proposes a singing match, in which the individual world views would be ordered and harmonized in 'songs,

/ Glees, catches, merry madrigals' (2.6.76–7) and madrigals in particular indicate that the voices, each retaining its individuality (its own words and line of melody), are nonetheless to be heard simultaneously, and in harmony. When the Devil repeats his proposal in act 3, he uses the word 'madrigal' but seems to be talking about airs: 'each / In turn should chaunt some love-lorn madrigal, / Some amorous ditty' (3.1.108–9). He who wins the contest will be rewarded with the unveiling of the lady. Language used in this way is, it seems, capable of discovery.

When we stand back from the whole of this unfinished play, we note that its action, at least as we have it in its fragmentary form, is framed by storm, woods, and night. One has a sense of a surrounding chaos, with a centre, Magus' cottage, where the chaos is at least intelligible because it is verbalized, and where there is the possibility of harmony and the unveiling of beauty. But Magus' powers are limited and he undertakes a journey, apparently to extend the powers of his language. He goes out into the storm on a voyage that is as much spiritual as it is physical, and the journey is, like that of the Ancient Mariner, a nightmare. Part of his experience is the hearing of his own name (3.2.111–12), and one has a sense that the key to increased power is the discovery of the self (the finding of one's own identity is the conventional goal of the romance quest). But the voyage is a failure: 'Some spells of darker Gramarie than mine, / Ruled the dim night and would not grant me passage' (3.2.136–7).

Though the voyage is a failure, and though the power of language to discover remains problematic, the power of language to create is very much in evidence. Each of the suitors has, after all, made his own world by appropriating the language characteristic of his profession (and, in this context, the fusion in the noun 'profession' of an occupation and a public declaration is richly suggestive). The link between speaking and creating is evident in some of Tennyson's early poems, the antecedent for such a link being God's creation of the world in the Genesis account: 'God said, Let there be light: and there was light.' Our speech is a repetition of this original act, a recreation that involves the shaping of nature, already created by God, into (to use Northrop Frye's metaphor) 'the envelope usually called culture or civilization.'[18] This verbal act is imaged in myth as the moving of stones and the building of cities, acts central to the story of Apollo, whose music built Troy, and to the story of Amphion, who (in Carlyle's words) 'built the walls of Thebes by the mere sound of his

Lyre.' And indeed, as Carlyle goes on to insist in the climactic chapter of *Sartor Resartus*, 'without the music of some inspired Orpheus was no city ever built, no work that man glories in ever done.'[19] Tennyson alludes to both Apollo and Amphion. His poem on the latter (published in 1842) is a jocular one in which Amphion creates a garden rather than a city. The poet laments his own inability, 'in such a brassy age' (65) as the nineteenth century, to do anything more than a not-very-good gardener does, and he parodies Wordsworth ('Better to me the meanest weed' 93) in an amusing way. His use of Apollo is more serious. He has Œnone link her lament with the song of Apollo ('I will speak, and build up all / My sorrow with my song, as yonder walls / Rose slowly to a music slowly breathed,' 38–40), and he has Tithonus liken Aurora's whispering to 'that strange song I heard Apollo sing, / While Ilion like a mist rose into towers' (62–3). The poem 'Ilion, Ilion,' unpublished during Tennyson's lifetime, uses the same myth, but it casts the act in the future ('When wilt thou be melody born?' is the refrain): the poem itself, with its repeated vowel sounds, seems to be the chant that will bring the city into being. The repeated sounds are the vowels of the word 'Ilion,' and their use suggests that the name of the city and its being are one. The speaker has only to chant the name and the city will appear – though the question that is the refrain casts a shadow of doubt on the timing of this act of creation.

As important as the link between voice and creation is the link between voice and the sustaining of an art or culture, once it has been established. This second link Tennyson explores in 'The Hesperides' (1832), where the daughters of Hesperus guard the golden apple by singing. So long as they sing 'evermore' and 'without stop' (56), the apple is safe, and the ceaseless singing is, as Ricks says in his preface, 'a basic notion of the Song' (1:462). Hence the voyager Hanno hears 'voices, like the voices in a dream, / Continuous' (12–13). The voices continuously create the garden and sustain its nature, all in the garden itself being 'mute' (18). The root of the tree is 'charmèd' – held in thrall, that is, by the song (the root of charm being the Latin *carmen*, song). 'Held up' by the song might be a more accurate way of describing the action, since this way links the song with Coleridge's (and Kant's) account of understanding that we explored in chapter 1: the song stands under the world of the garden and sustains its shape.

The sustaining of creation by singing parallels God's sustaining of the world by his divine energy, conventionally imaged as breath. Breathing is a kinesthetic rhythm, moving in time, and we note that the rhythms of the song match the rhythms of nature. Indeed, it is essential that they do so, for the vowel sounds alone will not guard the apple. The sisters will lose their treasure not only 'If ye sing not' but also 'if ye make false measure' (23), and to lose the rhythm is to allow the garden to collapse. The rhythm matches and controls the pulsing energy of nature, and a passage in part 1 of the song images the music calling forth the vital sap:

> For the blossom unto threefold music bloweth;
> Evermore it is born anew;
> And the sap to threefold music floweth,
> From the root
> Drawn in the dark,
> Up to the fruit,
> Creeping under the fragrant bark,
> Liquid gold, honeysweet, through and through. (30–7)

The unusual metre of the last line – three amphimacers – suggests the pulsing of the sap in time to the rhythm of the song, produced by the breathing of the sisters. 'Redolent breath' rises from 'Every flower and every fruit' (83), and the west wind is 'breathing afar' (90). The breath of nature, like the sap of part 1, is called forth by the song, and a line like 'Holy and bright, round and full, bright and blest' (93), with its strong initial accents in each phrase, its units of equal time (whether with one or two unaccented syllables), and its strong pauses, suggests the gentle steady beat of respiration.

In Tennyson's experience with his own name, then, we can detect two assumptions that are central to his theory of language: first, that there is in him an 'I' who is one and unique, a unified self, the first person pronoun participating, mysteriously but surely, in the divine 'I am that I am'; secondly, that his language ultimately comes out of and is the expression of this 'I,' each word finding its meaning in a pattern of relationships (like Coleridge's 'Noetic Pentad') which make up a verbal universe that is imperfect and often paradoxical, but that sustains the world of our actual experience. The first assumption is one questioned or rejected in the twentieth century and, if George Steiner is right in seeing in Rimbaud's '*Je est un autre*' and in his decon-struction of the first person singular of all verbs a fundamental break which defines modernity, then Tennyson's thinking is a late example of a kind of self-perception which would be under attack from the

1870s on.[20] The second assumption involves what Steiner calls a 'covenant between word and object' (90), and in Tennyson this covenant takes the form of the mind's shaping or framing of its experience of the world outside us. Mallarmé, Steiner argues, broke this covenant, and De Saussure gave the break 'canonic and systematic form' (95). Tennyson's understanding of language, then, is a paradigm that allows us to see clearly the kind of thinking the modernists were reacting against, but that thinking retains its validity in the same way that the Ptolemaic view of the universe retained its validity after the Copernican revolution. Though we know that the earth revolves around the sun, we still talk about the sun rising and setting; so, too, we will continue to say 'I' and to assume, for the purposes of ordinary life, that our words are not empty signs. This kind of trust in language is related in a fundamental way to Tennyson's faith, its central concern also being our ordinary quotidian existence, and in *In Memoriam* Tennyson explores all the complexities of that relationship.

Chapter Five

# 'Heart-affluence in
discursive talk':
*In Memoriam*

'Heart-affluence in discursive talk' is the first line of section cix of *In Memoriam*, and it is the first item of the poet's catalogue of Hallam's character in that lyric. The phrase neatly sums up two kinds of language in the poem, 'heart-affluence' being the expression of feelings and emotions while 'discursive talk' is the product of the understanding. Ideally, the feelings and the understanding should work in harmony, and indeed there is the suggestion in the prologue that they did so in the poet's own experience before Hallam's death; his death destroyed that harmony, and the poet must struggle to achieve it again. Hence his prayer in the prologue 'That mind and soul, according well, / May make one music as before, / But vaster' (27–9) defines his program. His model for this undertaking is Hallam himself, and the poet's successful achievement of a new and larger harmony is suggested both in section cxiv (where knowledge and desire, springing from the emotions and instincts, together make up wisdom) and in section xcvi, which picks up the music image of the prologue:

> one indeed I knew
> In many a subtle question versed,
> Who touched a jarring lyre at first,
> But ever strove to make it true:
>
> Perplext in faith, but pure in deeds,
> At last he beat his music out.                    (5–10)

Tennyson said that the 'one' was Hallam, but Hallam is the poet's model, and one can read the 'one' as at least an oblique reference to the 'I' of the poem and to the progress he has made. The lines from the prologue, quoted above, also define the structure of the elegy. Its movement is not, as some critics still insist, a movement from doubt to faith. If such were the shape of the poem, the prologue ought to be the epilogue, and all the stubborn affirmations of faith that Tennyson makes in the early sections of the poem (such as his indication in section iii that Sorrow's picture of a blind amoral nature comes from a 'lying lip') are misplaced. But affirmations of faith, statements of doubt, and expressions of grief all appear in the early sections of the poem, and such a mingling of contrary reactions is psychologically accurate, and true to anyone's actual experience of a death. The problem is not to affirm faith and eliminate doubt, but to harmonize all these feelings and thoughts into a working relationship that will enable the 'I' to get on with his life. The process is by no means a systematic one. The 'I' proceeds by fits and starts, with much reconsideration, backsliding, and repetition that often turns out to be an advance. Contrary feelings mingle with the darting of the mind in thought, and the result is a poem where there is plenty of evidence of moral and spiritual progress (imaged in the 'I' who grows to heroic stature in section ciii and confirmed by the statement in the 'marriage lay' at the end that 'I myself ... have grown / To something greater than before,' 19–20), but it is progress which is not steady and continuous, but rather unsystematic and intermittent. Hence the poet does not trust 'a larger lay,' as he says in section xlviii, but rather 'Short swallow-flights of song,' and these 'brief lays' are the primary elements of the poem. From 1833 on, Tennyson referred to the growing number of lays as the 'Elegies,' and in the late 1840s he considered calling the work 'Fragments of an Elegy.'[1] The fragment, I want to argue, is the essential form of the work, and this form is bound up with the language theories that lie behind the poem. The most obvious theory – it is the one that one would expect in an elegy – is expressionism, and it is with that theory that we must begin.

An elegy is conventionally the expression of grief, but the conventions of the genre were strengthened for Tennyson by the dominant role the Romantics had given to expression. Poetry is 'the spontaneous overflow of powerful feelings' – and *In Memoriam* may be seen as such a stream. But we note that there is often something that checks the flow, some hesitancy, some reticence. This restraining force may have something in common with Wordsworth's insistence, in his qualifying clause following his statement about the spontaneous overflow of powerful feelings, that good poetry also depends upon the poet's having thought 'long and deeply,' but in Tennyson the restraint seems to be as much psychological as it is intellectual, so that the expressionism that shapes this poem has more in common with Keble's theory than it does with Wordsworth's. That theory Keble set out in his Oxford lectures on poetry, delivered in Latin between 1832 and 1841. Tennyson had a copy of these lectures in his library, as well as the seventh edition (1831) of Keble's popular *The Christian Year*.

'We are all so framed by nature,' Keble says in his first lecture, 'that we experience great relief, when carried away by any strong current of thought or feeling, if we are at last able, whether by speech or gesture or in any other way, to find an expression for it.'[2] By nature, then, we want to make outer (to utter) that which is inner, and this movement from interiority to exteriority, based on a strong human need, is the essence of expressionism. But this movement has its opposite in the turning back on us of those things we have made outer, so that they affect us by leading us to recreate the original feelings and thoughts, now made manageable by this circular process. Verbal expression, says Keble, involves 'measure and a definite rhythm of sound' as well as images, and because of these two elements poetry has a 'wonderful efficacy in soothing men's emotions and steadying the balance of their mind' (1:21). But the 'strong current of thought or feeling' is not unrestricted in its first flow. In addition to the desire for relief there is also 'a higher and better instinct, which counsels silence as to many things,' and so we 'are altogether restrained by a sort of shame, far from discreditable, nay rather, noble and natural, from any such relief' (1:20). 'Healing relief' and 'modest reserve' – the one the overflowing of 'secret mental emotion,' the other, 'while giving scope to enthusiasm,' yet ruling it 'with order and due control' (1:22) – these are the two foundations of Keble's poetics, which he uses to account for the origin of poetry and for its various genres. But the second, which Keble sometimes calls reserve (thus linking it to theology and the practice of indirectly and gradually revealing the mysteries of faith) and sometimes reticence (when he is more concerned with human psychology as the source of irony) is, he insists, 'the very pivot on which our whole theory turns' (1:73). Reticence manifests itself in hints and suggestions; the poet's utterances will express passion, 'and yet not quite plainly and openly' (1:73):

The chief effect of this modesty, as we may call it, of poets, will thus be seen to be that they hint at very many things rather than are at pains to describe and define them. For they are under no necessity to delineate in minute detail; neither to assist recollection of the thing itself (for that is treasured up in their own mind and soul); nor to rouse the feeling of hearers, who, when everything is methodically insisted upon, either lose interest or admire the skill of the narrator, not the story told. Judicious writers, therefore, lightly touch the special points to be impressed on the reader; and an author, like a host, shows his ability most surely if his readers are dismissed with an appetite whetted but not satisfied. (1:77)

This passage could be taken as a theory of the fragment, in so far as it praises hints that prod the mind to complete them. Keble himself does not deal with the fragment, but he does, following Quintilian, divide emotion into *pathos* and *ethos*. The former is the 'very whirl and rush of passion' (1:88) and 'as an eager spirit generally burns itself out quickly, poems which arise through intense feeling and are thrown off in a single jet, as it were, will probably be shorter than the other kind and of simpler form' (1:90); they will be lyrics and elegies and satires, though hardly even one of these is 'a pure and simple outcome of passion' (1:90). Nonetheless, Keble is making the same point that Mann would later make in his defence of *Maud*, that (in Mann's words) 'impulsive utterances' will appear in 'fitful and broken strains'[3] rather than a lengthy and fully worked out structure. 'Breaking into song by fits' (section xxiii) is Tennyson's own phrase in *In Memoriam*.

Relief and reticence are both very much parts of Tennyson's poetics, especially in *In Memoriam*. His emotion at Hallam's death finds relief in expression – 'verse that brings myself relief' is a clause in section lxxv – but the overflow is never unchecked. Indeed, unchecked emotion is likely to overwhelm words, as it does in 'The Two Voices' (written at least in part after Hallam's death) when the 'I' involuntarily ends the first phase of the debate by being unable to speak:

I would have said, 'Thou canst not know,'
But my full heart, that worked below,
Rained through my sight its overflow. (43–5)

' "The artist is known by his self-limitation" was a favourite adage of his,'[4] Hallam Tennyson records of his father, and self-limitation is the Tennysonian equivalent of Keble's reserve. The son prints in his *Memoir* (490–1) an unfinished poem called 'Reticence' from 1869.

Reticence appears as a goddess in a shrine, 'with right hand / Moving toward her lips, and there / Hovering, thoughtful, poised in air.' Half the poem is given over to a description of the setting for this shrine, a landscape in which a river is the chief feature. The river (which is of course the conventional image for expression) 'never overflows,' but is always 'murmuring' and 'lightly lisping'; when it does 'break away,' it 'Showers in a whisper o'er the world.' *In Memoriam* suggests the same restraint, and indeed the 'I' there, like the 'I' in 'The Two Voices,' affirms that he can speak only when his feeling is not at its strongest. Tennyson's central image in section xix is the same conventional image he would use in 'Reticence,' his sorrow being identified with a river:

> The Danube to the Severn gave
> 　The darkened heart that beat no more;
> 　They laid him by the pleasant shore,
> And in the hearing of the wave.

> There twice a day the Severn fills;
> 　The salt sea-water passes by,
> 　And hushes half the babbling Wye,
> And makes a silence in the hills.

> The Wye is hushed nor moved along,
> 　And hushed my deepest grief of all,
> 　When filled with tears that cannot fall,
> I brim with sorrow drowning song.

> The tide flows down, the wave again
> 　Is vocal in its wooded walls;
> 　My deeper anguish also falls,
> And I can speak a little then.

There are 'lesser griefs that may be said' (section xx), but the saying is unsatisfactory, and the verb Tennyson uses for it in xix – 'babbling' – is the verb he elsewhere (in his own conversation as well as in his poetry) uses to denote talk that undermines the social structure. Greater griefs may only be hinted at, sporadically. As Tennyson says in section v, 'that large grief which these [words] enfold / Is given in outline and no more.' But in addition to the natural inability of greater griefs to find expression in words, there was in the poet himself an instinct of reserve. His son says that Tennyson 'spoke with the greatest reserve of what he called "these unfathomable mysteries,'' as befitting one who did not dogmatise, but who knew that the Finite can by no means grasp the Infinite.'[5] In *In Memoriam* Tennyson himself talks about reserve in much the same way as Keble: his personified sorrow

> holds it sin and shame to draw
> The deepest measure from the chords:

> Nor dare she trust a larger lay,
>     But rather loosens from the lip
>     Short swallow-flights of song, that dip
> Their wings in tears, and skim away.                    (xlviii: 11–16)

'A sort of shame ... noble and natural' are Keble's words, and this shame makes poetry hint at emotion, a hinting that Tennyson images in the 'swallow-flights' that are quick, brief, and evanescent.

The fleeting nature of the voice in *In Memoriam* – the poem's orality is the fiction by which it presents itself – is the primary element of the poem's fragmentary character, and this voice expresses its grief in fits and starts rather than in a continuous and fully worked out discourse or narration. But expressionism alone does not wholly account for the fragments. Another of Tennyson's titles for his 'Elegies' was 'The Way of the Soul,' and this was a title that Tennyson sometimes used, his son tells us, even after the publication of the poem.[6] Did Tennyson know that 'way' is a word that had a special meaning for Coleridge, that it signified an open and living method as opposed to a closed and static system? One can only answer, 'Probably.' Coleridge's essays on method are in the third volume of the 1818 edition of *The Friend*, and if Tennyson did know them or at least the ideas in them, the knowledge would have come to him through Hallam and the Apostles. (The copy of *The Friend* in Tennyson's library, the fourth edition of 1844, had belonged to Emily Tennyson before her marriage.) Certainly Hallam knew *The Friend*. In an 1828 letter to John Frere he tells a funny story about going into a bookseller's, asking for 'Mr. Coleridge's Friend,' and being directed to the post office.[7] Some lines in Hallam's poem 'Timbuctoo' were suggested to him (as he himself acknowledges in a note) by *The Friend*, and by a passage in the third volume of the 1818 edition. So it seems likely that Tennyson was aware of Coleridge's understanding of method, both from the 1818 essays on it, and from the embodiment of it in *Aids to Reflection*. He uses the word 'landing-place' in section xlvii of *In Memoriam* in the same sense as Coleridge uses it in *The Friend* (as Ricks points out in his notes 2:365), and, I think, his 'way' in 'The Way of the Soul' is also a reflection of the particular meaning Coleridge gives to that word. 'Method,' Coleridge writes in the first of his 'Essays on the Principles of Method,' 'implies a *progressive transition*, and it is the meaning of the word in the original language. The Greek Μεθοδος is literally *a way*, or *path of Transit*.'[8] The form of this 'way' is essentially fragmentary.

The fragment, as the embodiment of the method Coleridge is teaching, is descended from Bacon's initiative style and his use of the aphorism. Coleridge quotes from Bacon's *Advancement of Learning* and clearly was aware of the method Bacon recommends for the expanding of knowledge as opposed to its consolidation and application. In his reaction against deduction, Bacon began with data from experience, and these observations, embodied in statements or propositions, had to be accounted for in terms of more embracing truths. In moving from particulars to universals Bacon insisted upon the value of 'Writing in Aphorisms': 'Aphorisms, representing a knowledge broken, do invite men to enquire farther,'[9] and thus to push back the boundaries of knowledge. The initiative style is characterized by juxtaposition, and by the absence of conjunctions and subordination; it is abrupt and suggestive, as opposed to the magistral style, which provides more connections, explanations, and illustrations. Coleridge's 'art of METHOD' or 'Science of Method' – he uses both labels – is also concerned with advancement (moral and spiritual for him, as well as intellectual), and he praises Plato's dialogues as an example of this art, Plato's purpose being

not to assist in storing the passive mind with the various sorts of knowledge most in request, as if the human soul were a mere repository or banqueting-room, but to place it in such relations of circumstance as should gradually excite the germinal power that craves no knowledge but what it can take up into itself, what it can appropriate, and re-produce in fruits of its own. (1:473)

The 'art of METHOD' is the art of relating things, and 'To enumerate and analyze these relations, with the conditions under which alone they are discoverable, is to teach the science of Method' (1:451). Method is continuous and progressive, as opposed to 'a mere dead arrangement, containing in itself no principle of progression' (1:457). For this 'mere dead arrangement' Coleridge sometimes uses the word 'system.' One manifestation of 'system' is 'abstract knowledge,' when 'we think of ourselves as separated beings, and place nature in antithesis to the mind, as object to subject, thing to thought, death to life' (1:520). Frederick Denison Maurice, a disciple of Coleridge and friend of Tennyson, follows his master in commenting on the difference between method and system in his *The Kingdom of Christ* (1838), and the book itself – the first volume was in Tennyson's library – is the realization of method: not, Maurice insists in his preface, a 'learned treatise' but 'a collection of hints' in the form of letters.[10] Dwight Culler draws attention to the usefulness of the terms 'method' and 'system' in nineteenth-century studies, particularly when one is searching for ways of distinguishing between process and product,[11] and surely Culler is right to link *Guesses at Truth, Aids to Reflection,* and *In Memoriam,* and to ask of the last two, 'Is it any accident that both works are fragmentary or composite in form?' (156).

One antecedent for the theory of this fragmentary and composite form is the concept of Romantic irony, associated primarily with Friedrich Schlegel and his *Dialogue on Poetry,* published in 1800 in the last volume of the periodical *Athenaeum.* The artist always strives for complete expression, and always finds such expression impossible, Schlegel says; hence his work will always be fragmentary in character. His own *Dialogue* is a good example. Made up of an earlier essay and a letter as well as dialogue proper, it includes 'previous philosophical and critical positions' as well as present ones. 'By including such contradictory stages,' say Schlegel's English translators, Ernst Behler and Roman Struc, 'the work mirrors thinking-in-progress, the continuous struggle to overcome former positions in the manner in which thinking actually proceeds.'[12] The translators link the *Dialogue* to Schlegel's aphorisms, their form also being a rejection of systematic order, and the rejection in turn being based upon the assumption that the 'organized chaos' of the literary work reflects the 'chaos' of the created universe. 'One of the most subtle observations of Romantic irony,' Behler and Struc point out, 'is that the original order of things is chaotic. Systematic order has been superimposed on the original state of existence, diminishing the primeval richness of Being. In other words, chaotic order mirrors life and genuine Being, while systematic order is a mere shadow of life.'[13] Tennyson may not have known Schlegel, but he shared these assumptions about Being and the representation of it in words. His purpose in *In Memoriam* is (to use his figure) to sing, to 'make one music as before, / But vaster' ('Prologue' 28–9), and even though he does at last beat his music out, that music still falls short of Being, and can only hint at it. Tennyson's phrase for Being in section lxxxviii is 'the sum of things,' and his music is not even as full as that of the 'Wild bird' in whom 'fierce extremes' mingle, 'the senses mix,' and 'the passions meet':

> I cannot all command the strings;
>   The glory of the sum of things
> Will flash along the chords and go. (10–12)

Nonetheless, the 'way' that he chooses, with all its advances and backslidings, its contrary feelings and its contradictory positions (often presented in *In Memoriam*, as in 'The Two Voices,' in dialogue or, as in section xxxv, with several voices) is more natural and finally more fruitful than a systematic arrangement. Peter Allan Dale is surely right to make the account of the form of the poem in section cxxv the key to his criticism of the poem's language:

> Whatever I have said or sung,
>   Some bitter notes my harp would give,
>   Yea, though there often seemed to live
> A contradiction on the tongue,
>
> Yet Hope had never lost her youth;
>   She did but look through dimmer eyes;
>   Or Love but played with gracious lies,
> Because he felt so fixed in truth:
>
> And if the song were full of care,
>   He breathed the spirit of the song;
>   And if the words were sweet and strong
> He set his royal signet there;
>
> Abiding with me till I sail
>   To seek thee on the mystic deeps,
>   And this electric force, that keeps
> A thousand pulses dancing, fail.

The key words are 'A contradiction on the tongue' and 'gracious lies,' and they sum up Tennyson's 'way' with language. 'What seems particularly to fascinate him about words,' Dale argues,

> is the *hiddenness* of their power. Like the dead body of Hallam or the dead body of nature with which the dead Hallam is associated, words only *appear* as if they were bereft of a saving spiritual presence. In the end, they turn out to be a treasure house of divine spirit, to which the poet under the dulling influence of grief was temporarily blind. Thus, he tells us throughout the poem of the deceptive appearances of language, of the need to penetrate its surface to find out its true meaning.[14]

Words 'half reveal / And half conceal the Soul within' (section v), but the language which is most opaque is that which tries to fix truth in a final form.

The 'I' of the poem regularly voices his distrust of fixed and systematic arrangements of words. 'Her care is not to part and prove,' Tennyson says of Sorrow, his Muse in section xlviii, and the infinitives point to systematic thinking of the kind associated with Bentham. Mill, in his 1838 essay, praised Bentham as a seminal thinker, not for his ideas but for 'his mode of arriving at them':

> Bentham's method may be shortly described as the method of detail; of treating wholes by separating them into their parts, abstractions by resolving them into Things, – classes and generalities by distinguishing them into the individuals of which they are made up; and breaking every question into pieces before attempting to solve it.[15]

Elsewhere, Tennyson calls this kind of systematic analysis 'truth in closest words' (section xxxvi), and this truth 'shall fail.' Less likely to fail, but still inadequate, are creeds. In section xxxiii, the speaker contrasts 'thy sister' and her 'faith through form' with the 'thou' whom the poem addresses, 'Whose faith has centre everywhere, / Nor cares to fix itself to form.' He admonishes the 'thou' to 'fail not ... for want of such a type' as the sister. Nonetheless, the actual living of a moral and spiritual life in society is 'the creed of creeds' (section xxxvi), and its model is the life of Christ, which resists reduction to a system. The attitude toward system in the poem reflects Tennyson's own. Hallam Tennyson in the *Memoir* quotes the Bishop of Ripon as saying that the poet 'had a sympathy with those who were impatient of the formal statement of truth,' and this 'reverent impatience of formal dogma may be but the expression of the feeling that the truth must be larger, purer, nobler than any mere human expression or definition of it.'[16] Of his father Hallam Tennyson himself writes, 'His creed, he always said, he would not formulate':

He thought, with Arthur Hallam, that 'the essential feelings of religions subsist in the utmost diversity of forms,' that 'different language does not always imply different opinions, nor different opinions any difference in *real* faith.' 'It is impossible, ' he said, 'to imagine that the Almighty will ask you, when you come before Him in the next life, what your particular form of creed was: but the question will rather be, "Have you been true to yourself, and given in My Name a cup of cold water to one of these little ones?"'[17]

The metaphor Tennyson uses for the language of this living faith is a conventional one: words are coins.

The trope appears in a complicated context in the first two stanzas of section xxxvi:

> Though truths in manhood darkly join,
>     Deep-seated in our mystic frame,
>     We yield all blessing to the name
> Of Him that made them current coin;
>
> For Wisdom dealt with mortal powers,
>     Where truth in closest words shall fail,
>     When truth embodied in a tale
> Shall enter in at lowly doors.

The identification of words and coins appears in Latin literature, in Quintilian's *Institutio Oratoria*, for instance, and in Horace's *Ars Poetica*, where 'coin' is a verb imaging the making of new words that bear 'the stamp of the present day.'[18] Minting a word continued to be a commonplace – it turns up in Arnold's 'Sohrab and Rustum,' when Rustum contemptuously describes Sohrab as a 'Curl'd minion, dancer, coiner of sweet words!' (458) and in Trench's *On the Study of Words* – but more often the image suggests the role of words in our actual existence and daily life, and their worth in that context. Bacon made words one of the chief Idols of the Market-place in his *Novum Organum*, and he uses the coin image in the *Advancement of Learning*, where he says (in W.A. Wright's nineteenth-century translation) that 'words are the tokens current and accepted for conceits, as moneys are for values' (2.16.3).[19] Their value lies not in themselves but in their relations, words being images of things (*imagines rerum*). Words, like coins, can be used wisely or foolishly, and Hobbes' use of the metaphor is a natural extension of Bacon's complaint that men study words and not matter: 'For words are wise mens counters, they do but reckon by them: but they are the mony of fooles, that value them by the authority of an *Aristotle*, a *Cicero*, or a *Thomas*, or any other Doctor whatsoever, if but a man' (1.4).[20] In Tennyson's use of the metaphor, the context of 'current coin' is the same as Bacon's: our actual daily existence. Tennyson is like Bacon and Hobbes in affirming the value of words as a medium of exchange or communication, and we can infer that he, like them, rejects the elevating of individual words into absolute authority. His focus is on their arrangement and their context. 'Truth in closest words' – a philosophical system, perhaps, or Benthamite analysis – 'shall fail,' while 'truth embodied in a tale' finds its way more effectively in our actual daily lives. The tale is, I think, the life of Christ, but the wording is such that the reference may also be to the tales – parables – by which Christ taught. Whichever tale is meant, truth is clearly accommodated to limited human understanding, this accommodation being the realization of the principle of reserve, which prods the believer to puzzle his way to greater truth.

The principle that governs that way is analogy, and analogy is as important for Tennyson as it is for the Tractarian poets (explored in G.B. Tennyson's *Victorian Devotional Poetry* 1981) and for a large number of thinkers and writers whom W. David Shaw discusses in *The Lucid Veil* (1987). William Knight, Professor of Moral Philosophy at St Andrew's, tells of an 1870 conversation with Tennyson, in which the poet asked the philosopher to define his discipline: 'I want to know how we are to unite the One with the Many, and the Many with the All.' Knight records part of the conversation *verbatim*: '"Well," he said, "we must get to some height above phenomena. We must climb up, and we can't ascend a ladder without rungs. Isn't the ladder of analogy very useful in metaphysics?"' Then Tennyson moved away from abstractions to the materials of interest to him as a poet, 'the outward world, where the ladders and symbols are.'[21] These 'ladders and symbols' 'half reveal / And half conceal,' analogy being, as G.B. Tennyson remarks, 'God's way of practising Reserve,'[22] and language is part of God's scheme of analogy. Language, in Tennyson's thinking about it, is never hollow or empty, never a function of matter alone, never the 'Magnetic mockeries' (section cxx) of the brain as understood by the materialist. Instead, it suggests a likeness, partly revealed and partially grasped, between things below and things above. (Tennyson's ladder image, derived from Neoplatonism, involves these spatial metaphors.) Hence one ought to pay close attention to words, for 'a few little words' may, as Hallam had said in 1831, flash upon us 'a world of meaning.' Trench argues for the same view in his lectures on words and explicitly links this approach to words with analogy: 'Many a single word ... is itself a concentrated poem, having stores of poetical thought and imagery laid up in it. Examine it,' he says in the spirit of Coleridge's injunctions in the preface to *Aids to Reflection*, 'and it will be found to rest on some deep analogy of things natural and things spiritual; bringing those to illustrate and to give an abiding form and body to these.'[23] Trench links the coin metaphor we have been examining with analogy. Words may seem 'nothing more than the current coin of society,' but 'God having pressed such a seal of truth upon language, that men are continually uttering deeper things than they know, asserting mighty principles.'[24] In *Aids to Reflection*, Coleridge makes a widely known and influential distinction between analogy and metaphor, tautegorical expression and allegorical expression. Of analogy he says: 'The language is analogous, wherever a thing, power, or principle in a higher dignity is expressed by the same thing, power, or principle in a lower but more known form.' Analogies are the material or base of symbols, 'the nature of which is always *tau*tegorical' – same speaking – rather than '*alle*gorical' – other speaking.[25] Words are thus part of the reality to which they point. Hence Trench, following Coleridge, argues, in his *Notes on the Parables of Our Lord*, that a 'parable or other analogy to spiritual truth appropriated from the world of nature or man, is not merely illustration, but also in some sort proof,' both language and nature 'being throughout a witness for the world of spirit, proceeding from the same hand, growing out of the same root, and being constituted for that very end.'[26] The witnessing is not without difficulties. The principle of analogy does not provide clear and unassailable proof, but rather probable argument. 'Probability' is a key word for Bishop Butler, whose *The Analogy of Religion* (1736) was, as much as *Aids to Reflection*, a source for the Apostles. Butler was one of the thinkers they discussed,[27] and there was a copy of the 1813 edition of his *Analogy* in the library at Somersby. In his introduction Butler quotes Origen: 'he who believes the Scripture to have proceeded from him who is the Author of

Nature, may well expect to find the same sort of difficulties in it, as are found in the constitution of Nature.'[28] But just as God gives brutes instincts, so he gives us not only instincts but also reason to judge the probability of the imperfect and doubtful evidence presented to us.

The purpose of this account of analogy is to introduce the theory that underpins Tennyson's statements of faith. Briefly, that theory rests upon the assumptions that language and nature are analogous because both proceed from God; that nature gives imperfect evidence of providence; that language is likewise ambiguous and inadequate; and that these inadequacies in both nature and language make necessary our judgment, which sorts out degrees of probability where clear and unequivocal evidence is not to be had. Such assertions of probability are statements of faith, and their language is, to use Coleridge's adjective, tautegorical. Without using Coleridge's term, Trench suggests that language works in this way:

It is not merely that these analogies assist to make the truth intelligible, or, if intelligible before, present it more vividly to the mind, which is all that some will allow them. Their power lies deeper than this, in the harmony unconsciously felt by all men, and which all deeper minds have delighted to trace, between the natural and spiritual worlds, so that analogies from the first are felt to be something more than illustrations, happily but yet arbitrarily chosen.[29]

'Arbitrarily' is a key word. Usually associated with the capricious, with individual preferences and decisions loosely or wilfully related to the actual nature of things or situations, the word is in fact derived from the Latin *arbiter*, a judge. In a world that seems to be governed by the principle of analogy, judgment, aided by instincts and reason, is the essential human faculty.

Statements of faith often seem to be arbitrary – based on mere opinion or preference, that is – and it is easy to take the affirmations of *In Memoriam* as something less than they are: conventional statements expected by the age, for instance, or desperate attempts to convince the self, or to sound hopeful where little hope is felt. But opinion, and the judgment and feelings upon which it is based, are not small things in Tennyson's thinking. Indeed, a right understanding of opinion is crucial to a right understanding of the distinction Tennyson makes, throughout his career, between knowledge and faith; and to a right understanding of his affirmation that, in matters of faith, human needs are authoritative. The language question bound up with opinion is a question about the truth of propositions: what kind of truth or how much truth may assertions about the existence of God or immortality claim? I want to explore these issues by discussing, first, Locke's approach to them, and then Coleridge's.

A reader of the early Victorian period would have found Locke an unlikely thinker for anyone to call on as a defender of faith. Though Cambridge made the *Essay Concerning Human Understanding* part of the study of moral philosophy which was meant, at the time when Tennyson was an undergraduate, to provide a religious education, Locke himself was generally charged with undermining religious belief. Hans Aarsleff's essay 'Locke's Reputation in Nineteenth-Century England' describes in detail the curious mixture of misuse and misunderstanding of the *Essay*. Of special note for Tennyson is Maurice's condemnation of Locke in *The Kingdom of Christ* – the *Essay*, Maurice says, led Locke's followers 'to denounce all notion of a communication to the heart of man, but what comes through words and letters, and the organs of sense'[30] – and Aarsleff mentions other rejections of Locke: Carlyle's charge, in his essay on Goethe (1828), that Locke 'paved the way for banishing religion from the world,' Coleridge's well-known 'dislike and even contempt for Locke,' and the attacks on Locke by William Whewell and Adam Sedgwick at Cambridge.[31] Sedgwick took Locke to task for his 'contracted view ... of the capacities of man' and for his fathering 'many a cold and beggarly system of psychology.'[32] No wonder John Stuart Mill, in his 1840 essay on Coleridge, summed up the philosophy against which Coleridge was reacting as 'infidel.'[33] Practically everyone was familiar with one part of Locke's epistemology – that our ideas are derived from sensation, and that (in Mill's summary) 'all knowledge consists of generalizations from experience'[34] – but most paid insufficient attention to the purpose and total shape of the *Essay*, and Locke's reasons for writing it. Those reasons are deeply involved with the life of faith, and with the spirit of English Protestantism. Ricardo Quintana has remarked that 'the extent to which Locke's theory of knowledge reflects the spirit of the Anglican *via media* and its basic pattern has not always been appreciated.'[35] The extent to which Locke's theory of knowledge helps us define the spirit of the Broad Church movement in the Victorian period is worth investigating, too, as is Dwight Culler's observation that 'Tennyson is often called the poet of the Broad Church Movement.'[36]

In his admirable summary of Locke's life, Quintana indicates how profoundly the upheavals of the seventeenth century affected the purpose and shape of the *Essay Concerning Human Understanding*. He makes the telling point that, while Locke was deeply involved in the political conflicts of his day, and deeply interested in religious issues, the disorders and extremes of his age 'disturbed him profoundly,' and made him determined to find an orderly and reasonable way in which to live.[37] In particular, he wanted to mark the boundaries of knowledge and opinion, so that factions and sects might be discouraged from claiming inappropriate authority for assumptions that, however necessary for daily life, lacked full and demonstrable proof. Locke does not provide a creed or a body of doctrine. His concern is not with knowledge and beliefs *per se*, but with the way in which we hold them, and with their place in the actual living of our lives. In his Introduction, Locke writes:

When we know our own *Strength*, we shall the better know what to undertake with hopes of Success: And when we have well survey'd the *Powers* of our own Minds, and made some Estimate what we may expect from them, we shall not be inclined either to sit still, and not set our Thoughts on work at all, in Despair of knowing any thing; nor on the other side question every thing, and disclaim all Knowledge, because some Things are not to be understood. 'Tis of great use to the Sailor to know the length of his Line, though he cannot with it fathom all the depths of the Ocean. 'Tis well he knows, that it is long enough to reach the bottom, at such Places, as are necessary to direct his Voyage, and caution him against running upon Shoals, that may ruin him. Our Business here is not to know all things, but those which concern our Conduct.[38]

'My *Purpose*,' Locke says in the Introduction to book 1, is 'to enquire into the Original, Certainty, and Extent of humane Knowledge; together, with the Grounds and Degrees of Belief, Opinion, and Assent' (1.1.2). The scale which is central to the *Essay*, from certainty down through degrees of probability, is already apparent here, and Locke will later link knowledge with certainty, faith with probability (4.15.3). The scale is directly related to choosing, willing, and acting. 'It is ... worth while,' Locke writes, 'to search out the *Bounds* between Opinion and Knowledge; and examine by what Measures, in things, whereof we have no certain Knowledge, we ought to regulate our Assent, and moderate our Perswasions' (1.1.3). Locke wants to avoid having his readers 'intemperately require Demonstration, and demand Certainty, where Probability only is to be had, and which is sufficient to govern all our Concernments' (1.1.5).

The scale which Locke constructs in book 4 is worth looking at in some detail. It is not from highest to lowest, or from best to worst, but from most certain to least probable. At the top of the scale is what Locke calls 'intuitive Knowledge': 'For in this, the Mind is at no pains of proving or examining, but perceives the Truth, as the Eye doth light, only by being directed toward it. Thus the Mind perceives, that White is not Black, That a Circle is not a Triangle, That Three are more than Two, and equal to One and Two' (4.2.1). This kind of knowledge, Locke says, 'is the clearest, and most certain, that humane Frailty is capable of' (4.2.1), and 'leaves no room for Hesitation, Doubt, or Examination' (4.2.1). The next degree is 'Demonstrative' (4.2.1) or 'Rational Knowledge' (4.17.15). Here, the mind does not immediately perceive the agreement or disagreement of ideas, but requires intervening ideas or proofs, through which the mind progresses toward certainty. Nonetheless, 'This Knowledge by intervening Proofs, though it be certain, yet the evidence of it is not altogether so clear and bright, nor the assent so ready, as in intuitive Knowledge' (4.2.4). Nonetheless, Intuition and Demonstration provide certainty; 'whatever comes short of one of these, with what assurance soever embraced, is but Faith, or Opinion, but not Knowledge, at least in all general Truths' (4.2.14).[39]

From such certainty, Locke passes on to 'the several degrees and grounds of Probability, and Assent or Faith' (4.15.2), and distinguishes knowledge from faith thus:

And herein lies the difference between Probability and Certainty, Faith and Knowledge, that in all the parts of Knowledge, there is intuition; each immediate Idea, each step has its visible and certain connexion; in belief not so. That which makes me believe, is something extraneous to the thing I believe; something not evidently joined on both sides to, and so not manifestly shewing the Agreement, or Disagreement of those Ideas, that are under consideration. (4.15.3)

The highest degree of probability is based on 'the conformity of any thing with our own Knowledge, Observation, and Experience' (4.15.4), and is our ordinary attitude toward 'all the stated Constitutions and Properties of Bodies, and the regular proceedings of Causes and Effects in the ordinary course of Nature' (4.16.6). The next degree of probability is based on the testimony of others, 'when I find by my own Experience, and the Agreement of all others that mention it, a thing to be, for the most part, so; and that the particular instance of it is attested by many and undoubted Witnesses' (4.16.7). 'Thus far the matter goes easie enough' (4.16.9), so long as testimony squares with common experience; but when testimony questions the validity of such experience, or contradicts it, we are, after the mind has examined all such matters, in the realm of 'Belief, Conjecture, Guess, Doubt, Wavering, Distrust, Disbelief, etc.' (4.16.9). In this realm, the grounds for giving or withholding assent are, when judged by the criterion of knowledge, shaky or insubstantial. But in many matters which are of concern to us, knowledge is partial or unattainable.

This brings us to a central theme in the Essay: the limitations of knowledge, and its inadequacy as a guide for conduct. Locke announces this theme in his Introduction (1.1.5), and comes back to it again and again in book 4, his favourite adjective for knowledge being 'narrow' ('But how much these few and narrow Inlets are disproportionate to the vast whole Extent of all Beings' [4.3.23]). The opening paragraph of 4.14 is the fullest statement of this theme:

The Understanding Faculties being given to Man, not barely for Speculation, but also for the Conduct of his Life, Man would be at a great loss, if he had nothing to direct him, but what has the Certainty of true Knowledge. For that being very short and scanty, as we have seen, he would be often utterly in the dark, and in most of the Actions of his Life, perfectly at a stand, had he nothing to guide him in the absence of clear and certain Knowledge. He that will not eat, till he has Demonstration that it will nourish him; he that will not stir, till he infallibly knows the Business he goes about will succeed, will have little else to do, but sit still and perish. (4.14.1)

But we do not, in fact, 'sit still and perish'; we go about our daily business without the aid of proof, and on the basis of assumptions which are obviously necessary. Knowledge is sufficient for the purpose of preserving our physical being, and the pleasure and pain which we experience through our senses guide our actions (4.11.8), but, in moral and spiritual matters, we have the aid of judgment, 'the Faculty, which God has given Man to supply the want of clear and certain Knowledge in Cases where that cannot be had' (4.14.3). Judgment is our guide in this 'State of Mediocrity and Probationership' (4.14.2), so that we may 'spend the days of this our Pilgrimage with Industry and Care, in the search, and following of that way, which might lead us to a State of greater Perfection' (4.14.2). Locke identifies judgment with assent or dissent (4.14.3), but he might also have used the terms faith and doubt, for judgment determines the degree of probability, 'from full *Assurance* and Confidence, quite down to *Conjecture, Doubt*, and *Distrust*' (4.15.2).

Faith, then, consists of assumptions, the truth of which is probable but not certain. It is faith by which we actually live our lives, for knowledge is limited and revelation is extraordinary (though both are parts of a continuity of human concerns): 'for the state we are at present in, not being that of Vision, we must, in many Things, content our selves with Faith and Probability' (4.3.6). The central concern of faith is not the next world, but this one, and faith itself is not a body of doctrine, but a way of life.

This same spirit, this same concern with the actual living of our lives, is apparent elsewhere in the empiricist tradition, such as in Hume's *An Inquiry Concerning Human Understanding* (1748). 'Philosophical decisions,' writes Hume, 'are nothing but the reflections of common life, methodized and corrected.'[40] But when these decisions are removed from human experience, they lose their force, and vanish 'when the philosopher leaves the shade and comes into open day' (16).

The great subverter of Pyrrhonism, or the excessive principles of skepticism, is action, and employment, and the occupations of common life. These principles may flourish and triumph in the schools, where it is indeed difficult, if not impossible, to refute them. But as soon as they leave the shade, and by the presence of the real objects which actuate our passions and sentiments are put in opposition to the more powerful principles of our nature, they vanish like smoke and leave the most determined skeptic in the same condition as other mortals. (167)

There is no need to fear that Hume's own scepticism, and 'the Academic or Skeptical philosophy' to which it is related, 'should ever undermine the reasonings of common life and carry its doubts so far as to destroy all action as well as speculation. Nature will always maintain her rights and prevail in the end over any abstract reasoning whatsoever' (55). Hume's motto sums up this spirit: 'Be a philosopher, but, amidst all your philosophy, be still a man' (18).

This same spirit pervades Tennyson's poetry, and is particularly evident when Tennyson talks about the relation between knowledge and faith, about the limitations of knowledge, and about faith as the basis of conduct. The failure of this spirit makes the speaker of 'Supposed Confessions' the 'Second-Rate Sensitive Mind' that Tennyson's title indicates. When confronted with the atonement – 'Men say that Thou / Didst die for me' (2–3) – the speaker can only continue to ask for a sign, though he is ashamed of such a desire:

> That even now,
> In this extremest misery
> Of ignorance, I should require
> A sign! and if a bolt of fire
> Would rive the slumbrous summer noon
> While I do pray to Thee alone,
> Think my belief would stronger grow!                    (7–13)

In Lockeian terms, the speaker is confronting the testimony of others ('Men say' is the operative phrase) and finds that it does not fit his own experience. The definitive solution is knowledge; the sign would be evidence, available to the senses, of the existence of God. But such knowledge is not forthcoming, and the alternative is the life of faith, in which the individual assumes the existence of God and the efficacy of the atonement, though he cannot prove either.[41] 'And what is left to me, but Thou, / And faith in Thee?' (18-19), the speaker asks, and he indicates the value of such an affirmation in his description of the Christian community (19-32). But when he comes to affirm his faith – 'Why not believe then?' (123) – he lacks the strength to do so, and he remains, Hamlet-like, unable to act, in a 'damnèd vacillating state!' (190) – the Tennysonian parallel to Locke's sitting still and perishing.

The young man in the late poem 'The Ancient Sage' is not in quite so enervated a state, but he, too, fails to understand the relation between knowledge and faith. The young man says, in his lyric, that 'The nameless Power, or Powers, that rule / Were never heard or seen' (29–30), and the sage answers by telling the young man to turn within himself, where

> thou
> Mayst haply learn the Nameless hath a voice,
> By which thou wilt abide, if thou be wise,
> As if thou knewest, though thou canst not know.        (33–6)

The young man assumes that, because he cannot prove the existence of a deity, the concept ought to have no part in his life. But the sage knows that, in the absence of such proof, it is just as legitimate to affirm the existence of God as it is to deny it, and he knows, too, that the choice between affirmation and denial has a bearing on the whole course of one's life. Denial, in Tennyson's scheme of things, is likely to lead to materialism and its undermining of all human concerns. Affirmation leads to a sense of the mystery of all things. Like Locke, the sage emphasizes the limitations of knowledge. 'Thou canst not prove the Nameless, O my son' (57), he says, and he proceeds with a litany of things that cannot be proved. 'For nothing worthy proving can be proven, / Nor yet disproven' (66–7). The limitations of human knowledge are an inescapable part of our existence, but they ought not to prove a barrier to the affirmations which our lives require. Hence the advice of the sage:

> wherefore thou be wise,
> Cleave ever to the sunnier side of doubt,
> And cling to Faith beyond the forms of Faith! (67–9)

Faith and doubt are both, in Locke's term, opinion, and lack the certainty of knowledge; but for Tennyson, the choice between them is crucial. The 'sunnier side of doubt' is faith, and faith consists of all those assumptions which make life worth while. Creeds – 'the forms of Faith' – are limited things, and Tennyson's typical concern is with conduct, not doctrine.

In the prologue to *In Memoriam*, the distinction between faith and knowledge is insistent, not because Tennyson sees the two, finally, as opposed, but because, like Locke, he is keenly aware of the role of faith in making up for the limitations of knowledge. 'Believing where we cannot prove' (4) is the basis of every human life. Even our knowledge, finally, is a mystery based on faith:

> We have but faith: we cannot know;
> For knowledge is of things we see;
> And yet we trust it comes from thee,
> A beam in darkness: let it grow. (21–4)

How do we know that our senses are not deceiving us, and giving us a false picture of the world outside us – those very senses which provide us with data, which in turn are the bases of knowledge of which we are certain? We cannot prove, in any final way, that our senses are not deceiving us; we assume that they are not, and Tennyson indicates such faith by using the verb 'trust.' Locke makes *'the notice we have by our Senses, of the existing of Things without* us' the third degree of knowledge, but Locke clearly indicates in this passage from the *Essay* (4.11.3) that the assumption 'that our Faculties act and inform us right' is indeed an assumption by using words like 'assurance,' 'confidence,' and 'persuade' rather than 'certainty.' Even our knowledge, finally, is based on assumptions which are not provable, so that faith becomes the basis of practically everything that is of concern to us as human beings.

In this context, the much maligned ending of 'The Two Voices' becomes a good deal more acceptable. The poem is a debate and, at least initially, each voice strives to prove its arguments. At the end of the first stage of the debate, the self is ready to say to the still small voice, 'Thou canst not know' (43), but is prevented from doing so by tears. The charge could be turned against himself, since he has no certain answer for the voice's materialist arguments. Instead, he repeats his earlier charges:

'If all be dark, vague voice,' I said,
'These things are wrapt in doubt and dread,
Nor canst thou show the dead are dead.'

(265–7)

Charge and countercharge indicate the end desired by the debaters: certainty. And yet it is evident that the issues in the debate – the value of life, moral and spiritual progress, immortality – are not, in Locke's terms, matters of knowledge, and there can be no certainty about them. When the self wants to undermine the voice's arguments, he says that he finds in the words 'No certain clearness, but at best / A vague suspicion of the breast' (335–6); when the still small voice wants to undermine the arguments of the self, he labels them 'dreams' (386). Clearly there can be no resolution to the debate, so long as the argument is cast in these terms. The only resolution can be a turning away from the debate to the actual living of life. So the dialogue ceases, dawn breaks, and the self looks out to see a family going to church. The scene itself proves nothing, but the speaker's response to it is crucial: 'I blest them' (424). The blessing is an affirmation of the values of life, especially of family life and of worship; such a conviction cannot be proved, but its efficacy in the speaker's life is already apparent. The point is clear enough: one lives, not by knowledge, but by faith. F.E.L. Priestley's comments on the conclusion are surely right. The ending, he says, brings 'a sudden reminder of the arid and academic nature of the argument. No one decides to live or not to live, or feels or fails to feel the value of existence, by this sort of logic or by search for this sort of proof.'[42] Locke's statement of purpose is worth quoting again in this context: we should not 'intemperately require Demonstration, and demand Certainty, where Probability only is to be had, and which is sufficient to govern all our Concernments' (1.1.5).

Tennyson never disparages knowledge. Rather, he desires its advance, as in section cxiv of *In Memoriam*. At the same time, he is aware that he must live his life now, when knowledge is imperfect, and the assumptions that necessarily complete knowledge are the substance of faith. The combination of knowledge and faith Tennyson calls wisdom, and wisdom involves the right ordering of the two, and the recognition of the nature and limitations of both. At the end of 'The Two Voices,' the self becomes wise; he does not reject knowledge, but he relates it and his faith to conduct – Locke's final concern, too – and so finds blessedness.

Like faith and opinion, language is arbitrary. God may have given us the capacity to speak, but he did not give us a vocabulary or tell us what to say, so that we must constantly use our judgment to make sense of our experience and to determine our conduct. As I pointed out in chapter 1, language is arbitrary, not because we are capricious in our response to our experience, but because we are selective; every word is, as Locke says, 'the free choice of the Mind, pursuing its own ends' (3.5.6). Our generalizations *'are the Inventions and Creatures of the Understanding*, made by it for its own use' (3.3.11). We do not provide names for everything, but only for those things that have a bearing on our physical, moral, and spiritual life. We do not make assertions about everything, but only about those things that bear upon our existence and our conduct. The statements we make about the evidence of our senses ought, in Locke's view, to correspond to the relations we actually observe in the world around us, so that propositions, in their 'agreement with the reality of Things' (4.5.8), are like windows or mirrors. But we must also make statements concerning things about which we cannot have certain knowledge, but which are nonetheless of concern to us. We are led to judge these statements as probably true by 'our own Knowledge, Observation, and Experience' and by the testimony of others (4.15.4). Hence, success in life depends upon good judgment, and in *In Memoriam* the model for good judgment is Hallam, presented in the poem as the master of discursive talk.

'If Arthur Hallam had lived he would have been "one of the foremost men of his time, *but not as a poet*,"' Locker-Lampson reports Tennyson as saying.[43] Instead, he would have been known – as he was at Cambridge – as a conversationalist, a public speaker, and a debater, his fame resting upon his judgment in using words. The 'clear-headed friend' of *Poems, Chiefly Lyrical* (1830; the poem, which is titled simply 'To ——,' is #74 in Ricks' edition) was at first Blakesley but anticipates the Hallam of *In Memoriam*. The controlling image is the mental fight, with words as weapons. The friend sets people free with his 'joyful scorn, / Edged with sharp laughter,' and he does so by indicating, in his talk, that words are a human creation, setting out conditional and changing rather than fixed and absolute truth. As usual, Tennyson associates this latter kind of truth with creeds, but the friend

> cuts atwain
> The knots that tangle human creeds,
> The wounding cords that bind and strain
> The heart until it bleeds ...                                    (2–5)

Language is more effective than flame and sword: 'A gentler death shall Falsehood die, / Shot through and through with cunning words' (16–17).

In *In Memoriam*, Hallam's skill appears in casual conversation, as it does in section lxxxix, an idyll in which the friends 'banquet in the distant woods' (32):

> Whereat we glanced from theme to theme,
> Discussed the books to love or hate,
> Or touched the changes of the state,
> Or threaded some Socratic dream ...                             (33–6)

But Hallam's skill reveals itself best in debate, the topic of section lxxxvii. The imagery, which is of some importance, is drawn from archery:

> When one would aim an arrow fair,
> But send it slackly from the string;

And one would pierce an outer ring,
    And one an inner, here and there;

And last the master-bowman, he,
    Would cleave the mark. A willing ear
    We lent him. Who, but hung to hear
The rapt oration flowing free

From point to point, with power and grace
    And music in the bounds of law,
    To those conclusions when we saw
The God within him light his face,

And seem to lift the form, and glow
    In azure orbits heavenly-wise ...                    (25–38)

Lying behind the figure of the master-bowman is Apollo, the god of light, whose arrows figure his rays, and also his words. In his early poem 'The Poet,' Tennyson uses the arrow image in this way; his words are the 'viewless arrows of his thoughts' (11), then 'arrow-seeds' (19) that turn the world into a garden. But in this section of *In Memoriam*, the emphasis is not so much on the arrows themselves as on their hitting the mark. The image signifies correct judgment. We remember, in passing, that the reversals suffered by the tragic hero frequently come about through *hamartia*, an error in judgment, the word itself coming from archery, and meaning literally 'missing the mark.' *Hamartia* is also the New Testament word for sin, that turning away from God through wrong choice. Human beings make wrong choices because their knowledge is limited, and the limitations of knowledge and its inadequacy as a guide for conduct are, as we have already seen, central themes in Locke's *Essay*. But, where knowledge is insufficient, human beings have the aid of judgment. Locke identifies judgment with assent or dissent when it is 'about Truths delivered in Words' (4.14.3), and truth involves, not discrete words, but words as related in propositions. For the proper use of words in such a context, judgment is crucial, for, as Locke insists in book 4, truth must be not only verbal but real, and '*real Truth*' is expressed 'when these signs are joined, as our *Ideas* agree; and when our *Ideas* are such, as we know are capable of having an Existence in Nature' (4.5.8). Thus we hit the mark. Locke does not use that image, but Socrates does in the *Cratylus*, and does so, interestingly enough, when he is asked about the etymology of the word 'opinion.' He suggests two possible roots, but 'the shooting of a bow' is the more likely one because it is, he says, also linked with words for thinking and deliberating. All these words 'involve the idea of shooting,' and their opposite is a 'missing, or mistaking of the mark, or aim.'[44]

The *real Truth* of Hallam's words is confirmed by the experience to which they give rise. The ecstatic moment of section xcv comes about when Tennyson reads the dead man's letters:

> But when those others, one by one,
>     Withdrew themselves from me and night,
>     And in the house light after light
> Went out, and I was all alone,
>
> A hunger seized my heart; I read
>     Of that glad year which once had been,
>     In those fallen leaves which kept their green,
> The noble letters of the dead:
>
> And strangely on the silence broke
>     The silent-speaking words, and strange
>     Was love's dumb cry defying change
> To test his worth; and strangely spoke
>
> The faith, the vigour, bold to dwell
>     On doubts that drive the coward back,
>     And keen through wordy snares to track
> Suggestion to her inmost cell.
>
> So word by word, and line by line,
>     The dead man touched me from the past,
>     And all at once it seemed at last
> The living soul was flashed on mine ...                    (17–36)

We can most clearly see the kind of response that these lines describe if we contrast it with another kind of communication earlier in the poem. In the explicitly pastoral section xxiii, the conventional animation of nature figures the unity of man with his surroundings, and that unity is matched by the oneness of man with man. Such oneness makes speech unnecessary, since poet and friend communicate, like the angels in *Paradise Lost*, by instant apprehension:

When each by turns was guide to each,
  And Fancy light from Fancy caught,
  And Thought leapt out to wed with Thought
Ere Thought could wed itself with Speech ...                    (13–16)

In section xxiv, Tennyson begins to question that idealized past, and turns instead to their ordinary relations. Here, instant apprehension gives way to comprehension, which is won with effort and through words. That comprehension can mature into inspiration is the discovery of section xcv, and in that lyric Tennyson is going considerably beyond Locke. Locke's chapter on particles is brief, and its brevity indicates that, for all he has to say about assent and dissent in book 4, his account of language is largely an atomistic one, with its emphasis on the word as the sign of an idea, and with its suggestion that propositions are no more than the sum of the ideas that make them up. The poet in section xcv begins with the atomistic approach, 'word by word': 'So word by word, and line by line, / The dead man touched me from the past' (33–4). But we note that he proceeds from words to lines, from parts to units of meaning, and the stanza clearly indicates that meaning is more than the sum of its parts, that the words gain full meaning and power from their context, and that the suggestiveness of the structure not only prods the mind to act, but sparks thoughts and experiences at which words can only hint. This shift from the consecutive to the simultaneous, from the discrete words to the whole that is greater than the sum of its parts, epitomizes the development of language theory in England between Locke and Coleridge.

This shaping power of the mind, as Tennyson presents it, gains its authority from the judgment of Hallam, the 'heavenly friend' described in section cxxix, and present in section xcv. The presence of an inspiring male figure is a situation not unique in Tennyson's work. For instance, has anyone noticed the extent to which Tennyson's Cambridge prize poem, 'Timbuctoo' (1829), anticipates the situation of section xcv of *In Memoriam*? Culler, who discusses the relationship between 'Armageddon' and 'Timbuctoo' in some detail, notes that the second poem deals with the central problem of expression ('to give / Utterance to things inutterable,' as 'Armageddon' puts it, 1.16–17) by shifting from 'objective, divine inspiration' to 'the subjective power of the imagination.'[45] This shift raises the same issue about propositions – what truth can they claim? – that we have been examining in relation to Hallam's judgment in *In Memoriam*, and the solution anticipates that of section xcv.

As in section xcv, the 'I' of 'Timbuctoo' is alone and gazing with desire on the scene before him, the desire being based upon memory and its preservation of 'legends quaint and old' (16). The elegiac note is obvious in the passage which uses the *ubi sunt* formula (40–53) and in the cry of desire (54–61). With that cry comes the moment of illumination, the sudden appearance of the Seraph who is the Spirit of Fable. Like Hallam, he is a male figure who inspires through his mastery of words, fable being story, and also (if we focus on its Latin root, *fabula*) talk. The central question is about the kind of authority to which fable can lay claim. The Seraph simply asserts the truth of fable – its vine, he says, is 'Deep-rooted in the living soil of truth' (221) – but not before he has presented an argument against the view that fable is simple fiction, and evidence of solipsism. The Seraph affirms that fable has its seat in 'the heart of man' (192), just as the poet had earlier affirmed that 'legends quaint and old' (16) 'had their being in the heart of Man' (19). But he also affirms that sensations are his allies. With these

> 'I play about his heart a thousand ways,
> Visit his eyes with visions, and his ears
> With harmonies of wind and wave and wood.'                    (201–3)

Clearly sensations come from without, and the shaping of them from within. Fable is thus not solipsistic, but participates in those aspects of creation that are of concern to us. In the moment of illumination, the poet sees atoms and galaxies, the smallest parts and the largest patterns of creation. He has not literally seen either, of course, but these are the probable affirmations that his mind provides for the data from his senses.

The statements of faith in the prologue to *In Memoriam* are highly self-conscious statements. Tennyson is just as concerned with the way in which human beings make affirmations as he is with their content. The content of his own faith was simple and consciously undogmatic. 'He constantly emphasized his own belief in what he called the Eternal Truths,' his son writes in his *Memoir*, 'in an Omnipotent, Omnipresent and All-loving God, Who has revealed Himself through the human attribute of the highest self-sacrificing love; in the freedom of the human will; and in the immortality of the soul.'[46] To friends, he stated his faith even more simply. 'Two things ... I have always been firmly convinced of,' he told William Allingham in 1884, ' – God, – and that death will not end my existence.'[47] Jowett recorded that Tennyson often spoke of God, free will, and immortality, and James Knowles says that he wrote down this statement '(with the date) exactly and at once': 'There's a something that watches over us; and our individuality endures: that's my faith, and that's all my faith.'[48] But more typically in the Memoir we find Tennyson reflecting on the nature rather than the content of faith, distinguishing faith from knowledge, and giving authority to our human needs and concerns: 'if faith mean anything at all it is trusting to those instincts, or feelings, or whatever they may be called, which assure us of some life after this,'[49] he told a correspondent in 1863. The same emphasis is apparent in the prologue, where the statements of faith are often framed by verbs that indicate (if we read them in a Lockeian context) that the statements are opinion. The verbs Tennyson often uses to indicate opinion are 'think' and 'trust,' and they usually appear as the main verbs in the syntactical units, while the affirmations of faith appear as noun clauses, the objects of those verbs: man 'thinks he was not made to die' (11); 'we trust it [knowledge] comes from thee' (23); 'I trust he [Hallam] lives in thee' (39). Where the affirmations of faith appear to stand on their own, as they do in the second and fifth stanzas, for instance, the pronouns ('Thine' and 'our,' 'Thou' and 'we') embody the human perspective from which these statements are made, so that even without the explicit 'He thinks' or 'I trust' the reader is conscious of human opinion and its partial glimpses of truth.

The giving of authority to our human needs and concerns can be understood in a Coleridgian as well as a Lockeian context, and, to complete this account of Tennyson's statements of faith, we must also consider Coleridge's teaching in matters of faith. For Coleridge reacted against the Christian apologetics of the eighteenth century, with its persistent use of external evidence – the design of nature, scripture, miracles, and testimony – and based his defence of Christianity on inner need. Graham Hough has already indicated some of the parallels between Aids to Reflection and In Memoriam,[50] and his article, we should remember, helps to answer Harold Nicolson's 1923 charge, that Tennyson's idea 'that God must exist because the human heart felt an instinctive need of His existence' is a 'pathetically inadequate formula.'[51] Its adequacy becomes apparent when we look at it in the context of the history of ideas.

As Hough points out, Coleridge was reacting against the apologetics of the eighteenth century, in which Christianity was defended on the basis of outer evidence. The best-known examples of such a defence were Paley's. His *Evidences of Christianity* (1794) and his *Natural Theology* (1802) were, as I have already said, required texts at Cambridge; in the former, Paley defends the historical truth of the Gospel narratives by examining the testimony of contemporary witnesses and pronouncing it credible; in the latter, his argument from design gains much of its power from the famous analogy – the watch and the watchmaker – with which he begins. The persuasiveness of the argument disguises the poverty of the faith which it purportedly strengthens, and there is no better account of the relation of such an argument to faith than Mark Pattison's. In his seminal essay, 'Tendencies of Religious Thought in England, 1688–1750,' which appeared in the controversial *Essays and Reviews* of 1860, Pattison says of the religious literature of the eighteenth century: 'Christianity appeared made for nothing else but to be "proved"; what use to make of it when it was proved was not much thought about. Reason was at first offered as the basis of faith, but gradually became its substitute. The mind never advanced as far as the stage of belief, for it was unceasingly engaged in reasoning up to it.' 'When an age is found occupied in proving its creed,' writes Pattison aphoristically, 'this is but a token that the age has ceased to have a proper belief in it.'[52] Coleridge's apologetics was, then, a necessary corrective. He recognized that evidence can be forceful and persuasive only if it meets a human need; that need is prior to the evidence, and gives it its value. Faith is not a quality of outward things, but a human capacity, and it is inherent in our actual human experience.

Again and again in *Aids to Reflection* Coleridge appeals to our inner experience. The existence of God, for instance, cannot be conclusively demonstrated. 'But I also hold, that this truth, the hardest to demonstrate, is the one which of all others least needs to be demonstrated' (121); 'the Truth which it is the least possible to prove, it is little less than impossible not to believe!' (121).[53] So, too, with the idea of redemption and the doctrine of the atonement: 'The most *momentous* question a man can ask is, Have I a Saviour? And yet as far as the individual querist is concerned, it is premature and to no purpose, unless another question has been previously put and answered ... namely, Have I any need of a Saviour?' (165–6). And in his Conclusion, Coleridge alludes to Paley in a passage often quoted: '*Evidences of Christianity!* I am weary of the word. Make a man feel the *want* of it; rouse him, if you can, to the self-knowledge of his *need* of it; and you may safely trust it to its own Evidence' (272).

Coleridge's reaction against the religious writers of the eighteenth century came directly to Tennyson through the Apostles. We know that they debated the question 'Is an intelligible First Cause deducible from the phenomena of the Universe?' and that on this question Tennyson voted 'No.'[54] Again and again Tennyson would confirm that vote. In section cxxiv of *In Memoriam*, for instance, he writes, 'I found Him not in world or sun, / Or eagle's wing, or insect's eye' (5-6). Instead, he appeals to 'A warmth within the breast' (13), to (what the self in 'The Two Voices' calls) the 'heat of inward evidence' (284). 'It is hard to believe in God,' Tennyson's son quotes him as saying, 'but it is harder not to believe. I believe in God, not from what I see in Nature, but from what I find in man.'[55] Tennyson's best-known images of human need are in *In Memoriam*: the child crying in the night at the end of section liv, and the poet groping with 'lame hands of faith' at the end of section lv. In both sections, Tennyson rejects the idea that nature provides evidence of a loving God but, as the elegy proceeds, he realizes that to turn outward for such evidence is to move in the wrong direction. The cry, which seemed so full of despair, is itself the evidence he is seeking, and the groping, doomed to fail, is itself an affirmation. The final stanzas of section cxxiv use both images to affirm faith:

If e'er when faith had fallen asleep,
　I heard a voice 'believe no more'
　And heard an ever-breaking shore
That tumbled in the Godless deep;

A warmth within the breast would melt
　The freezing reason's colder part,
　And like a man in wrath the heart
Stood up and answered 'I have felt.'

No, like a child in doubt and fear:
　But that blind clamour made me wise;
　Then was I as a child that cries,
But, crying, knows his father near;

And what I am beheld again
What is, and no man understands;
And out of darkness came the hands
That reach through nature, moulding men.                    (9–24)

The crying is an affirmation – the child 'knows his father near' – but it is easy to look at this affirmation, as Nicolson does, as 'pathetically inadequate.' The affirmation is far more persuasive for us when we examine it in the context of Coleridge's lifelong concern with the definitions of 'subjective' and 'objective,' and with the true relation of subject and object.[56] The proofs and evidences of eighteenth-century religious writers were based on the assumption of a sharp distinction between subject and object – subject being the believer, and object the thing believed – and on a second assumption that truth must be external and factual, and carefully separated from the fictions created by our minds. Coleridge would break down the distinction between subject and object, and make us participants in the very being of the universe. In *Aids to Reflection*, in a long footnote to the second of the 'Aphorisms on Spiritual Religion,' he sets about the task of reintroducing the adjectives 'objective' and 'subjective' not as exclusive terms but as 'correspondent opposites,' and he sets out the nature of *'objective* and *subjective reality'* in the verbal pattern I have already examined, the 'Noetic Pentad' (117–18). The point of the pattern alone need concern us here: it makes us not a disposable part of a world already made but an essential participant in creation; it makes human perception and human concepts a reflection or turning back of divine energy; and it makes the universe not a dead object but a living process. In this context, human needs are not empty dreams, but essential and revealing parts of creation itself. These needs are the basis of a dynamic relationship which Coleridge calls reflection.

At the beginning of the book, Coleridge tells us that his prime concern is not 'a full and consistent Scheme' of Christian doctrine, but a way of approaching it, a method which he calls 'the art of REFLECTION' (xix). This method is literally a turning back or bending back, an action which the mind ought to take with all things of which it is conscious: one's 'own thoughts, actions, circumstances' (xix), words themselves, and 'their birth, derivation and history' (xix), and all data which come to us through our senses, and for which the mind provides 'certain inherent forms' (149). Reflection in relation to spiritual matters can perhaps be best understood by the conventional metaphor which Coleridge uses: God is light, and, in a dynamic relationship with him, we turn back that light when we reflect. Coleridge says:

Nothing is wanted but the eye, which is the light of this house, the light which is the eye of this soul. This *seeing* light, this *enlightening* eye, is Reflection. It is more, indeed, than is ordinarily meant by that word; but it is what a Christian ought to mean by it, and to know too, whence it first came, and still continues to come – of what light even this light is *but* a reflection. This, too, is THOUGHT; and all thought is but unthinking that does not flow out of this, or tend towards it. (4)

The goal of reflection is 'a lively conviction' and a 'power of thinking connectedly' (xiii). The 'lively conviction' is not primarily in a system of beliefs, but in the reader's 'responsibility as a moral agent' (xiii). The purpose of *Aids to Reflection* is the development of virtue, and Coleridge (for whom reflecting on words is crucial) defines the word in its original sense, as 'Manhood or Manliness' (128). His purpose is clear in the full title of the first edition of 1825: *Aids to Reflection in the Formation of a Manly Character, on the Several Grounds of Prudence, Morality, and Religion.*

*In Memoriam* is, among other things, about 'the Formation of a Manly Character' in the speaker himself, and this development depends upon the poet's response to Hallam's death. That response is, in a broad sense, a reflection of Hallam himself, recognized in section cxxix as the 'heavenly friend' and in the epithalamium as 'a noble type / Appearing ere the times were ripe' (138–9). The poet's new sense of strength and wisdom is set out in section xcvi, and in the dream of ciii, where 'I felt the thews of Anakim, / The pulses of a Titan's heart' (31–2). Such passages indicate that reflection is not just imitation of a model; it is, rather, a dynamic relationship in which man is constantly appropriating and turning back the spiritual energy which comes from the being who is both the subject and object of attention. This energy manifests itself primarily as love.

The fifth of Coleridge's 'Moral and Religious Aphorisms' is from Leighton, who characterizes human love as a reflection of divine love: 'If, therefore, [God's children] can read the characters of God's image in their own soul, those are the counterpart of the golden characters of his love, in which their names are written in the book of life' (37). Such love is an active and living relation:

He that loves may be sure that he was loved first; and he that chooses God for his delight and portion, may conclude confidently, that God has chosen him to be one of those that shall enjoy him, and be happy in him for ever; for that our love and electing of him is but the return and repercussion of the beams of his love shining upon us. (38)

Leighton's words give the essential characteristics of love: it is an energy which provides us with assurance that we are not alone, and that assurance is faith; it is an energy which carries us out of ourselves, and yet at the same time it assures us that the otherness of its object is not an alienating thing, but a kindred being; it is the mark of a freely chosen relationship, and it goes hand in hand with the will and the moral action which is the will's chief concern. Coleridge insists on this last point, especially when he attacks the confusion of love with sensibility, with 'shapeless feelings, sentiments, impulses' (25); Love becomes Love, he writes, 'by an inward FIAT of the Will, by a completing and sealing Art of Moral Election, and lays claim to permanence only under the form of DUTY' (25–6). He quotes Leighton – the quotation is the twenty-third of the 'Introductory Aphorisms' – to the effect that the ceremonial law of the Old Testament was the letter, 'of which morality was the *spirit*': 'But morality itself is the service and ceremonial ... of the Christian religion' (13). And the spirit of that religion is love.

Similar views on love are to be found in Hallam's essays, 'On Sympathy,' 'Essay on the Philosophical Writings of Cicero,' and *Theodicaea Novissima*. In the essay on Cicero, Hallam defines love, 'in its simplest ethical sense, as a word of the same import with sympathy, [as] the desire which one sentient being feels for another's gratification, and consequent aversion to another's pain.'[57] This, says Hallam, is 'the broad and deep foundation of our moral nature' (157). Hallam is concerned with love, not just between beings who find themselves in similar circumstances, but between a human and a higher being. Here the human being meets with difficulties: 'Can he love what he does not know? Can he know what is essentially incomprehensible?' (161). 'But Christianity has made up the difference' (161) because the Son became flesh, and made known the Father. Hallam concludes in a manner similar to Coleridge and Leighton: 'Thus the Christian faith is the necessary complement of a sound ethical system' (161). Love is the spirit of which morality is the letter.[58]

Tennyson begins *In Memoriam* with an apostrophe to the Son as love:

'Strong Son of God, immortal Love.' The apposition, one notes, makes love the essential characteristic of the Son, and one notes, too, that the love here is not a love between equals, but rather a love between lower and higher. Throughout the elegy, Tennyson talks about his love for Hallam, and though (especially in the early sections) he portrays himself and Hallam as friends, he finally pictures Hallam as a higher being. Their love, then, is a love between unequals, and the pattern for this relation is the most essential of Christian relationships.

The link between reflection and faith is clear in the opening stanza of the prologue to *In Memoriam* – the same stanza which can be read in a Lockeian context – where the diction and sound patterns embody brilliantly the nature of reflection:

> Strong Son of God, immortal Love,
>   Whom we, that have not seen thy face,
>   By faith, and faith alone, embrace,
> Believing where we cannot prove ...

'Believing' is the expected word as the opposite of proving, but it is an especially appropriate word, since its Old English predecessor, the verb *geliefan*, is derived from a still older Teutonic root, *luð*, from which the word 'love' is also derived. In the 'Preliminary Essay' to his *A New Dictionary of the English Language* (1836–7) – this was the dictionary Tennyson owned and used – Charles Richardson traces 'love' to the Anglo-Saxon *Luf-ian*, and links it with *Hlif-ian*, to select, to prefer; he also links 'believe' and 'live,' but does not explicitly link 'believe' and 'love.'[59] Tennyson, however, makes the relation between 'Love' and 'Believing' in the stanza crucial. We note, first of all, that the love relation is a relation between unequals ('we' and the Son), and that our response to love is belief, our human realization of 'immortal Love'; we note, next, that the essential element in belief is love, so that our belief is a reflection (in Coleridge's sense) of 'immortal Love'; we note, finally, that divine love initiates a dynamic relationship in which we return that love in its human form. This act of reflection is complemented by the Lockeian sense of the middle two lines, where both alliteration and assonance link the words 'face' and 'faith.' 'Thy face' may not be apprehended by our senses, and we may not know it in an empirically demonstrable way; but where knowledge is limited, faith takes over, supplying assumptions which are necessary in our lives.

I have already referred to Tennyson's faith as unsystematic, and the lack of system is a greater virtue than may at first be apparent, if we examine it in the light of *Aids to Reflection*. The purpose of its method is to relate our thinking to our conduct, a purpose Coleridge insists on in his distinction, twice given, between 'abstract or speculative reason' and 'practical reason.' 'Speculative reason' is concerned with *'formal* (or abstract) truth' (143), with doctrine (such as the Trinity), and with creeds; 'practical reason' is concerned with *'actual* (or moral) truth' (143), with conduct, and with human needs. The latter comprehends 'the Will, the Conscience, the Moral Being with its inseparable Interests and Affections' (115); it is 'the Organ of *Wisdom*, and (as far as man is concerned) the source of living and actual Truths' (115). 'Let the believer never be alarmed,' Coleridge says elsewhere in this same section, 'by objections wholly speculative, however plausible on speculative grounds such objections may appear, if he can but satisfy himself, that the *result* is repugnant to the dictates of conscience, and irreconcilable with the interests of morality' (111). In the fourth of the 'Aphorisms on Spiritual Religion,' there is an attack on speculation which is abstracted from conduct: 'This was the true and first apostasy – when in council and synod the Divine Humanities of the Gospel gave way to speculative Systems, and Religion became a Science of Shadows under the name of Theology, or at best a bare Skeleton of Truth, without life or interest, alike inaccessible and unintelligible to the majority of Christians' (126). Coleridge, one hastens to add, is not opposed to theology and to systems of philosophy, as his comment on the second aphorism indicates (see 122–3), and he has much to say about doctrines like that of the Trinity. But his treatment of this doctrine is typical. After he discusses the concept, he says, in words that remind one of Hume's, 'I now pass out of the Schools, and enter into discourse with some friend or neighbour, unversed in the *formal* sciences, unused to the process of abstraction, neither Logician nor Metaphysician' (116). Here the question shifts from the nature of God to the needs of man, and to 'the economy of his own soul' (122). The shift leads Coleridge to define the criterion by which all doctrine is to be judged: 'Revelation must have assured it, my Conscience required it – or in some way or other I must have an *interest* in this belief. It must *concern* me, as a moral and responsible Being' (120). 'My object,' Coleridge says elsewhere in this same comment on the second aphorism, 'has been to establish a general rule of interpretation and vindication applicable to *all* doctrinal tenets' (114), and this 'general rule' is 'that all Revealed Truths are to be judged of by us, as far as they are possible subjects of human conception, or grounds of practice, or in some way connected with our moral and spiritual interests' (114). His description of his religion confirms this rule: 'Christianity is not a Theory, or a Speculation; but a *Life*; – not a *Philosophy* of Life, but a Life and a Living Process' (134).

'I found Him not in world or sun,' says Tennyson in section cxxiv of *In Memoriam*, 'Nor through the questions men may try, / The petty cobwebs we have spun.' In the prologue, these cobwebs are 'Our little systems' which are 'but broken lights of thee.' Tennyson places these 'little systems' in the context of an energetic and flexible response to the actual circumstances of our lives, so that his faith is indeed 'a Life and a Living Process.'

Faith as the expression of inner need has its counterpart in the language theory which locates the origin of speech in the natural but inarticulate cry. Tennyson's picture of himself in section liv of *In Memoriam* as 'An infant crying in the night: / An infant crying for the light: / And with no language but a cry' (18–20) is rich in suggestiveness, not least because, as Ricks points out in his notes (2:370), 'infant' is derived from the Latin *infans*, unable to speak. Tennyson's phrase 'with no language but a cry' is a periphrastic translation of the Latin word. Equally suggestive are the colons and the parallelism of lines 18 and 19: the colons point forward, linking units where the syntactical structure is the same but the prepositions and their objects are different, and thus suggesting relations beyond the discrete words. 'In the night' describes the child's circumstance (a word which, for Tennyson, meant – as Ricks points out, 1:271 – 'the totality of surrounding things'), a world not of the child's making and not corresponding in any obvious way to his needs and desires. 'For the light' is the child's active response to circumstance, the preposition indicating his desire. This desire, in Tennyson's thinking as in Coleridge's, is not an empty thing. The very fact that it is part of our makeup gives it some degree of authority, though this fact is no proof that the desire will be fulfilled. Nonetheless, it does provide both the motive and the energy for expression, and Tennyson often suggests a return to this source as a first step in renewal, or for the healing of the wound caused by grief. 'I cannot endure that men should sacrifice everything at the cold altar of what with their imperfect knowledge they choose to call truth and reason,'[60] Hallam Tennyson records his father as saying. Tennyson told James Knowles, when they were discussing *In Memoriam* in 1870 and 1871, that he was thinking of adding another poem to the elegy, 'a speculative one bringing out the thoughts of the higher Pantheism and showing that all the arguments are about as good on one side as the other – & thus throw man back more & more on the primitive impulses & feelings.'[61] Tennyson is not necessarily disparaging knowledge or suggesting that we ought not to reflect or speculate or construct arguments, but he is indicating that arguments are, paradoxically, both inconclusive and necessary to us because they grow out of a basic human need. The cry is the source and generating power of every possible argument for God and immortality, but defies complete articulation.

In using the inarticulate cry as his central image of human needs, instincts, and feelings, Tennyson draws upon a recurring image in accounts of the origin of language, that central question for philosophers of language in the eighteenth century, and still an important question in the nineteenth century. James Stam and Hans Aarsleff have given us detailed accounts of this issue;[62] at the centre of much of this philosophical speculation are the *cris naturels*, the interjections which expressed some feeling or passion – hunger, fear, lust, and the like – and these natural cries are produced by most creatures, so that bird and animal sounds are conventional analogies for inarticulate but expressive human sounds. In his great work *Of the Origin and Progress of Language* (1773–92), Lord Monboddo makes natural inarticulate cries the source of human language, art and invention being necessarily based on nature; and in his *Lectures on Rhetoric and Belles Lettres* (1783), Hugh Blair presents the same view. Though language may have a divine origin, Blair says, God did not give us a fully developed system all at once, but gave us rather capacities upon which we could enlarge and improve. So language began with 'cries of passion,' 'the only signs which nature teaches all men, and which are understood by all'; these 'Interjections, uttered in a strong and passionate manner, were, beyond doubt, the first elements or beginnings of Speech.'[63] The theory was hardly new. Tennyson could have encountered it not only in Blair and in other eighteenth-century writers, but also in Lucretius, since he was thoroughly familiar with the *De Rerum Natura*. There are four different editions of this work in Tennyson's library, and three of them are marked in various ways, with underlining, sidelining, x's, and occasional marginal notes. The passage on natural cries is at 5:1010–90 in the poem, and Tennyson was aware that Horace in one of his satires (1.3.99–111) paraphrased these lines from Lucretius; in his student's copy of Horace, Tennyson underlined line 99 and wrote beside it, 'Vide

Luc. l.v.'[64] In the passage, Lucretius draws a parallel between the expressive cries of human beings and those of creatures. We could not simply have invented language, but built upon gestures both vocal and physical ('vocibus et gestu cum balbe significarent,' 1022), so that the names of things are the result of *utilitas* making use of *natura*. Language thus has a wholly natural origin – it begins as a function of our physical makeup – but Tennyson takes a quite different view of this primal cry, hearing in it the expression of a mysterious, spiritual, and unique self. His son's wail in 'De Profundis' is such a cry, and the poet articulates this holophrastic sound in 'The Human Cry' with which the poem ends, the abstract nouns there being a reflection or turning back toward God of the voice God has given to man. Hence, when Tennyson's Lucretius cries out ('O ye Gods, / I know you careless, yet, behold, to you / From childly wont and ancient use I call,' 207–9), his cry is more than the vocal gesture he himself had written about, and suggests a need that might compensate for the inadequacy of his Epicurean philosophy.

Like Lucretius, Tennyson parallels human cries – specifically his expressions of grief – and the inarticulate cries heard in nature, but again he goes beyond the materialism of Lucretius and suggests a divine purpose working both in the cries themselves and in his articulation of them. In section xxi, for instance, where the 'I' pictures himself in a pastoral mode, taking grasses from the grave and making them into pipes to express his grief, he responds to criticism of his concern with his private emotions thus:

> I do but sing because I must,
> And pipe but as the linnets sing:
>
> And one is glad; her note is gay,
>   For now her little ones have ranged;
>   And one is sad: her note is changed,
> Because her brood is stolen away.       (23–8)

Towards the end of the elegy – in sections cxv and cxvi – bird songs will be associated with consolation, which is not a rejection of the past but an integration of it in the present; not a putting aside of his grief but a conscious building upon it. Tennyson takes his inarticulate cry and makes it a fully articulated poem. So when the linnet sings again in section c, the sound awakens memory, but it is a 'gracious memory,' and has power to heal. And the 'wild bird' who sings with such passion in lxxxviii is a mystery ('O tell me where the senses mix, / O tell me where the passions meet, / Whence radiate'), and its voice seems oracular. This move from the natural expression of emotion to the artful articulation of it to the suggestion of the mysteries of existence is a move that goes beyond the account of the development of language in Monboddo and Blair, where art and invention and practical considerations build upon the interjection. Tennyson seems to be suggesting that his task is to articulate fully the implications of those natural cries, a task at which, by its very nature, he will fail: 'I cannot all command the strings; / The glory of the sum of things / Will flash along the chords and go' (lxxxviii:10–12). Thus the 'natural magic' that Kerry McSweeney has shown so clearly operative in *In Memoriam*[65] has a significance not limited to the observable aspects of physical nature. In an 1832 letter to Emily Tennyson, Hallam had insisted that the voice of the emotions was not only natural and expressive but also mysterious and oracular:

Sure I am that these emotions are not themselves idle, fleeting and insignificant; they passed indeed as all within us passes, at least in form; but the voice they uttered, as their sad & solemn presences hurried by us into indefinite gloom, that voice was oracular; it spoke the significance of life, the form of the riddle of the world; its tones have maddened into tremendous inspiration the souls of all poets & philosophers, since the world began – for, where the Ideas of Time & Sorrow, the one as cause, the other as effect, are not & sway not the soul with power, there is no true knowledge, and therefore no true organ of knowledge in poetry or philosophy.[66]

The highest kind of speech, therefore, is that speech which retains (principally through its tones) the power of the expressive cry while articulating, or at least attempting to articulate, the full implications of that cry. This highest kind of speech Tennyson links with Hallam's voice, and for every human being the highest form of such speech is prayer.

The 'I' of the elegy may long for Hallam's physical presence, the wished-for reunion being imaged in the clasping of hands, but Hallam's voice is a much more important power for him to recover, and it seems to have been the focus of Tennyson's earliest responses to Hallam's death. The voice (followed by the hands) is the first concern of 'some fragmentary lines, which proved to be the germ of

"In Memoriam.'" They date from the winter of 1833–4, and appear in the *Memoir*: 'Where is the voice I loved? ah where / Is that dear hand that I would press?'[67] The same question about the voice appears in various ways in the finished poem. In section xiii, the 'I' laments the fact that Hallam is now 'A Spirit, not a breathing voice' (12), and in lvi, in the midst of the distress caused by recent discoveries in geology and palaeontology, he longs for 'thy voice to soothe and bless!' He has no quarrel with Death, he says in lxxxii, except for one fact: 'He put our lives so far apart / We cannot hear each other speak' (15–16), and in lxxxv he quotes his earlier lament: 'in dear words of human speech / We two communicate no more' (83–4). Section xcv is the turning point, when he does in fact recover Hallam's voice through his letters; they are 'silent-speaking words,' and the oxymoron indicates, not that Hallam's voice has been lost, but that the 'I' has to learn to hear it through new means. The 'I' does learn, the letters being the immediate way to recover the voice, but more problematic is the 'I's' assertion that he hears Hallam's voice in nature, particularly when Tennyson affirms, in well-known passages, that nature is 'red in tooth and claw / With ravine' and gives no evidence of a loving God or a purposeful creation. Nonetheless, in section cxxx he celebrates the recovery of Hallam's voice through nature: 'Thy voice is on the rolling air; / I hear thee where the waters run' (1–2), and Hallam himself is 'mixed with God and Nature' (11). The affirmation here anticipates the affirmation in 'In the Valley of Cauteretz' (1864), where the voice of the stream is the central feature of a setting associated with Hallam. In the climactic four lines, the poet likens the stream's voice to Hallam's voice, and then identifies them, so that the 'dead' is in fact the 'living':

> For all along the valley, down thy rocky bed,
> Thy living voice to me was as the voice of the dead,
> And all along the valley, by rock and cave and tree,
> The voice of the dead was a living voice to me.

The fullest account of the role of Hallam's voice in *In Memoriam* is in a 1988 essay by Elizabeth Hirsh.[68] Her concern is the distinction between speech and writing, speech being considered, in nineteenth-century language theory, primary, while writing was secondary and no more than the record of the spoken word. Frederic Farrar, in his *An Essay on the Origin of Language* (1860), gives the conventional view of this relationship: the sound wave 'reaches but a little distance, and then vanishes like the tremulous ripple on the surface of the sea,' but writing, 'when graven on the stone or painted on the vellum ... passes from one end of the earth to the other for all time; it conquers at once eternity and space.'[69] J.W. Donaldson, Hirsh argues, accepted the view that writing is secondary but gave it new meaning by viewing language as logos, and by arguing that the striving after outward expression produced first speech and then letters, speech being inward and original while writing is outward and secondary. Both, however, proceed from human understanding and, where the voice is lost, letters are indispensable to its recovery. Donaldson argues that the invention of alphabets and of writing was the first step in the overthrow of idolatry, and the invention of the printing press made possible the renewal of Christianity: 'The letter did not kill but gave life, for it was by the letter that the spirit lived again.'[70] So Hallam's letters play a crucial role in section xcv, as do the wedding vows and the parish register in the epithalamium.

The identification of Hallam's voice with the voice of nature is, as I have said, more problematic. An understanding of it is bound up with the view that Tennyson called 'the higher pantheism,' and 'the higher pantheism,' as it appears in the 1869 poem of that title, is profoundly Berkelean in its nature. For though Berkeley was not a pantheist, his philosophy, as Thomas McFarland has pointed out, 'is not a defence against pantheism, and in its implications actually favours pantheism,' the implications being bound up with Berkeley's attempt to establish the monism of mind.[71] Pantheism ordinarily identifies God and the universe or God and nature, but 'the higher pantheism' identifies nature with 'the Vision of Him who reigns,' so that the universe and God's perception of it are one. This reading makes the pronoun in 'vision of Him' a subjective genitive rather than an objective genitive; this reading of the line also helps us to understand the impressions of James Knowles and William Knight, both of whom remark in their reminiscences that Tennyson was a Berkelean.[72] Human perception is far more limited ('the ear of man cannot hear, and the eye of man cannot see') and the world is therefore 'dark' to us. This darkness manifests itself as physical nature, solid and heavy and opaque: 'Earth, these solid stars, this weight of body and limb, / Are they not sign and symbol of thy division from Him?' But in spite of all that the poem has to say about seeing and its limitations, speaking is the means of overcoming the division caused by narrow human sight: 'Speak to Him thou for He hears.' The poem affirms that the voice of nature – it appears here as thunder – is in fact the voice of God, even though our hearing of it is problematic (is God law, or law God?). The limitations of human perception (both sight and hearing) are imaged as 'a straight staff bent in a pool.' Our judgment leads us to assert that the staff is straight, in contradiction to the eye, which sees it as bent. Monboddo uses this image in *Of the Origin and Progress of Language* to make the same point,[73] the point being based on Berkeley's insistence on our distinguishing judgments of the mind from observations of the senses. Berkeley's own examples deal with our judgments of distance and magnitude rather than shape, but the stick that looks bent is readily understandable in a Berkelean context. The data provided by the ear are just as much in need of interpretation as the sensations from the eye, and we may affirm that the voice of nature and the voice of Hallam both proceed from the same source – God, ultimately – and so they are same speaking or (to use Coleridge's adjective) tautegorical. This fact is not self-evident, however, but may be discovered only if we listen attentively and with discrimination. The voice may be oracular, but it is not definitive, and it still requires our judgment to make sense of it and to supply possible interpretations.

Hallam's voice derives its power not just from its ultimate source, which is the same as nature's, but (as I have already argued) from the discrimination or judgment of which it is the embodiment, and its fusion of emotion and reason is the ideal in the poem. Hallam himself had already suggested that ideal in his 1831 'Essay on the Philosophical Writings of Cicero,' where he attacks 'the common use of language, which sets reason or reflection in one scale, and impulse or feeling in the other, and appropriates a right course of conduct to the former alone,' when in fact 'in the eternal harmony of things, as it subsists in the creative idea of the Almighty, the two separate worlds of intellect and emotion conspire to the same end, the possible perfection of human nature.'[74] The phrase that heads this chapter – 'Heart-affluence in discursive talk' – may be, as Alan Sinfield has observed, itself evidence of 'a failure to achieve an adequate form of expression,'[75] but it does, in a rather flat-footed and unpoetic way, define the ideal for speech, an ideal Tennyson identifies with Hallam's talk, and for which he himself is striving. Other phrases in section cix suggest this same fusion of emotion and correct judgment, such as 'Impassioned logic' (7) and, less obviously, 'Seraphic intellect' (5; the seraphs, we remember, were distinguished from the other orders of angels by the intensity of their love of God). But the first phrase is a useful one because it points clearly to the kinds of speech underlying this fusion, expression (the Lincoln manuscript of the poem begins with 'Heart-effluence' rather than 'Heart-affluence') and discursive talk, propositions which are the result of judging in the absence of firm evidence. Tennyson expresses this same fusion in other ways in other sections, as 'sweetness' and 'skill' in cx, for instance, or in the more complex wording of the second stanza of lxxv, where he is striving to describe Hallam's conversation:

> What practice howsoe'er expert
>   In fitting aptest words to things,
>   Or voice the richest-toned that sings,
> Hath power to give thee as thou wert?

Here both judgment ('In fitting aptest words to things') and emotional range (conveyed, as in the poetry of sensation, through tones of voice) are necessary for anyone who would describe Hallam's talk adequately. The highest form of this fusion of feeling and thought, of emotion and judgment, is prayer.

If we return again to 'some fragmentary lines, which,' in Hallam Tennyson's words, 'proved to be the germ of "In Memoriam,"' we find that, even at this very early stage, Tennyson already conceived of Hallam as the type of the perfect (complete) man – 'Larger than human' is his phrase in this fragment – and images him in a posture that links him with prayer: he 'clasps his hands, as one that prays!'[76] The posture is, perhaps, not surprising, since the Apostles had discussed the nature of prayer and were evidently fascinated with it. Hallam Tennyson prints in the *Memoir* a 'remarkable sentence' on prayer by Arthur Hallam, rejecting the usefulness of distinguishing 'the operations of God in me from motions in my own heart'[77] – 'how do you know there is any distinction?' he asks – and Tennyson later made a statement parallel to this question when he was asked about prayer ('I believe that God reveals Himself in each individual soul') and talked about it as the reflection or literally the turning back toward God of this revelation: 'Prayer on our part is the highest aspiration of the soul.'[78] At a gathering at Thomas Woolner's in 1865, Tennyson went further in his talk about prayer: 'The human soul seems to me always in some way – how, we do not know – identical with God,'[79] though in *In Memoriam* the identity is not quite complete: 'The likest God within the soul' gives rise to the wish for immortality (lv:4). When

Tennyson uses images for prayer, the images are those conventionally associated with expressionism, and involve in various ways the flowing of water. He had already had his Arthur tell Bedivere to pray, and 'let thy voice / Rise like a fountain for me night and day' ('Morte d'Arthur' 248–9), and in the *Memoir* his son quotes him as saying, 'Prayer is, to take a mundane simile, like opening a sluice between the great ocean and our little channels when the great sea gathers itself together and flows in at full tide.'[80] He repeated the sluice image at Woolner's in 1865 and, because we so easily associate the conventional flowing with the emotions, we may easily miss the fact that the words springing from within are as much the expression of our judgment as they are of our feelings.

The opening part of *In Memoriam*, untitled by Tennyson but labelled the 'Prologue' by Bradley in 1901, and so called by critics since then, is in fact a prayer, and it is a combination of propositions, the expression of both judgment and feelings, and entreaties, mostly for forgiveness. The forgiveness is for the fault of separating his grief from his intellect, the result of which is 'these wild and wandering cries' (41). The mirror-image fault – intellect separated from feeling – is perhaps suggested by 'our little systems' (17). At any rate, his entreaty is 'That mind and soul, according well, / May make one music as before, / But vaster' (27–9). The prayer is addressed to Love, and the elegy ends with a celebration of love, a reaffirmation of the propositions of the opening prayer, but fuller as a result of the poet's own embracing of sorrow as his wife. Kenneth McKay, in his complex analysis of the role of sorrow in the poem, argues that the structure of *In Memoriam* is circular, and that (as in 'The Palace of Art') 'Love is realized in human life in mourning and prayer – through Sorrow.'[81] McKay links poetry, song, crying, and prayer in a complex pattern that defines the vaster music for which Tennyson is striving.

The elegy's narrative of loss and recovery is a version of the biblical myth of language, which rests upon three episodes: Adam's naming of the beasts in Genesis, the confusion of tongues at Babel, and the command of tongues given to the Apostles at Pentecost. In Tennyson's version of this myth, Adam's language finds its parallel in the early communication of the poet and his friend, communication which takes place in an ideal pastoral setting, and which is characterized by the harmony of mind and mind. With Hallam's death, the poet loses his ability to speak to Hallam, and is unable to speak to anyone else when his grief is deepest. In this second stage, his words are the expression of 'My lighter moods' (xx.9), and are inadequate anyway, separated as they seem to be from his strongest and most important feelings. The complaint at the beginning of section lii is typical of this stage:

> I cannot love thee as I ought,
>    For love reflects the thing beloved;
>    My words are only words, and moved
> Upon the topmost froth of thought.                    (1–4)

The Pentecostal wind of section xcv makes possible a more substantial language, though it is one not free of the difficulties and limitations he had earlier complained of, as I have tried to indicate in my analysis of 'matter-moulded forms of speech.' For just as the rushing mighty wind and the tongues of fire did not bring the world back to a single language but instead enabled the Apostles to speak to every man in his own language, so too the breeze of section xcv does not change the poet's existing language, or return him to 'days of happy commune dead' (cxvi.14). Instead, it gives him greater command over the words he has been using all along. The 'contradiction on the tongue' (cxxv.4) may still be present, but now the poet is aware of a relationship between his words and Love, a relationship explored in some detail in section cxxv, where words, unlike those of section lii, are no longer 'only words.' The full realization of this new relationship is the 'marriage lay' with which the poem ends, a celebration of love which repeats, in its sequence of events, the sequence of section xcv. 'Streaming cloud' and 'rising fire' replace the breeze and inspire the words. 'The dawn, the dawn' – the words spoken by the breeze in xcv – is the herald of a greater unity, but in the 'marriage lay' the words are not those of some separate agent but of the inspired poet himself, who prophesies the 'one far-off divine event, / To which the whole creation moves.'

If we stand back from the language of *In Memoriam* and try to gain some perspective on its multiple concerns, two matters emerge to pattern the picture more than others: the arbitrary and the interjectional. Both of these Tennyson borrows from philosophical positions he would not so much reject as transform: the arbitrary comes from the Lockeian view of language, the interjectional from the Lucretian view. Tennyson cleared away the clutter of caprice and wilfulness with which the arbitrary had become associated, and revived its original Lockeian meaning, a judgment made by the mind where empirical evidence is partial or lacking. This judgment – it is opinion in Locke – became faith in Tennyson, and verbal propositions are its embodiment, such propositions being not final truths but ones contingent on our daily lives, assumptions by which to live. Such propositions Tennyson linked with inner human needs, expressed by the voice in inarticulate cries. Tennyson would affirm, like Lucretius, that such cries are natural, but would also affirm, like Coleridge, that they are the expression of a self both unique and (in some mysterious way) one with God. The cry thus develops into the ability to say 'I.' When the 'I' affirms its faith, when judgment and expression fuse harmoniously – Hallam is the model for such melding – the poet achieves the highest level of human speech. He identifies such speech with prayer, and there is a sense in which all such speech is prayer, a reflecting or turning back toward God of the powers and capacities which he has given us. Such acts are the shapers of our daily lives, and characterize a way of life that is ongoing and vital rather than a system that is fixed and dead. *In Memoriam* itself is the record of such a way.

# Chapter Six

# 'Man's word is God in man': *Idylls of the King*

*Idylls of the King* is permeated with a sense of the new philology which gained ground rapidly in England from 1830 on.[1] It was new in part because it transformed the study of classical languages and literature so that Donaldson, for instance, could claim that his *The New Cratylus* (1839) is a contribution, as he says in his subtitle, 'towards a more accurate knowledge of the Greek language' because he has rendered 'the resources of a more comprehensive philology available for the improvement of the grammar and lexicography of the Greek language, and for the criticism and interpretation of the authors who have written in it.'[2] *Idylls of the King* is, similarly, the new Malory, and though Tennyson's aim is not scholarly, he does, like the fictional poet Everard Hall in 'The Epic,' hold that 'a truth / Looks freshest in the fashion of the day' (32). The philological fashion of the day is manifest in Tennyson's style, and in the central thematic place he gives to language in the poem.

When Tennyson commented on the style of the *Idylls*, he had clearly come to share in the preference for a Germanic purism in his language. 'He would remark on his use of English – in preference to words derived from French and Latin,' his son records for 1872; 'he revived many fine old words which had fallen into disuse: and I heard him regret that he had never employed the word "yarely."'[3] So, if one looks at the idyll first published in 1872 ('Gareth and Lynette'), one finds, even in a cursory reading, words such as 'gyve' (362, a shackle), 'boon' (327 and elsewhere, a gift but also a petition or request), and 'doom' (314, judgment); compounds such as 'dragon-boughts' (229; Tennyson glosses this in the Eversley edition as 'folds of the dragons' tails'); and other compounds that sound Germanic, though one of the words may be of French origin (like 'kitchen-vassalage,' 157, or the near-compound 'beef and brewis,' 447). Coventry Patmore had already praised the purism of Tennyson's language in his review of the four idylls of 1859 – 'no poetry has been written with so small an admixture of Latin as the "Idylls of the King,"' and ... no language has surpassed in epic dignity the English of these poems'[4] – and T. Kington Oliphant would, as a passing comment in his 1873 book, *The Sources of Standard English*, praise Tennyson for having 'done much for the revival of pure English among us';[5] and indeed Tennyson's interest in the resources of his own language is already apparent in the 'Morte d'Arthur' of 1842. There he uses words like 'mere,' 'brand,' and 'lief,' and exploits the harsh consonants and sibilants of English to suggest the harshness of the landscape: Bedivere steps down 'By zig-zag paths, and juts of pointed rock' (50), and even 'zig-zag,' French in origin, sounds like those strongly alliterative double words ('riff-raff' is an example) whose homeliness and vigour Trench would later praise as a curious but rich part of our language.[6]

Tennyson 'had a strong sense of the force and rhythm of words, and his knowledge of old English and of vivid provincial expressions was very great'[7] – so W.E.H. Lecky, the historian, remembers from conversations of the period 1874–80. This double interest, in the origins of the language and in its various dialects, is typical of the new philology, with its emphasis on common language rather than literary or courtly language, and with its opposition to standard speech and to the kind of grammatical correctness which could be derived from a dead language like Latin but which was inappropriate to the living languages of modern Europe and the living dialects of modern England. This interest in the language of the folk Tennyson probably associated with Jacob Grimm, whose work was vigorously championed in England by Tennyson's friend and fellow Apostle John Mitchell Kemble, who, with others, made Grimm's *Deutsche Grammatik* (1819–37) known to English readers. Tennyson also owned two books by William Barnes, an outspoken proponent of purism in English, and the double emphasis, on origins and on dialects, is evident in these volumes: the dialect in Barnes' *Poems of Rural Life in the Dorset Dialect* (1848), and word origins in his *Notes on Ancient Britain and the Britons* (1858), which is full of information on place names and other words derived from Welsh. The authority that the new philology gave to dialects and spoken (as opposed to literary) language is the context in which we must read Tennyson's poems in the Lincolnshire dialect. 'The deathbed musings of his Northern Farmer' is the one Tennyson poem Oliphant specifically mentions in 1873, when he describes Tennyson as 'a countryman of Robert Manning' of Brunne – also a Lincolnshire man – and thus links purism with an interest in regional speech.[8]

Tennyson shared the view that language is the expression of the character of the folk or people. The Grimms had operated on this principle, and to preserve their national linguistic heritage was the motive behind their collecting of folk tales and fairy stories for their *Nursery and Household Tales* (1812, 1815). When Wilhelm Grimm revised the tales for a second edition (1819), in response to criticism of the coarse language of the original edition, Jacob Grimm objected, saying that the stories were not meant specially for children. In England, the Hares had already absorbed Jacob Grimm's views, and were repeating them in the aphorisms of *Guesses at Truth* (1827), a book almost as important for the Apostles as *Aids to Reflection*: 'Languages are the barometers of national thought and character' (Augustus Hare); 'every language must be the print of the national mind' (Julius Hare).[9] So, too, Richard Garnett in an essay of 1835: 'a scientific acquaintance with a language cannot fail to throw some light on the origin, history, and condition of those who speak or spoke it,'[10] and Trench, in his *On Some Deficiencies in our English Dictionaries*, argues for a knowledge of the history of words: 'It was a remark of Coleridge, that you might often learn more from the history of a word than from the history of a campaign; and this is true.'[11] In his 'Introductory Lecture' in *On the Study of Words*, Trench asserts that language is 'the embodiment, the incarnation, if I may so speak, of the feelings and thoughts and experiences of a nation.'[12] His particular emphasis is 'On the Morality in Words' – this is the title of his third lecture – and in it he repeats Augustus Hare's barometer metaphor, but with the addition of a crucial adjective: language is 'a moral barometer indicating and permanently marking the rise or fall of a nation's life'; in language 'the mighty moral instincts which have been working in the popular mind have found therein their unconscious voice.'[13] Maurice held the same view, and in the ninth of his twenty-one lectures on *Social Morality* (1869) – he presented a copy of the book to Tennyson – he explores the links between 'national morality' and language, a nation being held together by words, and the words in turn representing – at least they should represent – 'the purpose of him who speaks them.'[14] Tennyson's view is like that of Trench and Maurice. Language as the expression of national character is a central theme in *Idylls of the King*, and Tennyson gives it a strongly moral dimension. 'Man's word is God in man' ('The Coming of Arthur' 132), Arthur says to Lancelot on the battlefield where he establishes his kingdom; the line reappears as Arthur's civilization declines, at the beginning of 'Balin and Balan' (8), and in variant form in 'Guinevere,' where one of the vows is 'To honour his own word as if his God's' (470). This view is implicit in the early 'Morte d'Arthur' where, in Arthur's great farewell speech to Bedivere, prayer is 'man's word' and is his expression of 'knowing God':

> For what are men better than sheep or goats
> That nourish a blind life within the brain,
> If, knowing God, they lift not hands of prayer
> Both for themselves and those who call them friend? (250–3)

And this same sense of men's knowing God in their words Tennyson was still expressing at the very end of his life, in lines he wrote for the acting version of *Beckett*, and specifically for Irving, who was playing the title role; the 'anthem-speech' begins, 'The voice of the Lord is in the voice of the people.'[15]

In a recent essay, Linda Dowling has drawn attention to the doubts and anxieties fostered in the Victorians by the new philology, and particularly by the premise (Dowling is here drawing upon Foucault) 'that language was organized on purely linguistic principles independent of both human control and of representation.'[16] Language was thus coming to seem more like nature, also independent, essentially, of human control, and also, to all appearances, nothing other than itself – certainly not symbolic (not the 'Living Garment of God,' as Carlyle's Teufelsdröckh, quoting Goethe, had finally asserted), not the manifestation of divine purpose or, as Tennyson wants to affirm in section lvi of *In Memoriam*, of 'Creation's final law,' which is love. Tennyson was agonizingly aware of the opacity of nature – to the eye it seemed, in his famous phrase, only 'red in tooth and claw / With ravine' (lvi: 15–16) – but he seems to have been little affected by the possible autonomy of language, though he (like Locke) makes much of our misuse of words. Instead he finds in language (as he ultimately does in nature) the working out of a divine purpose, and in language, as in all other aspects of human life, 'God fulfils Himself in many ways' ('Morte d'Arthur' 241). The speaker of 'Locksley Hall' (1842) says, 'Yet I doubt not through the ages one increasing purpose runs' (137), and

Tennyson himself, though often doubting, would make the same affirmation. Certainly Jowett linked this statement with Tennyson himself when, in 1858, he sent the poet a copy of Hegel's *Philosophy of History*, which, Jowett wrote, 'is just "the increasing purpose that through the ages runs" buried under a heap of categories.'[17] The new philology may, from our late twentieth-century perspective, have suggested the autonomy of language, but to Tennyson and his circle it suggested something quite other. Both the old and new philology, J.W. Burrows points out in a 1967 essay, 'were interpreted in the light of a Romantic, anti-materialist theory of knowledge, and comparative philology was placed in the service of a providential theory of history.'[18] The subtext of much of the new philology confirms this providential view.

To any observer with scholarly interests but not himself a scholar, like Tennyson, the new philology was an astonishing accomplishment. The ancient languages, and the languages of the modern world, many in number (Max Müller estimated in 1861 that 'their number can hardly be less than nine hundred')[19] seemed (to borrow Matthew Arnold's words) a vast multitude of facts, most of them unconnected, and likely to be inaccessible to anyone who knew, from his schoolboy struggles with Greek and Latin, how much effort the learning of even one or two languages required. The new philology made possible the comprehension of this vast multitude of facts, so that they became (as Trench says of the discovery that words are 'living powers') 'not, like the sands of the sea, innumerable disconnected atoms, but growing out of roots, clustering in families, connecting and intertwining themselves with all that men have been doing and thinking and feeling from the beginning of the world till now.'[20] The family metaphor is pervasive in the new philology, and Trench uses it freely. 'Of whole groups of words, which may seem to acknowledge no kinship with one another,' he says, 'it will not be difficult to show that they had the same parentage, or, if not this, a cousinship in common.' 'Words have now an ancestry ... Words are now a nation, grouped into tribes and families, some smaller, some larger.'[21] For many in Victorian England and for Tennyson in particular, marriage and family life meant participation in a divine purpose – I have explored the implications of family life at length elsewhere – and this same sense of participating in a divine purpose simply by speaking is suggested frequently in Trench's lectures. In every word there is 'some deep analogy of things natural and things spiritual'; 'men are continually uttering deeper things than they know, asserting mighty principles'; 'there is a law here at work,' (this in the context of a discussion of words becoming obsolete) 'however hidden it may be from us.'[22] For others, this 'law' could be frightening in its implications; it could suggest that language is independent of human control, and that we are powerless to change it. (Max Müller makes the implication explicit: 'As man is the lord of nature only if he knows her laws and submits to them, the poet and the philosopher become the lords of language only if they know its laws and obey them.')[23] But for Trench there is, finally, no separation of man from language, or of language from the onward-moving cycle which is the master-pattern of all earthly life. Languages 'have their youth, their manhood, their old age, their decrepitude, their final dissolution ... [O]ut of their death a new life comes forth; they pass into new forms, the materials of which they were composed more or less survive, but these now organized in new shapes and according to other laws of life.'[24] Moreover, as Carlyle teaches through his organic filaments in *Sartor Resartus*, advance and decline proceed together. 'In states and languages,' Trench says,

it would be a serious mistake to assume that all up to a certain point and period is growth and gain, and all after, decay and loss. On the contrary, there are long periods during which growth in some directions is going hand in hand with decay in others; losses in one kind are being compensated, or more than compensated, by gains in another; during which a language changes, but only as the bud changes into the flower, and the flower into the fruit.[25]

Earlier, Trench had used the organic metaphor to suggest that language is not an invention of ours but an essential power in us, not a house we have built but a growth out of our nature: 'Man makes his own language, but he makes it as the bee makes its cells, as the bird its nest; he cannot do otherwise.'[26]

Nor was Trench alone in suggesting that language is a manifestation of divine purpose, of unrecognized laws and of an ultimate unity. Kemble, like Trench, uses the family metaphor for languages and nations. He praises Grimm's *Deutsche Grammatik* for laying open the 'hidden laws' that connect the various Teutonic tongues. About origins he writes, 'This, indeed, is the sum of our knowledge, that different peoples exist in the world in different places, and with languages apparently different; that nevertheless some secret and mysterious bond does exist between them, which evidently proves the common influence of some law working among them.' This 'mysterious bond' suggests a state of original perfection (perfection being understood, as its Latin root indicates, as completion): 'man or men did exist complete from the first, complete in bodily form, complete in understanding, complete in language, every one of whose most hidden springs is a hidden spring of the understanding also.'[27] When Robert Chambers dealt with language as part of his popular synthesis of contemporary science in 1844, he placed his account of the language families – he too uses this crucial metaphor – in the context of a creation characterized by design, by a fundamental unity, and by progress which is the expression of the divine will, all of creation advancing upward through 'a nobler type of humanity' to 'the grand crowning type.'[28] Tennyson, who echoes these phrases in his 'the crowning race' and 'a noble type' in the epithalamium of *In Memoriam*, sent for Chambers' book soon after it came out.[29] Chambers deals with the new philology in his chapter on the 'Early History of Mankind,' his principal argument being for a primal unity of all human beings. He supposes 'that all the great families of men are of one stock,' and turns immediately to modern philology: 'The tendency of the modern study of the languages of nations is to the same point' (283). And even Müller, for all his talk about the 'science' of language, is in fact, as Linda Dowling points out, quite unscientific (or at least not 'scientific' as his opponent, Whitney of Yale, thought he should be), and held language to be 'necessary, internal, and expressive in origin.'[30] He called the final stage of any scientific study 'the theoretical, or metaphysical' stage, and said, in his very first lecture of 1861, that

If the work of classification is properly carried out, it teaches us that nothing exists in nature by accident; that each individual belongs to a species, each species to a genus; and that there are laws which underlie the apparent freedom and variety of all created things. These laws indicate to us the presence of a purpose in the mind of the Creator; and whereas the material world was looked upon by ancient philosophers as a mere illusion, as an agglomerate of atoms, or as the work of an evil principle, we now read and interpret its pages as the revelation of a divine power, and wisdom, and love.[31]

I have quoted thus from Trench and Kemble, Chambers and Müller, all of whom Tennyson knew or read, to indicate that, in the accounts of the new philology with which he was familiar, language was firmly placed in a providential view of creation and in a progressive view of history. There would indeed be periods of loss and decline, as Trench suggests, but these periods were only parts of an all-embracing circular movement spiralling upward, 'measured arcs,' in Tennyson's words in section cv of *In Memoriam*, that 'lead / The closing cycle rich in good.' In *Idylls of the King*, we have the story of a single arc in the rise and decline of the vows, the words that establish the Order of the Round Table and then separate themselves from it. And behind the many voices that we hear in the *Idylls* we also hear, but do not comprehend, 'The voice of days of old and days to be' ('The Passing of Arthur' 135).

This voice is Tennyson's way of presenting the Logos and, as we shall see, it is to be understood ontologically (it is the continuing ground of all existence, and the energy that sustains all creation) as well as epistemologically (our affirmations are the imperfect human expression of the Word). In his chapter on *Idylls of the King* in his *Memoir*, Hallam Tennyson gives an account of his father's conception of Arthur in relation to the Logos:

Guided by the voice within, the Ideal Soul looks out into the Infinite for the highest Ideal; and finds it nowhere realized so mightily as in the Word who 'wrought With human hands the creed of creeds.' But for Arthur, as for every one who believes in the Word however interpreted, arises the question, 'How can I in my little life, in my small measure, and in my limited sphere reflect this highest Ideal?'[32]

In the *Idylls*, 'this highest Ideal' is reflected in the vows.

It is Bellicent who gives the first account of the vows in the poem, and she does so in 'The Coming of Arthur' in response to Leodogran, who is wrestling with the question of Arthur's authority. 'Then,' she says,

'the King in low deep tones,
And simple words of great authority,
Bound them by so strait vows to his own self,
That when they rose, knighted from kneeling, some
Were pale as at the passing of a ghost,
Some flushed, and others dazed, as one who wakes
Half-blinded at the coming of a light.'       ('The Coming of Arthur' 259–65)

The King's 'low deep tones' sound like the cosmic voice with which Tennyson identifies the Logos – its sound is like that of the sea, and its source is 'the great deep,' as in Bellicent's story of Arthur's birth on the wave, 'a ninth one, gathering half the deep / And full of voices' ('The Coming of Arthur' 379–80) – and that voice is the source of Arthur's authority. That authority manifests itself in 'simple' words, words, that is, that are univocal, not equivocal. The root of 'simple' is *sem*, and in both Latin and Greek *sem* is one. Trench comments on 'simple' in his lecture 'On the Morality in Words': 'The "simple" is one properly of a single fold' (he thinks the word has two roots, 'semel' and 'plico'), 'and, indeed,' he continues, 'what honour can be higher than to have nothing *double* about us, to be without *duplicities* or folds?'[33] But the dominant metaphor in Tennyson's account of the vows is not the fold but the bond or tie: Arthur 'Bound them by so strait vows to his own self.' The image is in the verb 'bound' itself, and 'strait' is related etymologically to *strictus*, the past participle of *stringere*, to tighten, to bind tightly. The image ties these two words to the word 'religion,' which is (the *Oxford English Dictionary* tells us) of doubtful etymology, but seems connected with *religare*, to bind. 'For so the whole round earth is every way / Bound by gold chains about the feet of God' ('The Passing of Arthur' 422–3) – in these lines from his farewell speech Arthur is in effect defining religion. When Tennyson was first considering the Arthurian material and thinking of it in terms of its 'allegorical drift,' he allegorized Arthur as 'Religious Faith' – this in a memorandum dating from 1833.[34] Tennyson would later reject reading the *Idylls* 'too allegorically,'[35] but the bond image suggested by the word 'religion' remains central to the finished poem, and is associated primarily with the vows. The bonds are liberating, not constraining. At Arthur's wedding, the knights are present and 'glorying in their vows' ('The Coming of Arthur' 457), and their attitude indicates the true sense of the word 'religious' as Trench describes it in *On the Study of Words*: 'any one who felt and owned the bonds that bound him to God and to his fellow-men.' Trench goes on (speaking from a Protestant point of view) to discuss 'religious' as an example of a word that preserves a record of a perversion of the moral sense, since, in the Middle Ages 'and indeed in many parts of Christendom still' the 'religious' person is not a member of a Christian household, but 'one who had taken peculiar vows upon him, the member of a monastic Order, of a "religion" as it was called.'[36] The bonds by which Arthur ties his knights to him are, in Tennyson's treatment of them, perverted in the same way. At the beginning of 'Merlin and Vivien,' the minstrel of Caerleon tells of 'perfect virgin knights' who are 'So passionate for an utter purity / Beyond the limit of their bond' (26–7) that they worship Guinevere, whom they cannot have, rather than maidens whom they might themselves marry. It is only a step from such perverted bonds to Pellam's court, with its monastic life and its rejection of women as 'polluted' ('Balin and Balan' 105), and one more step to the Red Knight and his parodic vows: 'whatsoever his own knights [Arthur's, that is] have sworn / My knights have sworn the counter to it' ('The Last Tournament' 79–80). So words – the vows – degenerate. Once (to use Trench's words) 'the veritable transcript of [man's] innermost life, the genuine utterance of the faith and hope which is in him,' they come to be scorned, and Trench gives examples of 'the contemptuous use which words expressive of goodness gradually acquire.' One of his examples is 'simple.'[37]

But in the springtime of Arthur's reign, the knights are one with their king, and Arthur's words and voice hold them together. Here is Bellicent's account of that oneness:

> 'But when he spake and cheered his Table Round
> With large, divine, and comfortable words,
> Beyond my tongue to tell thee – I beheld
> From eye to eye through all their Order flash
> A momentary likeness of the King.'    ('The Coming of Arthur' 266–70)

Bellicent hears Arthur's voice but cannot repeat his words, so that her relation to his voice parallels the relation of all of us to the cosmic voice, heard but 'Beyond my tongue to tell thee.' But if the voice is not comprehended, it *is* heard, and its power is felt and assimilated. The three adjectives Bellicent uses to describe Arthur's words indicate the nature of this power. 'Large' suggests bounty and munificence, the generous giving of a benefit (Malory uses the word in this sense); 'divine' suggests that the words (as in Coleridge's 'Noetic Pentad') participate in the nature of the Logos; and 'comfortable' (as in the *Book of Common Prayer*'s reference to the 'comfortable words' of Christ) means 'strengthening.' In his *Select Glossary*, Trench includes the word 'comfortable' and writes, 'The verb "confortare," not found in classical Latin, but so frequent in the Vulgate, is first, as is plain from the "fortis" which it embodies, to make strong, to corroborate, and only in a secondary sense, to console.'[38] Tennyson is using the word in its older sense, but he also uses the verb in its modern sense (to console) in Bellicent's account of her childhood with Arthur: 'he was at my side, / And spake sweet words, and comforted my heart' ('The Coming of Arthur' 347–8). But the chief emphasis in this account of Arthur's words is on their relation to the Logos, felt and assimilated by the knights, though it is to be imperfectly articulated by them. In their song at Arthur's wedding, they give full assent to his authority, in part because 'God hath told the King a secret word' ('The Coming of Arthur' 488). The principle they are suggesting is reserve, and the vows for them are the partial revelation of this word.

When a reader traces the vows through the *Idylls*, he or she discovers that they become more explicit and specific, and that, as they do so, they move farther and farther away from the spirit that inspires them. This shift is yet another manifestation of Tennyson's distrust of creeds and systems, his distrust being expressed, as it is in the *Idylls*, through the spatial metaphor of interior and exterior. So long as the vows are internalized – so long as there is, in each of the knights, at least 'a momentary likeness of the King' – the vows are a living power, full of potential. When they are externalized, as they are by Tristram ('we sware but by the shell,' 'The Last Tournament' 270), they are easily dismissed as mere words. Interiorizing is Tennyson's version of the biblical Word-made-flesh, which is then expressed in actual human words and in human acts. In his 1969 book on the *Idylls*, John R. Reed uses syntax as a metaphor for the relation of spirit, words, and deeds in the poem, one of Tennyson's purposes being, Reed says, 'to establish the subject and predicate of existence': 'In the ideal is the subject, the predicate is the act, and utterances the multiform modifiers.'[39] Reed's words suggest an Aristotelian syntax, but Donaldson and Farrar, with their distinction between Form-words and Matter-words, provide us with a related and, I think, better metaphor, Arthur being the pronoun 'I' shaping the world around him by being part of the words and deeds of his knights. At first, both words and deeds are the effective externalizing of the Logos; as time goes on, both become a parody of it. Tennyson characteristically links the decline with vows that are increasingly explicit and defined – and separated from those who make them.

When Arthur himself gives an account of the vows in 'Gareth and Lynette,' the second of the *Idylls* in Tennyson's final ordering of them, he describes the vows in terms of human virtues rather than as particular do's and don't's, as inner qualities rather than specific acts. 'My knights,' he tells Gareth,

'are sworn to vows
Of utter hardihood, utter gentleness,
And, loving, utter faithfulness in love,
And uttermost obedience to the King.'      ('Gareth and Lynette' 541–4)

The repetition of 'utter' makes Arthur's words sound strict, but his sense is that these virtues are to be pursued without reservation or qualification. Gareth protests his own fitness by giving specific examples of these virtues in his own conduct – and, indeed, he must rely on these virtues and not on any rules in his quest, when he is confronting his strange antagonists, and when he is dealing with the petulant Lynette. The vows only confirm the ideals already in him, and already expressed to his mother:

> 'Man am I grown, a man's work must I do.
> Follow the deer? follow the Christ, the King,
> Live pure, speak true, right wrong, follow the King –
> Else, wherefore born?'      ('Gareth and Lynette' 115–18)

By the time we reach 'The Last Tournament,' this unity of vows and actions has receded into the past. Isolt of Cornwall would like to believe Tristram's protestations, and would even like him to lie to her, and at least to act out the vows in kneeling and swearing. The past now seems astonishing to her:

> 'My God, the power
> Was once in vows when men believed the King!
> They lied not then, who sware, and through their vows
> The King prevailing made his realm ...'      ('The Last Tournament' 643–6)

But Tristram has no such nostalgia for the past: 'The vow that binds too strictly snaps itself' (652), he says, carrying the bond or tie image to its logical conclusion. 'I swore to the great King, and am forsworn' (656). Tristram's polyptoton neatly sums up the decline that has taken place. The active ('I swore') gives way to the passive ('am forsworn'), and there is a suggestion that words, separated from the speaker, and mouthed but not believed by him, turn upon him and destroy him.

So the vows, once a joyful affirmation of unity, turn upon man and become his accuser, like the Ten Commandments in a fallen world, and like Arthur's speech for Lancelot, 'Round whose sick head all night, like birds of prey, / The words of Arthur flying shrieked' ('The Last Tournament' 138–9). And indeed, it is when his kingdom is crumbling that Arthur gives the fullest account of the vows. The scene is in the 'Guinevere' idyll, where it is Arthur's responsibility to bring Guinevere to a conviction of sin:

'I made them lay their hands in mine and swear
To reverence the King, as if he were
Their conscience, and their conscience as their King,
To break the heathen and uphold the Christ,
To ride abroad redressing human wrongs,
To speak no slander, no, nor listen to it,
To honour his own word as if his God's,
To lead sweet lives in purest chastity,
To love one maiden only, cleave to her,
And worship her by years of noble deeds,
Until they won her; for indeed I knew
Of no more subtle master under heaven
Than is the maiden passion for a maid,
Not only to keep down the base in man,
But teach high thought, and amiable words
And courtliness, and the desire of fame,
And love of truth, and all that makes a man.'  ('Guinevere' 464–80)

There is nothing in Arthur's speech that is not implicit in all the earlier actions in the *Idylls*, but this explicit statement of the vows appears only at the end of his reign. The vows as Arthur describes them here are not quite fixed in the form of a creed, but they have become almost a dead form in Camelot, and Tennyson characteristically links this verbal explicitness with a decline of genuine belief.

The fact that the vows move toward the fixed form of a creed is not the only symptom of the fall of Camelot. If the reader focuses simply on the story of the *Idylls* as Tennyson shapes it, and attempts to explain why Arthur's order fails, the explanation that the poem itself most obviously suggests is slander or gossip. Tennyson deliberately leaves vague the point at which Guinevere and Lancelot actually commit adultery, and although that act may be the 'one sin' that Tennyson himself said ruined 'the dream of man coming into practical life,'[40] the poem itself raises the question as to whether the act gives rise to the gossip, or the gossip gives rise to the act. The weight of suggestion in the *Idylls* is on the latter. For if words have the power to create, as Arthur's vows create a kingdom, words also have the power to destroy, and the explicit theme of many of the *Idylls* is the destructive nature of slander.

From the very beginning, slander is the chief threat to Arthur's order. In 'The Coming of Arthur,' the plain-speaking Bedivere is

Arthur's champion against the destructive power of words: 'For bold in heart and act and word was he, / Whenever slander breathed against the King' (175–6). But it is in the two Geraint idylls that we watch slander actually creating the situation about which it talks. The precipitating cause of Geraint's actions is 'a rumour … about the Queen, / Touching her guilty love for Lancelot' ('The Marriage of Geraint' 24–5), and this rumour gives rise to his suspicions of Enid: has she suffered 'any taint / In nature' (31–2)? His suspicions affect his conduct, and people

> Began to scoff and jeer and babble of him
> As of a prince whose manhood was all gone,
> And molten down in mere uxoriousness. (58–60)

This babble is not untrue – Enid in fact sorrows over the change in Geraint – and (as is conventional in romance) he now hears what he is afraid of hearing. Only by confronting, in externalized form, the neuroses born of gossip and babble is Geraint able to conquer them: Edyrn is, among other things, a slanderer ('The Marriage of Geraint' 450), and Limours is the embodiment of duplicity ('Geraint and Enid' 290–2). In 'Balin and Balan,' slander receives its emblem. It is the tongue, and it has a central place in the blazon of Balin's shield, which is a 'rough beast … / Langued gules, and toothed with grinning savagery' (192–3). Hallam Tennyson glosses 'langued gules' as 'red-tongued,' and the redness, associated with madness and bloodshed in this idyll, will soon become linked with the fire of wider destruction. But in this idyll gossip destroys the brothers. Balin is the more susceptible to it: he was exiled from court because he had struck a man who 'had spoken evil' (56) of him, and Garlon's gossip about Guinevere, plus Vivien's repetition of it, drives Balin to a second, and fatal, exile.

Up to this point, Tennyson's story has focused on the effects of gossip, but in 'Merlin and Vivien,' the sixth of the *Idylls* in the final ordering, the slanderer herself becomes the central figure, and her talk is more vigorously destructive. Beginning as 'faintly-venomed points / Of slander' (170–1), it becomes a holocaust: she

> let her tongue
> Rage like a fire among the noblest names,
> Polluting, and imputing her whole self,

Defaming and defacing, till she left
Not even Lancelot brave, nor Galahad clean.                    (799–803)

The fire image reappears in 'Lancelot and Elaine,' when Gawain, whom Tennyson characterizes as a gossip, 'buzzed abroad / About the maid of Astolat, and her love' (717–18): 'So ran the tale like fire about the court, / Fire in dry stubble a nine-days' wonder flared' (729–30). Gawain's gossip is not so fiercely malicious as Vivien's (Bedivere will later characterize him as 'Light ... in life, and light in death,' 'The Passing of Arthur' 56) but it is just as disruptive and ultimately destructive, – or more so, perhaps, because it is thoughtless.

Tennyson's verb for such thoughtless talk is 'babble,' and it turns up at several points in the *Idylls*, as when Limours misreads Enid and 'babbled to his men, / How Enid never loved a man but him' ('Geraint and Enid' 362–3), or when the courtiers look with puzzlement (like the 'wellfed wits at Camelot' in the 1832 version of 'The Lady of Shalott') at the dead Elaine and 'babbled of the King' ('Lancelot and Elaine' 1252). In 'The Last Tournament,' Dagonet accuses the knights of babbling about Arthur, 'all to show your wit' (340), and Guinevere's experience at Almesbury is a repetition of her experience in Camelot, when she is beset by the 'babbling heedlessness' of the little novice ('Guinevere' 149). The same verb turns up in Hallam Tennyson's *Memoir*, for instance, when Tennyson complains of the curiosity of the public about a poet's private life ('It is all for the sake of babble');[41] his synonyms are 'gabble,' 'gabblements,' and 'blab' (as in his indictment of his time as 'this horrible age of blab').[42] His use of 'babble' may owe something to Carlyle, who, in an 1842 letter to Tennyson, defends his criticism of Tennyson's poems by saying, 'This is not babble; it is speech.'[43] The context of Carlyle's nouns suggests the nature of the distinction between them: speech is based upon judgment, and on the effort to judge correctly; babble indicates not so much a failure in judgment as it does a slight or inadequate effort to judge at all.

The reader begins to realize, then, that the words that destroy Camelot are of two kinds: there is the slander of Vivien, who is actively evil, and there is the babble of Gawain, who is 'light' in all his thinking and, as Arthur says of him in 'The Holy Grail,' 'too blind to have desire to see' (868). Of the two kinds, Gawain's is the more destructive. Vivien's slander succeeds because others' judgment of it is too easy, and so their responsibility for the fall is greater than hers. The narrator even suggests that Vivien, like Satan in *Paradise Lost*, ultimately serves

God's purposes, and he does so through the leavening image, which is an image of organic growth and development. In the narrator's syntax, Arthur and Vivien appear together in the scheme of antithesis, which depends upon parallel verbal structures pivoting on the verb 'leavened':

> then as Arthur in the highest
> Leavened the world, so Vivien in the lowest,
> Arriving at a time of golden rest,
> And sowing one ill hint from ear to ear,
> While all the heathen lay at Arthur's feet,
> And no quest came, but all was joust and play,
> Leavened his hall.                 ('Merlin and Vivien' 138–44)

But the narrator does not suggest that babble, like slander, is a part of the cycle of organic growth and decay. It is, rather, the manifestation of something intractable in human nature, a carelessness or indifference that finally undermines all thinking and all values.

*Idylls of the King* begins with an intense struggle to arrive at a decision: Leodogran must assess Arthur's claim to be king. As the *Idylls* proceed, the will to strive toward such judgments slackens, and Arthur's authority dwindles in the growing babble around him. Bedivere's struggle to make a decision in 'The Passing of Arthur' suggests a painful return to correct judgment. The central place that Tennyson gives to judgment in the poem does not come out of the new philology, but rather out of earlier thinking about language which I have already explored. In the new philology, there is an increasing emphasis on language as an independent power not to be controlled by the individual. Language, says Trench, 'is too entirely the collective work of a whole people, the result of the united contributions of all, it obeys too immutable laws, to allow any successful tampering with it.'[44] And Müller, talking about 'continuous change in language,' says that

it is not in the power of man either to produce or to prevent it. We might think as well of changing the laws which control the circulation of our blood, or of adding an inch to our height, as of altering the laws of speech, or inventing new words according to our own pleasure.[45]

Language thus comes to seem more like nature, an immutable power with a disheartening indifference to human concerns. But Tennyson does not share this view of language. We must use our judgment when we are dealing with nature, and to 'follow nature' is, as a general rule, just as dangerous as thinking about the laws of language as identical with truth. It may not be possible to change the laws of nature, or of language, but one 'does not necessarily *guide* himself by them,' as Mill said of nature.[46] When one considers the truth of any statement or proposition, it is soon apparent that language can be manipulated to an even greater degree than nature. Tennyson may ultimately affirm that nature is the living garment of God and language is the embodiment of the Logos, but our ordinary experience is with a nature and a language that give little evidence of a divinity in them.

In section xxxvii of *In Memoriam*, Tennyson contrasts his muse – 'my Melpomene' – with the heavenly muse, Urania. Urania has 'prevailing mysteries' while Melpomene, 'but an earthly Muse,' can only murmur 'Of comfort clasped in truth revealed.' 'Truth revealed' is rare, while the truth which is opinion, hard-won through the operations of the understanding and the judgment, is more usual. I have already suggested how much Tennyson's treatment of opinion and of the judgment through which it is arrived at is like Locke's treatment of those (necessary) human affirmations that go beyond knowledge, but Horne Tooke's treatment of opinion is an equally suggestive context for Tennyson's thinking, because Tooke, like Locke, relates opinion to the language which expresses it.

The problem, in Tooke as in Locke, is the nature of truth. Tooke, unlike Tennyson, denies the existence of absolute truth, and identifies truth with opinion by providing the etymology of the word. In the second book of *The Diversions of Purley*, 'F.' asks that recurring question in human thinking, 'What is TRUTH?' and 'H' (the author, Tooke himself) explains that 'true' or 'trew' is the past participle of the verb *treoþan*, to think or to believe firmly or to trow. Truth 'means simply and merely – That which is TROWED.' There is 'no such thing as eternal, immutable, everlasting TRUTH' but only opinion; 'TRUTH supposes mankind; *for whom* and *by whom* alone the word is formed, and *to whom* only it is applicable.' Hence truth is not, as is commonly assumed, 'a rare commodity upon earth,' and in fact 'there is nothing but TRUTH in the world' – 'except only in words,' he adds as a crucial qualification.[47] Aside from the denial of absolute truth, the human situation that Tooke is describing is very much like that in the *Idylls*: Merlin in his 'riddling triplets' says, 'And truth is this to me, and that to thee; / And truth or clothed or naked let it be' ('The Coming of Arthur' 406–7). He is not, I think, counselling indifference to truth, but rather a willingness to accept all its human forms. The variety of forms is apparent in the witnesses to Arthur's authority and to his claim to be king in 'The Coming of Arthur'; such a variety is also apparent in 'The Holy Grail,' where the repeated verb 'see,' with its suggestions of knowledge confirmed by the sense of sight, in fact indicates the opinions of the questing knights. It is Arthur who puts all their affirmations in the context of opinion, who shows that seeing cannot be separated from the particular eyes that look out and frame what is seen: 'But if indeed there came a sign from heaven,' Arthur says to the knights weakened by the quest (and his 'if' is crucial),

> 'Blessèd are Bors, Lancelot and Percivale,
> For these have seen according to their sight.
> For every fiery prophet in old times,
> And all the sacred madness of the bard,
> When God made music through them, could but speak
> His music by the framework and the chord;
> And as ye saw it ye have spoken truth.'　　　　('The Holy Grail' 869–76)

'Could but speak / His music by the framework and the chord' – the words are richly suggestive. 'Framework' suggests the perceiving mind, as in the ideas I traced in chapter 1 from Whewell and Donaldson back through Coleridge to Kant; 'chord' suggests the structure of language itself, its laws which, like the musical scale with its tones and semitones, we use but may not change. So truth is everywhere: 'as ye saw it ye have spoken truth.' Everywhere, 'except only in words.'

For human beings can and do lie, and lying is possible only if one conceives of the structures of language, its propositions and affirmations, as representational. If one focuses on language as an autonomous system with its own structures and laws, then its propositions are neither true nor untrue. Truth and falsehood become possible only if one thinks of words and syntax as referring to an order of things outside themselves. But our detection of a lie or our affirmation of a truth – our matching of a proposition with the things it purports to represent – is complicated by the fact that our knowledge of that order of things is problematic. As Locke had long before shown, our knowledge – the things of which we can be certain through the evidence of our senses – is limited, and we must rely to a large extent on opinion, with its varying degrees of certainty. Judging is always, thus, a difficult act, and likely to fail. The narrator begins the 'Geraint and Enid' idyll with this theme:

O purblind race of miserable men,
How many among us at this very hour
Do forge a life-long trouble for ourselves,
By taking true for false, or false for true;
Here, through the feeble twilight of this world
Groping, how many, until we pass and reach
That other, where we see as we are seen!                                (1–7)

The apostrophe and exclamation clearly apply to Geraint, who takes Enid as false when she is in fact true, and they apply as well to the first two idylls published in the trial edition of 1857. These were the 'Enid' idyll, subsequently divided into two, and the 'Nimuë' idyll, Nimuë being Tennyson's first name for Vivien. Tennyson called the 1857 volume *Enid and Nimuë: The True and the False,* and his subtitle indicates his central theme at this early stage.

'The true and the false' remains a central concern of the finished poem. At the beginning of Arthur's reign, lies are told, but the result is not the misery with which the narrator associates the misjudging of them. Arthur, the Seer tells Gareth, 'cannot brook the shadow of any lie' ('Gareth and Lynette' 287), yet Gareth lies to him about himself and his circumstances. His is a 'half-shadow of a lie' (316) and it 'sits like a little ghost / Here on the threshold of our enterprise' (291–2). The lie at this stage is associated with the romance convention whereby the champion fights in disguise (like Edgar in act 5 of *King Lear*) and remains nameless until he has forged his own identity through the quest. 'Let be my name until I make my name!' (562), Gareth asks Arthur. By the time we reach 'Balin and Balan,' the lie is not nearly so benign, and the 'little ghost' has become a substantial monster. Garlon gossips about Guinevere, and Balin rightly rejects his words as 'Felon talk!' (375); Vivien repeats the gossip and 'lied with ease' (517). Balin is devoted to truth – Arthur says to him that 'Thou hast ever spoken truth; / Thy too fierce manhood would not let thee lie' (70–1) – but, like Geraint, he takes false for true, and turns into a monster more violent than Geraint. He matches the talk with his own chance witnessing of Lancelot and Guinevere in the garden, and, in his judgment, the gossip seems to him to represent all that he has seen and heard, to be, in short, true. As he is dying, he learns from his twin brother that he has misjudged the relation between words and circumstances: 'Foul are their lives; foul are their lips; they lied. / Pure as our own true Mother is our Queen' (605–6). But the reader cannot be so sure, and Tennyson manages his narration in such a way that his reader's situation parallels that of his characters: like them, the reader has limited knowledge, and hence must use his judgment to arrive at an opinion. We are fully ready to think of Vivien as false and her gossip as lies, but is it? At this stage, her talk, malicious though it is, seems not wholly untrue.

The web of lies, misjudgments, and misery receives its fullest treatment in the seventh idyll in the final ordering, 'Lancelot and Elaine.' It is here that the vows, the crucial words in Camelot, begin to look like lies, and that the later charge of Pelleas, 'the King / Hath made us fools and liars' ('Pelleas and Ettarre' 469–70), begins to sound plausible. The vows start looking like lies because those who swear them think that the words no longer correspond to anything outside themselves, and are in fact a misreading of human nature. Guinevere's indictment of Arthur, 'swearing men to vows impossible' (130), will later be taken up by Tristram, as will the bond image. The bonds snap with Tristram, and are already slackening with Guinevere in this idyll when she assures Lancelot that 'I am yours, / Not Arthur's, as ye know, save by the bond' (134–5). The context for this degeneration of the vows is a web of lies and deceptions, deception being the central theme of the idyll. It appears initially as benevolent. Lancelot's secret purpose, like Gareth's, is an innocent one: he intends to present the diamonds, awarded to him one by one in successive tournaments, to the Queen. But he misreads the Queen's look (the face as text is a motif in the idyll) and so lies to the King; then the Queen blames him for his decision, and Lancelot is 'vext at having lied in vain' (102). He cannot retract his words to the King, and so must deceive him:

'And with what face, after my pretext made,
Shall I appear, O Queen, at Camelot, I
Before a King who honours his own word,
As if it were his God's?'                                          (141–4)

The lines echo Eve's in *Paradise Lost* when she, having fallen, is planning to deceive Adam ('But to *Adam* in what sort / Shall I appear?' 9.816–17), and the comparison with Gareth, who also considered 'what face' to use in appearing before the King, is of some importance in the total design of the *Idylls*. Gareth is innocent (literally, lacking the will to harm) but Lancelot and Guinevere are not, and the diction Tennyson has Guinevere use indicates her fallen nature. She defines Arthur as 'A moral child without the craft to rule' (145), and in Shakespeare's diction 'craft' identifies the Machiavel (as does the word 'practice' which Tennyson associates with Vivien, who, in the midst of the storm, 'Nor yet forgot her practice in her fright,' 'Merlin and Vivien' 945). 'Craft' is the opposite of innocence and, from the perspective of 'craft,' the innocent seems only the 'moral child.' And indeed Arthur does not yet discern a sin in Lancelot, but he does condemn Lancelot's ruse, when discovered, as 'idly dallying with the truth' (587). His diction suggests the lightness of Gawain, and that lightness, as we have already seen, is as great a threat to Camelot as an actively evil nature. Lancelot's fault is not, in fact, idle dallying, but he knows that easy judgments characterize the world:

> 'the world, the world,
> All ear and eye, with such a stupid heart
> To interpret ear and eye, and such a tongue
> To blare its own interpretation ...'　　　　　　　　　(935–8)

Lancelot makes no such easy judgment. He does in fact judge correctly, but his will is defective.

In this idyll, the act of judging is presented in the metaphor of reading a face; sustained, intense, and loving scrutiny gradually reveals the meaning of the countenance. The observer may misjudge that meaning, as Lancelot does when he looks into Guinevere's eyes, 'thinking that he read her meaning there' (86), but nonetheless there is at least the possibility of discovering in the outer appearance something hidden and inward. Hartley, as we have already seen, uses the face as an example of the association between a visible appearance and an invisible emotion, but in Tennyson this pattern of visible and invisible, outer and inner, is held together not by association but (as in Carlyle) by something divine bodying itself forth in symbol or emblem. To those who idly dally with such things, the appearance is only an appearance and nothing more; to those who look intensely, the symbol becomes revelation. (So, in 'The Passing of Arthur,' Arthur instructs Bedivere to 'Watch what thou seëst,' 'seëst' indicating only the eye's receiving of sensations, but 'watch' indicating the mental attention which makes revelation possible.) Tennyson explicitly likens reading a face to reading a word, in the deathbed scene, when Elaine's father first hears her wishes for her funeral:

> As when we dwell upon a word we know,
> Repeating, till the word we know so well
> Becomes a wonder, and we know not why,
> So dwelt the father on her face ...                    (1020–3)

So the view that the word participates in the essential being of the thing it names appears here, linked by the simile to reading a face, which also manifests the essential being of the person behind it. And indeed, Lancelot and Elaine read each other's faces, and read them with an intensity of involvement that is revelatory. On Lancelot's first visit to Astolat,

> the lily maid Elaine,
> Won by the mellow voice before she looked,
> Lifted her eyes, and read his lineaments.
> The great and guilty love he bare the Queen,
> In battle with the love he bare his lord,
> Had marred his face, and marked it ere his time.      (241–5)

The passage involves the romance convention of showing the inner state of a character through his outer appearance, and how many heroines in nineteenth-century fiction watch a man's inner battles fought out on his face! But Tennyson makes the face a language, and suggests that it, like words, reveals not just passing actions but something essential. So, when Elaine dreams of Lancelot's face, she reads in it not the adultery but the noble nature:

> And all night long his face before her lived,
> As when a painter, poring on a face,
> Divinely through all hindrance finds the man
> Behind it, and so paints him that his face,
> The shape and colour of a mind and life,
> Lives for his children, ever at its best
> And fullest; so the face before her lived,
> Dark-splendid, speaking in the silence, full
> Of noble things, and held her from her sleep.         (329–37)

Similarly, Lancelot reads Elaine's essence – her love – in her face:

> his large black eyes,
> Yet larger through his leanness, dwelt upon her,
> Till all her heart's sad secret blazed itself
> In the heart's colours on her simple face ...           (829–32)

The discovery of something essential is also the discovery of a relationship between observer and observed, and in the idylls that relationship is usually imaged as a bond. In this particular idyll, the bond is associated with love, and comes increasingly to seem constricting rather than liberating. 'Free love will not be bound' (1368), Lancelot tells Arthur in their crucial conversation at the end of the idyll, and Arthur corrects him: "'Free love, so bound, were freëst,'' said the King. / ''Let love be free; free love is for the best''' (1369–70). But in Lancelot's experience the bond is indeed a constraint, and he must reject the possibility of Elaine becoming his wife:

> The shackles of an old love straitened him,
> His honour rooted in dishonour stood,
> And faith unfaithful kept him falsely true.           (870–2)

The oxymorons in this passage suggest that words have ceased to be simple, and are becoming duplicitous or equivocal, like the title of the last tournament, introduced in lines where the scheme of antithesis embodies the doubleness: the event is 'By these in earnest those in mockery called / The Tournament of the Dead Innocence' ('The Last Tournament' 135–6) – and the theme of this idyll turns upon the double meaning of the word 'fool.' Tennyson had earlier linked equivocal words with another lover, Limours in the 'Geraint and Enid' idyll, who

> told
> Free tales, and took the word and played upon it,
> And made it of two colours ...           (290–2)

Further, the narrator likens Limours' talk to 'a gem / Of fifty facets' (294–5). I quote this passage because it anticipates the scene in which Lancelot presents the diamonds to Guinevere, and does so with a sense that language has somehow degenerated: 'I sin / In speaking';

'Such sin in words / Perchance'; 'I hear of rumours flying through your court' (1179–80; 1181–2; 1183). There seems to be a need for the regeneration of language, and its renewal follows the same pattern as in *In Memoriam*: speech lapses into silence, but is preserved in letters and is heard again when a reader brings them to life.

The emblem of the lapse into silence is the dumb old man who rows Elaine's funeral barge. We meet him first when Lancelot does, for Lancelot is admitted to the Castle of Astolat by 'an old, dumb, myriad-wrinkled man' who is 'wordless' (169, 171). Elaine's father later explains to Lancelot that 'The heathen caught and reft him of his tongue' (272) because, conscious of his bond, he warned the family of 'bonds or death' (276). The new philology's conventional linking of changes in language with the life cycle of the individual lies behind this nameless figure, and we remember Trench's statement (quoted earlier in this chapter) that out of the death of a language 'a new life comes forth.'[48] His example is Latin, which perished only to live on in French, Italian, Spanish, and Portuguese. Tennyson, unlike Trench, gives letters a major role in this renewal. He assumes – and his assumption is typical of his age – that speech is primary, and that letters are essentially a recording of it, fixed and dead. So it is easy enough to allegorize Elaine's death and her floating down river in the funeral barge. Elaine asks her brother 'to write as she devised / A letter, word for word' (1096–7), and to place it in her hand on the funeral barge, which is to be rowed by 'our dumb old man alone' (1120). So the living words become the dead letter, held in a dead hand and guarded by a figure who is dumb. In this picture of 'the dead, / Oared by the dumb' (1146–7) we have an emblem of written language. The same emblem had already appeared in 'The Lady of Shalott,' for the Lady, we remember, had also turned herself into a text: 'And round about the prow she wrote / *The Lady of Shalott*' (125–6). But a text is written to be read, and reading, in Tennyson's scheme of things, is renewal. In 'The Lady of Shalott,' the lady 'floated by ... Silent into Camelot,' and 'Knight and burgher, lord and dame' read her name and also fall silent. The letters need the right kind of reader, and the Lady finds him in Lancelot, who 'mused a little space' and reads her face. In 'Lancelot and Elaine,' the right kind of reader is Arthur, and his response, like Lancelot's in the earlier poem, is in sharp contrast to that of his court. They gape and babble; he reads aloud Elaine's letter, and so brings the dead words to life.

And ever in the reading, lords and dames
Wept, looking often from his face who read
To hers which lay so silent, and at times,
So touched were they, half-thinking that her lips,
Who had devised the letter, moved again.                    (1275-9)

So Elaine's words, like 'the silent-speaking words' of Hallam's letters
in *In Memoriam*, become live speech. Earlier, Elaine herself had
apprehended in a dream Lancelot's face 'speaking in the silence' (336),
and that moment at Astolat foreshadows this moment at Camelot,
when Elaine's face 'which lay so silent' (1277) also finds its voice.

The pattern I have been exploring, of dead letters becoming living
speech, is also apparent in Tennyson's relations with Malory and his
other sources. The fiction by which Tennyson presents the *Idylls* is that
of a narrator telling the stories aloud, and repeating earlier stories
which, using his judgment, he modifies in renewing. The narrator has
a sense of himself as the latest of a long line of those who transmit the
stories, as at the end of 'Gareth and Lynette':

And he that told the tale in older times
Says that Sir Gareth wedded Lyonors,
But he, that told it later, says Lynette.                    (1392-4)

His stock reference to his predecessors is 'he that tells the tale'
('Geraint and Enid' 161), and he suggests that the living tradition is an
oral one, as in the clause 'as he speaks who tells the tale' ('The Coming
of Arthur' 94). Bellicent in the first idyll describes this oral Arthurian
tradition to Leodogran:

'so great bards of him will sing
Hereafter; and dark sayings from of old
Ranging and ringing through the minds of men,
And echoed by old folk beside their fires
For comfort after their wage-work is done,
Speak of the King ...'                    ('The Coming of Arthur' 413-18)

A literal (as opposed to an oral) version of these stories may be
necessary to preserve them, but they come to life only in the speaking.
So, in 'The Epic,' the frame Tennyson provided in 1842 for the 'Morte
d'Arthur,' the poet, Everard Hall, writes his epic of King Arthur and

then burns it, condemning it as 'faint Homeric echoes, nothing-worth' (39). But when he reads aloud the eleventh book, saved from the fire by his host, Francis Allen, the story comes alive: 'we / Sat rapt: it was the tone with which he read' (276–7) – and the 'I,' as a result of this reading, dreams the myth onward.

The word 'legend' belongs in this context. Tennyson uses it four times in the *Idylls*, once to refer to Arthur's coming ('that weird legend of his birth,' 'The Last Tournament' 664), once to refer to a saint's life ('holy Joseph's legend,' 'Balin and Balan' 358), and twice to refer to stories from the past (in 'Merlin and Vivien' 552 and 'The Holy Grail' 87). In all instances, the word suggests a written text, *legenda* being, in medieval Latin, what is read. It was once assumed that truth lay in the text; in the present time of the *Idylls*, that truth is problematic, and the act of reading or repeating aloud is crucial. Percivale locates the truth of the Holy Grail story in 'A legend handed down through five or six [old men], / And each of these a hundred winters old, / From our Lord's time' ('The Holy Grail' 87–9), and Ambrosius, who also appeals to 'old books' (59), says that they 'seem / Mute of this miracle, far as I have read' (65–6). The bringing of this legend to life is disastrous for Camelot, and the legend that Merlin tells Vivien – it is the story of the wizard whose book Merlin now has – does not save the teller from the fate of the *femme fatale* in his story. 'Legend' thus seems to have changed and declined, and its role in the *Idylls* parallels the history of the word as given by Trench in his *On the Study of Words*. Legends were once true stories. 'By this name of "legends" the annual commemorations of the faith and patience of God's saints in persecution and death were originally called; these legends in this title which they bore proclaiming that they were worthy to be read, and from this worthiness deriving their name.' But with the growing corruption in the church, stories worthy to be read became unworthy and truth became fiction; Trench mentions 'Luther's indignant turn of the word,' the 'legends' (*legende*) becoming 'lyings' (*lügende*).[49] So the repeating aloud of old stories is no guarantee of their usefulness or effectiveness, and the repetition must clearly be modified by our judgment of them in our present circumstances. Merlin's charms are powerful because their language changes.

We might carelessly assume that a charm is a fixed verbal formula, as it is, for instance, in Browning's 'An Epistle,' when the young Karshish and Abib 'would unadvisedly recite / Some charm's beginning' from their master's book. Merlin, too, has a book of charms, but their form is not fixed, and changes in a way that is analogous to the history of languages as revealed by the new philology. The book, which Merlin inherited from a wizard, is

> 'but twenty pages long,
> But every page having an ample marge,
> And every marge enclosing in the midst
> A square of text that looks a little blot,
> The text no larger than the limbs of fleas;
> And every square of text an awful charm,
> Writ in a language that has long gone by.'  ('Merlin and Vivien' 666–72)

This original text is surrounded by commentary (as an ancient and dead language transforms itself into newer and more recent languages that gradually replace the original):

> 'And every margin scribbled, crost, and crammed
> With comment, densest condensation, hard
> To mind and eye ...'  (675–7)

Merlin is like the modern philologist struggling with these languages and trying to make sense of the relations among them:

> 'And none can read the text, not even I;
> And none can read the comment but myself;
> And in the comment did I find the charm.'  (679–81)

Tennyson simply accepts the convention of charms (that words have power over people and things), and places them in the context that interests him, the relation of written text to spoken word. This particular text is not only dead but deadly. In the 'Merlin and Vivien' idyll, Merlin falls silent, and the seductress Vivien (in an act which we can see in retrospect as a parody of Arthur's bringing a written text to life) moves him to speak and reveal the charm to her. The written text, so carefully preserved by him, destroys him by condemning him to permanent silence. We might contrast this deadly text with the living speech of Arthur, 'the living words / Of so great men as Lancelot and our King' ('The Holy Grail' 709–10), as Percivale will later say, and we note that a written and silent text is linked here, as it is in 'The Holy Grail,' with losing the self. Romance convention identifies the place where such a loss is possible with a piece of furniture, like *le lit perilous* in the stories that lie behind *Sir Gawain and the Green Knight* (a version of that bed is in the pavilion where Pelleas discovers Gawain and Ettarre sleeping, and lays 'The naked sword athwart their naked throats,' 'Pelleas and Ettarre' 443). In 'The Holy Grail' that place is 'The Siege perilous,' a chair made by Merlin

> 'And carven with strange figures; and in and out
> The figures, like a serpent, ran a scroll
> Of letters in a tongue no man could read.'                    (169–71)

Percivale tells Ambrosius that 'once by misadvertence Merlin sat / In his own chair, and so was lost' (175–6). Once again Tennyson characteristically links a fixed and written text with loss and dissolution.

But a text may become again a living word, and we see such a renewal in Tennyson's account of Arthur's sword, Excalibur. Arthur receives it from the Lady of the Lake, and its design includes two texts:

> 'on one side,
> Graven in the oldest tongue of all this world,
> "Take me," but turn the blade and ye shall see,
> And written in the speech ye speak yourself,
> "Cast me away!"'                              ('The Coming of Arthur' 300–4)

'The oldest tongue of all this world' is perhaps an allusion to the debate about which language was the original human language, the claim of Hebrew being no longer tenable in the light of the new philology. At any rate, Tennyson again juxtaposes an ancient and a modern text, the problem for any reader being his responsibility to carry the text forward as a living power. This is essentially the problem facing Bedivere in 'The Passing of Arthur.' He would like to preserve Excalibur, 'Stored in some treasure-house of mighty kings' (269), its texts fixed and unchanging. But Arthur insists on realizing in action the imperative, 'Cast me away!', and it is he who challenges Bedivere to bring the text to life. The King's command is a rewording of the graven imperative ('take Excalibur, / And fling him far into the middle mere,' 204–5), and we remember that the chief manifestation of Arthur's authority throughout the *Idylls* is his voice. Then Bedivere must struggle with himself to give life to the words. The sword's jewels suggest the living gems of the Book of Revelation, but in Bedivere's eyes the truth is divided into myriad lights (like the 'gem / Of fifty facets' that Tennyson likens to Limours' talk), and, in the absence of sure and certain knowledge of the consequences of one decision or the other, Bedivere must use his judgment. Tennyson's description of Bedivere's state at this point is suggestive: he stood, 'This way and that dividing the swift mind, / In act to throw' (228–9). This picture of the mind moving swiftly back and forth in thought may be an allusion to Coleridge's etymology of the word 'mind' from the German *Mahnen* or *Mähen*, 'to move forward & backward, yet still progressively – thence applied to the motion of the Scythe in mowing,'[50] and, as James McKusick points out in his discussion of the passage, this concept of the mind 'is inextricably bound up with the concepts of memory, motion, and repetition.'[51] This etymology appears in the third of Coleridge's 1801 letters to Josiah Wedgwood, and if Tennyson is indeed alluding to it, he may have come to know it through Hallam, who, in an 1828 letter defending Coleridge, refers to 'the "mowing" crotchet' as 'very mad indeed.'[52] The editor of Hallam's letters, Jack Kolb, does not identify this crotchet, and Tennyson's knowledge of it – he wrote the lines in 1833–4 – must remain a matter of speculation (mainly about transmission through conversation and discussion and talk, perhaps from Coleridge himself). The point, so far as my present argument is concerned, has to do with Bedivere's revival of a dead text. The casting away of Excalibur becomes a part of his being, and Arthur reads the text in his face: 'Now see I by thine eyes that this is done' (317).

Speech which is renewed after silence finds its highest form in prayer, and Arthur, in his great farewell speech, advises Bedivere, who will soon be without a text ('If thou shouldst never see my face again') to 'Pray for my soul' (415). For silence has characterized the final stages of Arthur's civilization: at the end of 'Pelleas and Ettarre,' 'all talk died' and 'a long silence came upon the hall' (594, 596); in 'The Last Tournament,' the music associated with a springtime Camelot retreats to become 'a silent music up in heaven' (349); and, in 'The Passing of Arthur,' after the last great battle in the west, 'A dead hush fell' (122). But Arthur advises Bedivere to 'let thy voice / Rise like a fountain for me night and day' (416–17), and he had already enabled Guinevere to find her voice. Silent throughout their final meeting, she 'cried aloud' (603) when Arthur disappeared in the mist, and then 'Went on in passionate utterance' (607).

Prayer here, as in *In Memoriam*, is the highest form of human speech – 'More things are wrought by prayer / Than this world dreams of' (415–16), Arthur tells Bedivere – and why this should be so becomes apparent when we compare prayer as Arthur describes it with Maurice's account of prayer in *The Kingdom of Christ*. Tennyson would have reservations about Maurice's argument in favour of repeated verbal formulae (prayer, in Maurice's view, is not primarily an individual act but a communal one, and the fellowship on which it is based has its formal expression in the liturgy) but he would fully agree with Maurice's rejection of the Quaker understanding of prayer and the arguments that Maurice uses to lead up to his defence of the liturgy. For the Quaker, prayer is a matter of inspiration, and he does not pray until the Spirit moves him. For him, 'Forms of worship are not only no signs of the existence of a spiritual commonwealth; they are positively incompatible with it. The Spirit bloweth where it listeth. Prayer is given by the Spirit.'[53] Maurice does not deny 'that the Spirit of God is the author of prayer' (288), but he does deny that the man who prays is merely the passive instrument of the Spirit. The Spirit is the 'awakener' (289), and it calls forth our will and reason, so that we are active and conscious participants in the act. This act is a version of Coleridge's art of reflection, in which we turn back toward God the powers that God has given us. 'We do make prayer the utterance of the Will and Reason of man,' Maurice writes in contrasting his church's position with that of the Quakers; 'We consider [prayer men's] highest and most perfect utterance; that in which, and in which alone, they fully realize themselves' (288). More things are indeed wrought by prayer than this world dreams of, and those things are, initially at least, acts of our inner life by which we make ourselves fully human. Their basis is, as Arthur says, knowing God, and knowing that one knows, in contrast to the 'blind life within the brain' that characterizes animals:

> 'For what are men better than sheep or goats
> That nourish a blind life within the brain,
> If, knowing God, they lift not hands of prayer
> Both for themselves and those who call them friend?'     (418–21)

Maurice, too, contrasts man who knows God with 'unconscious animal utterers of certain sounds':

We believe that this knowledge is far more deep and awful than that which any one possessed who merely felt that he was the subject of *an* inspiration; but that being deep and awful, it is incompatible with excitement, with any distortions of manner or of voice, with the notion that we are merely the unconscious animal utterers of certain sounds which are imparted to us, instead of the living, conscious, voluntary, rational agents of One who, when He promised the Spirit to his disciples, said, 'Henceforth I call you not servants, but I have called you friends, for the servant knoweth not what his Lord doeth; but whatsoever I have heard and learned of the Father, I have made known unto you.' (289)

Arthur uses two principal images in his speech, and the second – 'For so the whole round earth is every way / Bound by gold chains about the feet of God' (422–3) – is a metaphorical picture of religion, if we understand the word as literally a tying again of creatures to their creator. The first – 'let thy voice / Rise like a fountain for me night and day' (416–17) – is a repetition of the conventional image for expression, but it is also one of the Bible's principal images. There, the life-giving fountain is a symbol of God's presence. 'God is in the midst of her,' as in Psalm 46, where the psalmist links this flowing water with God's voice. So, as in Coleridge's 'Noetic Pentad,' our speech is a turning back toward God of God's own word – his name – in the expression of which we participate through our will and reason.

The parallel in individual experience to society's falling silent and then regaining speech is the loss and recovery of one's own name. Names, as Tennyson treats them in the *Idylls*, participate in the essential being of the individuals they designate, though Tennyson does not go so far as to suggest that knowing a person's name gives one control over that individual. Rather, he ties the name to the romance convention whereby one result of the quest – the typical action in romance – is the quester's discovery of his own identity. Thus Childe Roland, for instance, can name himself only at the end of Browning's poem. In the *Idylls*, Tennyson's emphasis is not so much on the discovery of one's true identity as it is on the making of it – as Arthur says, it is the ambition of every young knight 'To win his honour and to make his name' ('Lancelot and Elaine' 1351) – but if one's name can be made, it can also be destroyed. Gareth's quest establishes the pattern of right conduct, and it is based on his request to Arthur, 'Let be my name until I make my name!' ('Gareth and Lynette' 562). Geraint has already made his name – 'Geraint, a name far-sounded among men / For noble deeds' ('The Marriage of Geraint' 427–8) – but nearly destroys it through his own folly. Pelleas actually loses his name. When Lancelot asks him, 'What name hast thou / That ridest here so blindly and so hard?' Pelleas shouts, 'No name, no name' ('Pelleas and Ettarre' 551–3). As the Red Knight in 'The Last Tournament,' Pelleas retains his distinctive voice, which Arthur recognizes, but 'the name / Went wandering somewhere darkling in [Arthur's] mind' (455–6). Like the conventional champion in romance, Lancelot enters the tournament unknown – his name, Guinevere had argued, was enough to conquer his opponents – and the emblem of his namelessness is his blank shield. He nearly destroys his name, as Pelleas does, but the crucial conversation with Arthur makes possible the renewal of it. Arthur draws his attention to 'the glory of thy name and fame, / My knight, the great Sir Lancelot of the Lake' ('Lancelot and Elaine' 1361–2), and Lancelot reflects on the discrepancy between his name and his actions: 'Why did the King dwell on my name to me? / Mine own name shames me, seeming a reproach' (1391–2):

'For what am I? what profits me my name
Of greatest knight? I fought for it, and have it:
Pleasure to have it, none; to lose it, pain;
Now grown a part of me: but what use in it?'                    (1402–5)

The name, like the vows, is in danger of separating itself from the inner man, but the repentance in these final lines of the idyll is the process by which name and self are once again identified. The separation of name and self is one aspect of Tennyson's treatment of the Tristram and Isolt story, Tristram losing Isolt of Cornwall to Mark and marrying the other Isolt because 'the sweet name / Allured him first' ('The Last Tournament' 397–8). 'Did I love her?' Tristram later asks in the presence of the first Isolt; 'the name at least I loved' (598).

The making of one's name – the realization of it in one's conduct, action, and deeds – suggests a different relationship between a word and its referent than that in Locke's language theory. Locke begins with sensations and moves to ideas by the process of abstraction, and to ideas sounds are arbitrarily attached; these generalizations from experience make up our knowledge. For all its appeal to the senses, then, empiricism quickly becomes, as Mill pointed out in his 1840 essay on Coleridge, 'abstract and metaphysical.'[54] The Germano-Coleridgian views move in the opposite direction, toward the 'concrete and historical.' In his conclusion to *Aids to Reflection*, Coleridge attacks the Lockeian view, 'the habit of attaching all our conceptions and feelings, and of applying all the words and phrases expressing reality, to the objects of the senses: more accurately speaking, to the images and sensations by which their presence is made known to us,' and then moving to abstractions. Christ's words are spirit, and the Lockeian position makes spirit seem to be an abstraction, unreal, remote, and even slightly ridiculous, as if part of a never-never land. Hence, writes Coleridge, we take Christ's words – 'Water, Flesh, Blood, Birth, Bread!' – and say that they are 'mere metaphors, figures of speech, oriental hyperboles! "All this means *only* Morality!" Ah! how far nearer to the truth would these men have been, had they said that Morality means all this!'[55] This same movement, from the metaphysical to the concrete, is apparent in Arthur's establishment of the Round Table, in his marriage to Guinevere, and in his own existence: 'Ideal manhood closed in real man' (38) is Tennyson's line in his dedication of the *Idylls* to the Queen, and Arthur himself defines his civilization as character-ized by 'noble deeds at one with noble vows' ('The Last Tournament' 123). The most important manifestation of this pattern is the movement from silence to speech, and the loss and recovery of the voice is a major aspect of 'The Passing of Arthur.'

The voices that Arthur hears before and during the last battle are the voices of destruction: Gawain's shrill cry about the vanity of the world, and the 'dim cries' 'As of some lonely city sacked by night, / When all is lost, and wife and child with wail / Pass to new lords' (43–5). On the battlefield are heard

> shrieks
> After the Christ, of those who falling down
> Looked up for heaven, and only saw the mist;
> And shouts of heathen and the traitor knights,
> Oaths, insult, filth, and monstrous blasphemies,
> Sweat, writhings, anguish, labouring of the lungs
> In that close mist, and cryings for the light,
> Moans of the dying, and voices of the dead.          (110–17)

Then silence: 'Save for some whisper of the seething seas, / A dead hush fell' (121–2). But beyond the sounds of the battle is another voice: 'rolling far along the gloomy shores / The voice of days of old and days to be' (134–5). Arthur hears this voice as the voice of destruction, and asks Bedivere:

'Hearest thou this great voice that shakes the world,
And wastes the narrow realm whereon we move,
And beats upon the faces of the dead,
My dead, as though they had not died for me?'                    (139–42)

In fact, however, Arthur is hearing only one phase of the voice, which presides not only over decline, but over all cycles, 'of days of old and days to be.' In effect, Tennyson substitutes voice for sight in a Berkelean scheme of things. Arthur's civilization comes into being, and is sustained, by his voice and the voices of his knights. And when those voices fall silent, the voice of God sustains his creation, just as, in Berkeley, the things which we perceive do have an independent existence because they are continuously perceived by God. The primary attribute of 'the Nameless' in 'The Ancient Sage' is the fact that it 'hath a voice' (34), and of that voice human speech is not only an echo, but a sharer in its creative and sustaining power.

At the lowest point in 'The Passing of Arthur,' both Arthur and Bedivere fear losing their voices, Arthur when his wound 'hath taken cold' (334) and Bedivere when he is overwhelmed with grief: he 'would have spoken, but he found not words' (340). Bedivere's renewal comes about through inner need and its expression, which begins with an interjection: 'Ah! my Lord Arthur, whither shall I go?' (395). Arthur's renewal begins with his great farewell speech, where he acknowledges that God sustains the entire cycle of creation and destruction, and where he advises Bedivere to 'let thy voice / Rise like a fountain' (416–17). We are not told that Bedivere prays, but 'when the man was no more than a voice / In the white winter of his age' (3–4) he continues to tell the story of Arthur, and thus his voice is the essential and defining power of his earthly existence, as he, like the poet, carries the story onward.

There is, then, at the end of the *Idylls* a conjunction of voices like that at the end of *In Memoriam*. There, Hallam's voice is merged with the voice of nature and both voices with the sustaining voice of God (in section cxxx), while the poet prays

That we may lift from out of dust
  A voice as unto him that hears,
  A cry above the conquered years
To one that with us works ...                    (cxxxi.5–8)

This voice is like Bedivere's cry of need, which is also the cry of faith, and it is Bedivere who, like the poet of the marriage lay in *In Memoriam*, has the last word. Like the poet who places the wedding in the context of all that has gone before, Bedivere links Arthur's end to his beginning (449–56), and the last sound he hears is the completion of the 'dim cries' Arthur dreamt of hearing from a sacked city. In fact, Tennyson describes the sound Bedivere hears as 'Like the last echo born of a great cry' (459), and the simile suggests not just its intensity but its origin in suffering. The many sounds become one, 'as if some fair city were one voice / Around a king returning from his wars' (460–1). The 'dim cries' that become the 'one voice' parallel the many witnesses of 'The Coming of Arthur' giving way to the single witnessing of Bedivere in 'The Passing of Arthur.' And so the voices – including Tennyson's – will continue to sound so long as Arthur's story is retold.

# Conclusion

The reader may find useful an attempt to summarize Tennyson's views of language. Those views have a place in the idealist philosophy which Tennyson's experience at Cambridge made his own – his informal education, as opposed to the official curriculum. His place among the Apostles, the 'Germano-Coleridgian' character of that society (a character established by Maurice and Sterling, and maintained by Hallam and Trench), and the reaction against Locke by Whewell and others, all contributed to Tennyson's understanding of the nature of words and of grammar. In the idealist position, the perceiving mind is primary. The shapes which it brings to our experience of the world outside us – a world which we know through our five senses – in fact make that experience possible. Kant is the source of this view and Coleridge the transmitter of it. A word, then, is not just, as Locke taught, a sound which is arbitrarily attached to a sensation, though the idealist does not deny to sensation a place in his epistemology, and indeed affirms that sensation calls forth the patterns that the mind brings to experience; sensation, though, is not the source of those patterns which, we realize, must have pre-existed to make the experience possible. In this context, a word is not essentially a sign which points to some phenomenon, some thing or action, in the world outside us; it does not simply have a content (the sensation to which it refers) but is the sign, rather, of shaping powers in the mind: the powers of perceiving likenesses and differences; of abstracting, generalizing, and classifying; of ordering our experiences in ways that realize our human concerns. These ways are natural; that is, they are born in us and characterize our human nature; they are God-given.

Such is Tennyson's theory of naming, one of the two major divisions of philology.

The other is the theory of grammar, which is concerned with the parts of speech and their relationship, and ultimately with the question of truth. The dominant theory of grammar in Western Europe was the Aristotelian one, with its characteristic pattern of naming a thing and making assertions about it; of beginning with the noun and proceeding to predication, such propositions being considered true when the asserted relations correspond to relations actually observed in the world outside us. But the idealist position modifies this picture or mirror theory of grammar by drawing attention to the perceiving consciousness which frames all experience and gives it shape, this consciousness finding expression in the ability to say 'I.' The new philology, with its empirical and historical investigation of languages, gave new importance to the pronouns and strengthened the reaction against Aristotelian grammar, a reaction implicit in Berkeley and Kant. The discovery that the inflections – the endings that make up the conjugations of verbs – were in fact the pronominal elements in a language led to a new division of the parts of speech: where the noun and the verb had once been considered primary, some philologists now realized that the two primary parts of speech were in fact pronouns – Farrar would call them 'Form-words' – and all others, including both nouns and verbs, which Farrar would call 'Matter-words.' The truth of propositions would now lie, not in a theory of correspondence, but in a theory of expression, the 'I' (in Tennyson's view) being (paradoxically) both unique and participating, in some mysterious way, in the 'I am that I am,' God's utterance to Moses from the burning bush. From this perspective, our language is symbolic, not because words themselves are synecdoches and participate in the essential being of the things they name (Tennyson toyed with this magic theory of language but did not hold it as his own), but because they are our contribution – this is the root meaning of the word 'symbol' – to an all-embracing Word, a Logos which we apprehend partially and imperfectly when we turn back toward God (or reflect) the power to speak that God has given us. Hence language, like nature, is hard to use and difficult to understand.

If our expression is, inevitably, imperfect, then we must constantly judge all assertions and propositions in an effort to determine their truth. In this context, the word 'arbitrary' is crucial. Locke had described the link between sound and sensation as an arbitrary one, and the word became associated with the capricious and the wilful. But etymology links the word with judgment, and judgment is a key faculty in Locke's account of the mind, arriving as it does at opinion where clear and certain evidence is lacking. Judgment involves human attention to specifically human concerns – the needs of our physical, civil, moral, and religious life – and is the basis of faith. Coleridge gave new authority to our deepest needs, and in Hallam's discursive talk Tennyson heard those needs most fully articulated, thanks to Hallam's judgment. The new philology rejected caprice and chance in language itself: nothing in language and in the history of languages – the changes in semantics, phonetics, and grammar – is arbitrary. Languages are the expression of the character of a people or nation, and Trench and others explicitly linked language with moral character, a link Tennyson explored in *Idylls of the King*. The new philologists also, however, loosened the link between individual judgment and language, so that language seems to be speaking through us rather than a power we wield, but Tennyson focuses on an individual's moral responsibility in speaking, and seems untouched by, or unaware of, the possibility that language might be independent of human control or that sounds might be empty of significance.

Instead, the voice, with its range of expressive tones and cadences as well as its ability to articulate, was for him the primary mode of language, while writing was secondary, a record (albeit a useful and valuable one) of speech, but still secondary. The voice expressed the 'I' and was analogous (in Coleridge's sense) to the divine voice Tennyson heard in nature, a voice which (like the perception of God which sustains the world in Berkeley's philosophy) holds up creation and maintains its vitality. That voice may be difficult to hear above specific sounds of nature or the empty (and hence dangerous) human speech that Tennyson calls 'babble,' but ultimately all these sounds find their place in an all-embracing, all-powerful voice that Tennyson most often imaged with the sound of the sea, rolling (like the sound of a cathedral organ) through every recess of the vast edifice of creation. In the voice Tennyson heard evidence for a providential view of history, history being a story (like the Arthurian legend) which must constantly be renewed in the retelling.

Tennyson differs from Coleridge in giving no evidence of an active hostility to Locke and, indeed, he seems to revive aspects of Locke's thinking that had been obscured by Locke's reputation in the early nineteenth century, particularly the crucial role of opinion in human affairs, based as it is on the distinction between knowledge and faith. This distinction is of considerable importance for Tennyson's views of the nature of propositions. Statements of which we can be certain mirror the relations we actually observe in the world outside us; other statements, essential in shaping and energizing our lives, may not picture much, or indeed anything, in the world we see, and must be subject to judgment, which guides us where evidence is incomplete or wholly lacking. Coleridge, and Tennyson too, ground such propositions in human needs and concerns (as Locke does also), and Tennyson affirms that the 'I' participates in the spirit of God, but he does not find such being a guarantee that the individual will utter truth, which in this world is inevitably fragmentary, incomplete, and circumstantial, and hence must always be judged – as Locke keeps reminding us. Tennyson's recognition of the essential role of opinion, of truth which is fragmentary and contingent rather than absolute and universal, is perhaps surprising in an idealist. His position gives language a crucial role in human affairs: it is a heuristic, helping us (if we learn to reflect on it) to move toward 'the Unseen, the Undiscovered, the as yet Unrevealed' – for all of which, H.M. Butler records in his 'Recollections of Tennyson,' the poet had 'a deep reverence.'[1]

Tennyson's logocentric view, then, though strongly based on the 'Germano-Coleridgian' tradition and on the new philology, does not exclude the philosophy of language that Locke had linked with empiricism. The logocentric view was soon – indeed, during Tennyson's lifetime – to be under attack from philosophers and critics, and De Saussure would, a little later, rethink the arbitrary nature of the sign. For Tennyson, however, there are 'real presences' in language – I am borrowing the phrase from George Steiner – and these presences are the three voices he teaches us to hear: that of the individual for whom all speech is finally the expression of the 'I,' that of the nation who share this speech and guarantee communication, and that of God, who voices himself, in some mysterious way, in every utterance.

# Notes

All quotations from Tennyson's poetry, unless otherwise noted, are from *The Poems of Tennyson* ed Christopher Ricks, 2nd ed, 3 vols (Harlow: Longman 1987). All references to Hallam Tennyson's *Alfred Lord Tennyson: A Memoir by His Son* are to the one-volume edition (London: Macmillan 1899), cited in the notes as *Memoir*.

INTRODUCTION

1 Patrick Greig Scott ' "Flowering in a Lonely Word": Tennyson and the Victorian Study of Language' *Victorian Poetry* 18 (1980) 371
2 Samuel Taylor Coleridge 'The Author's Preface' *Aids to Reflection* (London: Bell 1913) xix
3 John Ruskin *Sesame and Lilies* (London: Smith 1865) 29–30
4 Peter Allen *The Cambridge Apostles: The Early Years* (Cambridge: Cambridge UP 1978) 214
5 Hans Aarsleff *The Study of Language in England, 1780–1860* (Princeton: Princeton UP 1967) 214
6 Henry George Liddell and Robert Scott 'Preface' *A Greek-English Lexicon* (Oxford: Oxford UP 1845) ix

CHAPTER ONE

1 Hans Aarsleff *The Study of Language in England, 1780–1860* (Princeton: Princeton UP 1967) 165
2 Martha McMackin Garland *Cambridge before Darwin: The Ideal of a Liberal Education, 1800–1860* (Cambridge: Cambridge UP 1980) 4
3 *The Letters of Alfred Lord Tennyson* ed Cecil Y. Lang and Edgar F. Shannon Jr (Cambridge: Belknap 1981– ) 1:23

4 Hallam Tennyson *Alfred Lord Tennyson: A Memoir by His Son* (London: Macmillan 1899) 57. Hereafter cited as *Memoir*.

5 *The Letters of Arthur Henry Hallam* ed Jack Kolb (Columbus: Ohio State UP 1981) 244. Hereafter cited as Kolb.

6 Kolb 260–1

7 Peter Allen *The Cambridge Apostles: The Early Years* (Cambridge: Cambridge UP 1978) 76. For an account of Coleridge's influence, see Graham Hough 'Coleridge and the Victorians' *The English Mind: Studies in the English Moralists Presented to Basil Willey* ed Hugh Sykes Davies and George Watson (Cambridge: Cambridge UP 1964) 175–92. Hough points out that, while the Romantics valued Coleridge the poet and critic, 'his Victorian admirers were interested chiefly in the Coleridge of the Highgate days – the inspired table-talker, the speculative thinker, the religious and political philosopher' (177)

8 Qtd in *Memoir* 30

9 *Memoir* 37

10 Tennyson's words in an 1874 letter quoted by David Staines 'Tennyson's Mysticism: A Personal Testimony' *Notes and Queries* ns 24 (1977) 405

11 *Memoir* 42

12 William Allingham *A Diary* ed H. Allingham and D. Radford (Harmondsworth: Penguin 1985) 337

13 Kolb 233

14 Kolb 344

15 Ian H.C. Kennedy 'Alfred Tennyson's *Bildungsgang*: Notes on His Early Reading' *Philological Quarterly* 57 (1978) 82–103

16 All quotations from Locke's *An Essay Concerning Human Understanding* are from the edition by Peter H. Nidditch (Oxford: Clarendon 1975)

17 Charles Richardson 'Preliminary Essay' *A New Dictionary of the English Language* (London: Pickering 1836–7) 1:41

18 Richard Chenevix Trench *On the Study of Words* 18th ed (London: Macmillan 1882) 48, 321

19 Thomas Carlyle *Sartor Resartus* ed Charles Frederick Harrold (New York: Odyssey 1937) 73

20 Ralph Waldo Emerson *Nature; Addresses and Lectures* (1903; New York: AMS 1968) 25

21 G.B. Tennyson *Sartor Called Resartus: The Genesis, Structure, and Style of Thomas Carlyle's First Major Work* (Princeton: Princeton UP 1965) 266

22 Gordon N. Ray prints James Knowles' notes – 'made by me from Tennyson's dictation as he read the poem to me in August 1870 – & March 1871' – as an appendix to his Sedgewick Memorial Lecture,

*Tennyson Reads 'Maud'* (Vancouver: U of British Columbia 1968) 37–42.
'Great Soul' appears on page 40.

23 *Memoir* 268

24 Timothy Peltason *Reading 'In Memoriam'* (Princeton: Princeton UP 1985)
113

25 *Collected Letters of Samuel Taylor Coleridge* ed Earl Leslie Griggs (Oxford:
Clarendon 1956–71) 2:682. I am deeply indebted to Eleanor Cook for
first pointing out this passage to me.

26 Isobel Armstrong 'Tennyson, the Collapse of Object and Subject: *In
Memoriam*' in *Language as Living Form in Nineteenth-Century Poetry*
(Brighton: Harvester 1982) 177

27 Hans Aarsleff 'Locke's Reputation in Nineteenth-Century England' *From
Locke to Saussure: Essays on the Study of Language and Intellectual History*
(Minneapolis: U of Minnesota P 1982) 120–45

28 Samuel Taylor Coleridge *Aids to Reflection and The Confessions of an Inquiring Spirit* Bohn's Standard Library Edition (London: Bell 1913) xix

29 Trench *On the Study of Words* 240–1

30 *Coleridge on the Seventeenth Century* ed Roberta Florence Brinkley
(Durham: Duke UP 1955) 97

31 *Collected Letters of Samuel Taylor Coleridge* 2:682. All further quotations in
this paragraph (except the last one) are from this edition.

32 Samuel Taylor Coleridge *The Philosophical Lectures* ed Kathleen Coburn
(London: Routledge 1949) 378

33 John William Donaldson *The New Cratylus, or Contributions Towards a More
Accurate Knowledge of the Greek Language* (Cambridge: Deighton 1839) 42,
45

34 James C. McKusick *Coleridge's Philosophy of Language* (New Haven: Yale
UP 1986) 1–2

35 *Collected Letters of Samuel Taylor Coleridge* 1:626

36 Richard Chenevix Trench *On Some Deficiencies in our English Dictionaries.*
Being the substance of two papers read before the Philological Society,
Nov. 5, and Nov. 19, 1857 (London: Parker 1857) 35

37 Kolb 274

38 Hans Aarsleff 'Locke's Reputation in Nineteenth-Century England'
124

39 *Memoir* 32–3

40 *Memoir* 319

41 *Memoir* 475

42 William Whewell *The Philosophy of the Inductive Sciences* 'A New Edition' 2
vols (London: Parker 1847) 1:26

43 William Whewell *History of the Inductive Sciences* 'A New Edition' 3 vols (London: Parker 1847) 1:6

44 John Herivel, Introduction *The Philosophy of the Inductive Sciences* by William Whewell (1847; New York: Johnson 1967) xviii. See also Robert O. Preyer's excellent account of Whewell on naming, 'The Language of Discovery: William Whewell and George Eliot' *Browning Institute Studies* 16 (1988) 123–52

45 *Memoir* 37; Kolb 322

46 *Memoir* 549

47 René Wellek *Immanuel Kant in England 1793–1838* (Princeton: Princeton UP 1931) 18–21

48 Immanuel Kant *Prolegomena to every future Metaphysic, which can appear as a science* trans John Richardson (London: Duncan 1818) 51

49 William Knight 'A Conversation with Tennyson (1870)' *Tennyson: Interviews and Recollections* ed Norman Page (London: Macmillan 1983) 184

50 J.A. Symonds 'An Evening at Thomas Woolner's' *Tennyson: Interviews and Recollections* 83

51 *Collected Letters of Samuel Taylor Coleridge* 2:698

52 Stephen K. Land *From Signs to Propositions: The Concept of Form in Eighteenth-Century Semantic Theory* (London: Longman 1974) 2,v

53 Murray Cohen *Sensible Words: Linguistic Practice in England 1640–1785* (Baltimore: Johns Hopkins UP 1977) xx

54 James C. McKusick *Coleridge's Philosophy of Language* (New Haven: Yale UP 1986) 125

55 *The Table Talk and Omnia of Samuel Taylor Coleridge* (London: Oxford UP 1917) 62

56 McKusick *Coleridge's Philosophy of Language* 34–8

57 *The Philological Essays of the late Rev. Richard Garnett of the British Museum* ed [Richard Garnett] (London: Williams 1859) 87. Garnett's theory of naming, where nouns are 'used by a sort of synecdoche,' parallels that of Kemble. William A. Wilson argues that this theory is a source of Tennyson's sense of the inadequacy of language ('Victorian Philology and the Anxiety of Language in Tennyson's *In Memoriam*,' *Texas Studies in Literature and Language* 30 [1988]: 28–48)

58 Frederic William Farrar *Language and Languages*. Being 'Chapters on Language' and 'Families of Speech' (London: Longmans 1878) 107

59 W. David Shaw *The Lucid Veil: Poetic Truth in the Victorian Age* (London: Athlone 1987) 49

60 John William Donaldson *The New Cratylus* 4th ed (London: Longmans 1868) 76n

61 G.B. Tennyson *Victorian Devotional Poetry: The Tractarian Mode* (Cambridge: Harvard UP 1981) 45
62 *Memoir* 364
63 *Memoir* 362
64 Frederick Denison Maurice *The Friendship of Books and Other Lectures* ed Thomas Hughes, 2nd ed (London: Macmillan 1874) 36

CHAPTER TWO

1 *The Letters of Arthur Henry Hallam* ed Jack Kolb (Columbus: Ohio State UP 1981) 446. Hereafter cited as Kolb.
2 Arthur Hallam 'On Some of the Characteristics of Modern Poetry, and on the Lyrical Poems of Alfred Tennyson' *The Writings of Arthur Hallam* ed T.H. Vail Motter (New York: Modern Language Association 1943) 186. Hereafter cited as Motter.
3 Robert James Mann *Tennyson's 'Maud' Vindicated: An Explanatory Essay* (London: Jarrold 1856) 12–13
4 William Allingham *A Diary* ed H. Allingham and D. Radford (Harmondsworth: Penguin 1985) 330–1
5 Lawrence Poston 'Poetry as Pure Act: A Coleridgean Ideal in Early Victorian England' *Modern Philology* 84 (1986) 171, 162. Eileen Tess Johnston also reads the essay in a Romantic context ('Hallam's Review of Tennyson: Its Contexts and Significance' *Texas Studies in Language and Literature* 23 [1981] 1–26).
6 Kolb 520
7 Motter 188
8 Kolb 379
9 Kolb 520
10 Hans Aarsleff 'Locke's Reputation in Nineteenth-Century England' *From Locke to Saussure: Essays on the Study of Language and Intellectual History* (Minneapolis: U of Minnesota P 1982) 120–45
11 All quotations from Locke are from Peter H. Nidditch's edition of *An Essay Concerning Human Understanding* (Oxford: Clarendon 1975).
12 David Hume *An Inquiry Concerning Human Understanding*, ed Charles W. Hendel (New York: Liberal Arts 1955) 27,26
13 Motter 184. On the importance of sympathy in Hallam's poetics, see Johnston's reading of the essay in her 'Hallam's Review of Tennyson.'
14 John Stuart Mill 'Bailey on Berkeley's Theory of Vision' *Essays on Philosophy and the Classics* ed J.M. Robson (vol 11 of *Collected Works of John Stuart Mill.* Toronto: U of Toronto P 1978) 247

15 *The Works of George Berkeley, Bishop of Cloyne* ed A.A. Luce and T.E. Jessop, 9 vols (London: Nelson 1948–57) 1:171

16 John Ruskin *The Elements of Drawing* (New York: Dover 1971) 27. Lawrence Campbell quotes Monet's comment in his introduction to this edition, viii.

17 *Memoir* 524

18 William Knight 'A Conversation with Tennyson (1870)' *Tennyson: Interviews and Recollections* ed Norman Page (London: Macmillan 1983) 184

19 E.H. Gombrich *Art and Illusion: A Study in the Psychology of Pictorial Representation* (1960; London: Phaidon 1972) 251

20 If Tennyson had early absorbed Berkeley's ideas, he did so probably through Hallam. There is no evidence that Tennyson read Berkeley for himself until shortly after his marriage, when, according to his son, Berkeley was 'among the books added to his library.' Tennyson was reading 'different systems of philosophy' at the time, yet, his son cautions us, 'none particularly influenced him' (*Memoir* 258).

21 Kolb 401

22 Ray Frazer 'The Origin of the Term "Image" ' *ELH* 27 (1960) 149–61

23 Thomas Hobbes *Leviathan* ed C.B. Macpherson (Harmondsworth: Penguin 1968) 85–6

24 Stephen K. Land *The Philosophy of Language in Britain: Major Theories from Hobbes to Thomas Reid* (New York: AMS 1986) 39

25 See Land's analysis, 16.

26 McKusick *Coleridge's Philosophy of Language* 28–32

27 Land *The Philosophy of Language in Britain* 94

28 Motter 186

29 Motter 186

30 Motter 186

31 Motter 192

32 Edmund Burke *A Philosophical Enquiry into the Origin of our Ideas of the Sublime and Beautiful* ed James T. Boulton (Notre Dame: U of Notre Dame P 1968) 170

33 David Hartley *Observations on man, his frame, his duty, and his expectations* 2 vols (1749; New York: Garland 1971) 1:65.

34 Hans Arens *Aristotle's Theory of Language and Its Tradition: Texts from 500 to 1750* Amsterdam Studies in the Theory and History of Linguistic Science 29 (Amsterdam/Philadelphia: Benjamin 1984)

35 G.A. Padley *Grammatical Theory in Western Europe 1500–1700: Trends in Vernacular Grammar I* (Cambridge: Cambridge UP 1985)

36 Land *The Philosophy of Language in Britain* 129

37 Motter 184
38 Motter 187–8
39 Motter 192–3
40 Kolb 433
41 Kolb 579

CHAPTER THREE

1 Arthur Hallam 'On Some of the Characteristics of Modern Poetry, and on the Lyrical Poems of Alfred Tennyson' *The Writings of Arthur Hallam* ed T.H. Vail Motter (New York: Modern Language Association 1943) 186. Hereafter cited as Motter.
2 In a review of W.J. Bate's *From Classic to Romantic, University of Toronto Quarterly* 16 (1946–7) 96
3 James Anderson Winn *Unsuspected Eloquence: A History of the Relations between Poetry and Music* (New Haven: Yale UP 1981) 202
4 James Beattie *Essays* (1776; New York: Garland 1971) 443
5 *Memoir* 13
6 *The Works of Sir William Jones* 6 vols (London: Robinson 1799) 4:550
7 *The Letters of Alfred Lord Tennyson* ed Cecil Y. Lang and Edgar F. Shannon Jr (Cambridge: Belknap 1981– ) 1:2
8 *The Letters of Arthur Henry Hallam* ed Jack Kolb (Columbus: Ohio State UP 1981) 502. Hereafter cited as Kolb.
9 *Memoir* 80
10 Motter 192
11 Motter 194–5
12 Frederic William Farrar *Language and Languages* (London: Longmans 1878) 69
13 Motter 195
14 See Morris W. Croll 'The Cadence of English Oratorical Prose' *Style, Rhetoric and Rhythm: Essays by Morris W. Croll* ed J. Max Patrick and Robert O. Evans (Princeton: Princeton UP 1966) 303–59; and Norton R. Tempest 'Cadence' *The Rhythm of English Prose* (Cambridge: Cambridge UP 1930) 72–103.
15 Kolb 244
16 *Guesses at Truth* (London: Taylor 1827) 2:206–8
17 *Memoir* 169
18 *The Works of Sir Henry Taylor* 5 vols (London: King; Kegan Paul 1877–8) 3:329
19 William Allingham *A Diary* ed H. Allingham and D. Radford (1907; Harmondsworth: Penguin 1985) 158

20 *Memoir* 162
21 H.D. Rawnsley 'Memories of Farringford' *Tennyson: Interviews and Recollections* ed Norman Page (London: Macmillan 1983) 63
22 *Tennyson: Interviews and Recollections* 99, 112, 128, 172; *Memoir* 490
23 *Memoir* 244
24 *Memoir* 41. For the argument that Tennyson was 'confined within the limits of his personal voice,' see Francis Berry 'The Voice of Tennyson' *Poetry and the Physical Voice* (London: Routledge 1962) 47–65.
25 Eric Griffiths *The Printed Voice of Victorian Poetry* (Oxford: Clarendon 1989) 125, 103
26 Motter 195
27 *Memoir* 41, 16
28 *Memoir* 162
29 *Memoir* 68–9
30 Dwight Culler *The Poetry of Tennyson* (New Haven: Yale UP 1977) 8
31 *Memoir* 68–9
32 Dwight Culler 'Monodrama and the Dramatic Monologue' *PMLA* 90 (1975) 368
33 James Engell 'The New Rhetoricians: Psychology, Semiotics, and Critical Theory' *Psychology and Literature in the Eighteenth Century* ed Christopher Fox (New York: AMS 1987) 278, 285
34 Hugh Blair *Lectures on Rhetoric and Belles Lettres* 2nd ed 3 vols (London: Strahan 1785) 1:410
35 See Bennett Maxwell 'The Steytler Recordings of Alfred, Lord Tennyson – a History' *Tennyson Research Bulletin* 3 (1980) 150–7
36 *Memoir* 478
37 J. Hillis Miller 'Catachresis, Prosopopoeia, and the Pathetic Fallacy: The Rhetoric of Ruskin' *Poetry and Epistemology: Turning Points in the History of Poetic Knowledge* ed Roland Hagenbüchle and Laura Skandera (Regensburg: Pustet 1986) 403
38 *Memoir* 9
39 Printed by Robert Martin *Tennyson: The Unquiet Heart* (Oxford: Clarendon 1980) 22, from manuscript materials assembled by Hallam Tennyson for the *Memoir*
40 James McKusick *Coleridge's Philosophy of Language* (New Haven: Yale UP 1986) 29
41 Walter Ong *Orality and Literacy: The Technologizing of the Word* (London: Methuen 1982) 42–50
42 *Memoir* 484
43 *Memoir* 249. He had lost the earliest manuscript of *Poems, Chiefly Lyrical*

'out of his great-coat pocket one night while returning from a neighbour-ing market town' (*Memoir* 223).

44 *Memoir* 317–18
45 Ong *Orality and Literacy* 36–41
46 *Memoir* 428
47 *Memoir* 41, 305
48 James Knowles 'A Personal Reminiscence' *Tennyson: Interviews and Recollections* ed Norman Page (London: Macmillan 1983) 90–1
49 *Memoir* 158, 100
50 *Memoir* 145
51 *Memoir* 363, 394, 240, 440, 354, 323, 348, 311
52 *Memoir* 474

CHAPTER FOUR

1 Dwight Culler *The Poetry of Tennyson* (New Haven: Yale UP 1977) 4
2 B. Jowett, Introduction to *Cratylus*, *The Dialogues of Plato* trans B. Jowett, 4th ed, 4 vols (Oxford: Clarendon 1953) 3:3–4
3 *Memoir* 268. Tyndall's account is printed by Hallam Tennyson on 815–16.
4 Coleridge *Aids to Reflection* (London: Bell 1913) xix
5 John Stuart Mill 'Coleridge' *Essays on Ethics, Religion and Society* ed J.M. Robson (vol 10 of *Collected Works of John Stuart Mill*. Toronto: U of Toronto P 1969) 126. In Tennyson's library, Coleridge's statement appears in *The Literary Remains of Samuel Taylor Coleridge* ed Henry Nelson Coleridge, 2 vols (London: Pickering 1836) 1:326n.
6 *The Letters of Arthur Henry Hallam* ed Jack Kolb (Columbus: Ohio State UP 1981) 718
7 Thomas Carlyle *Sartor Resartus* ed Charles Frederick Harrold (New York: Odyssey 1937) 219
8 *Memoir* 144
9 *The Table Talk and Omnia of Samuel Taylor Coleridge* (London: Oxford UP 1917) 62
10 James McKusick deals at length with this controversy in *Coleridge's Philosophy of Language* (New Haven: Yale UP 1986).
11 Coleridge *Aids to Reflection* 118
12 Bernard Anderson *Understanding the Old Testament* 3rd ed (Englewood Cliffs: Prentice 1975) 54–6
13 Qtd in McKusick *Coleridge's Philosophy of Language* 137
14 J.A. Symonds 'An Evening at Thomas Woolner's' *Tennyson: Interviews and Recollections* ed Norman Page (London: Macmillan 1983) 83

15 *Memoir* 493
16 Anya Taylor *Magic and English Romanticism* (Athens: U of Georgia P 1979) 13
17 Culler *The Poetry of Tennyson* 9
18 Northrop Frye *Creation and Recreation* (Toronto: U of Toronto P 1980) 5
19 Thomas Carlyle *Sartor Resartus* ed Charles Frederick Harrold (New York: Odyssey 1937) 263
20 George Steiner *Real Presences* (Chicago: U of Chicago P 1989) 87–116

CHAPTER FIVE

1 *Memoir* 249, 244
2 *Keble's Lectures on Poetry 1832–1841* trans Edward Kershaw Francis, 2 vols (Oxford: Clarendon 1912) 1:19. For an authoritative and detailed account of Keble's poetics, see G.B. Tennyson *Victorian Devotional Poetry: The Tractarian Mode* (Cambridge: Harvard UP 1981).
3 Robert James Mann *Tennyson's 'Maud' Vindicated: An Explanatory Essay* (London: Jarrold [1856]) 8
4 *Memoir* 99
5 *Memoir* 265
6 *Memoir* 331
7 *The Letters of Arthur Henry Hallam* ed Jack Kolb (Columbus: Ohio State UP 1981) 261
8 *The Friend* ed Barbara E. Rooke, 2 vols (vol 4 of *The Collected Works of Samuel Taylor Coleridge*. London: Routledge; Princeton: Princeton UP 1969) 1:457
9 Francis Bacon *Works* ed James Spedding, Robert Leslie Ellis, and Douglas Denon Heath, 7 vols (London: Longman 1858–61) 3:405
10 Frederick Denison Maurice *The Kingdom of Christ* 3 vols (London: Darton 1838) 1:xxii, vii
11 Dwight Culler *The Poetry of Tennyson* (New Haven: Yale UP 1977) 158–9
12 Ernst Behler and Roman Struc, Introduction *Dialogue on Poetry and Literary Aphorisms* by Friedrich Schlegel (University Park: Pennsylvania State UP 1968) 12
13 Introduction 11
14 Peter Allan Dale ' "Gracious lies": The Meaning of Metaphor in *In Memoriam*' *Victorian Poetry* 18 (1980) 154–5
15 John Stuart Mill 'Bentham' *Essays on Ethics, Religion and Society* ed J. M. Robson (vol 10 of *Collected Works of John Stuart Mill*. Toronto: U of Toronto P 1969) 83

16 *Memoir* 259
17 *Memoir* 259
18 Walter Jackson Bate's translation in his *Criticism: The Major Texts* (New York: Harcourt 1952) 52
19 Francis Bacon *The Advancement of Learning* ed William Aldis Wright (1868; Oxford: Clarendon 1957) 167
20 Thomas Hobbes *Leviathan* ed C.B. Macpherson (Harmondsworth: Penguin 1968) 106
21 William Knight 'A Conversation with Tennyson (1870)' *Tennyson: Interviews and Recollections* ed Norman Page (London: Macmillan 1983) 182
22 *Victorian Devotional Poetry: The Tractarian Mode* (Cambridge: Harvard UP 1981) 47
23 Richard Chenevix Trench *On the Study of Words* 18th ed (London: Macmillan 1882) 6
24 Trench *On the Study of Words* 7
25 Samuel Taylor Coleridge *Aids to Reflection and The Confessions of an Inquiring Spirit* Bohn's Standard Library Edition (London: Bell 1913) 136
26 Richard Chenevix Trench *Notes on the Parables of Our Lord* (New York: Appleton 1883) 12–13
27 *Memoir* 37
28 Joseph Butler *The Analogy of Religion, Natural and Revealed, to the Constitution and Course of Nature* (London: Hamilton 1813) 5–6
29 Trench *Notes on the Parables of Our Lord* 12–13
30 Frederick Denison Maurice *The Kingdom of Christ* 3 vols (London: Darton 1838) 1:50
31 Hans Aarsleff 'Locke's Reputation in Nineteenth-Century England' *From Locke to Saussure: Essays on the Study of Language and Intellectual History* (Minneapolis: U of Minnesota P 1982) 120–45. The quotations are on 121 and 125 respectively.
32 Qtd in Martha McMackin Garland *Cambridge before Darwin: The Ideal of a Liberal Education, 1800–1860* (Cambridge: Cambridge UP 1980) 6
33 John Stuart Mill 'Coleridge' *Essays on Ethics, Religion and Society* ed J.M. Robson (vol 10 of *Collected Works of John Stuart Mill*. Toronto: U of Toronto P 1969) 125
34 Mill 'Coleridge' 125
35 Ricardo Quintana *Two Augustans: John Locke, Jonathan Swift* (Madison: U of Wisconsin P 1978) 41
36 Dwight Culler *The Poetry of Tennyson* (New Haven: Yale UP 1977) 156. See also Melvin G. Williams 'In Memoriam: A Broad Church Poem' *Costerus* 4 (1972) 223–33

37 Quintana *Two Augustans* 27
38 John Locke *An Essay Concerning Human Understanding* 1.1.6. All quotations are from the edition by Peter H. Nidditch (Oxford: Clarendon 1975).
39 To these two kinds of knowledge, Locke adds a third, sensitive knowledge, which is 'of the existence of particular external Objects, by that perception and Consciousness we have of the actual entrance of *Ideas* from them' (4.2.14). 'The confidence that our Faculties do not herein deceive us, is the greatest assurance we are capable of, concerning the Existence of material Beings' (4.11.3).
40 Hume *An Inquiry Concerning Human Understanding* ed Charles W. Hendel (New York: Liberal Arts 1955) 170
41 Tennyson differs from Locke, who makes the existence of God a matter of demonstrative knowledge. We have intuitive knowledge of our own existence, and our reason leads us from our own being to a Being who is eternal, powerful, and knowing (4.10). '*How far the* Idea *of a most perfect Being*, which a Man may frame in his Mind, does, or does not prove the *Existence of a* GOD, I will not here examine' (4.10.7).
42 F.E.L. Priestley *Language and Structure in Tennyson's Poetry* (London: André Deutsch 1973) 169
43 *Memoir* 476. Hallam Tennyson records a similar comment, *Memoir* 32.
44 I here use Jowett's translation 420b–420c.
45 Culler *The Poetry of Tennyson* 20
46 *Memoir* 261
47 William Allingham *A Diary* ed H. Allingham and D. Radford (1907; Harmondsworth: Penguin 1985) 329
48 Benjamin Jowett 'Notes on Characteristics of Tennyson' *Tennyson: Interviews and Recollections* ed Norman Page (London: Macmillan 1983) 193; James Knowles 'A Personal Reminiscence' *Tennyson: Interviews and Recollections* 91
49 *Memoir* 416. See *The Letters of Alfred Lord Tennyson* ed Cecil Y. Lang and Edgar F. Shannon Jr (Cambridge: Belknap Press of Harvard UP 1981– ) 2:350.
50 Graham Hough 'The Natural Theology of *In Memoriam*' *Review of English Studies* 23 (1947) 244–56
51 Harold Nicolson *Tennyson: Aspects of His Life, Character and Poetry* (London: Constable 1923) 252
52 Mark Pattison 'Tendencies of Religious Thought in England, 1688–1750' *Essays and Reviews* (London: Parker 1860) 259–60, 264
53 All quotations from *Aids to Reflection* are from Bohn's Standard Library edition (London: Bell 1913).

54 *Memoir* 37. See also Allen *The Cambridge Apostles: The Early Years* 142; and *The Letters of Alfred Lord Tennyson* 1:43.

55 *Memoir* 732

56 On this complicated topic, Owen Barfield's book *What Coleridge Thought* (Middletown, Conn: Wesleyan UP 1971) is especially useful.

57 Arthur Hallam 'Essay on the Philosophical Writings of Cicero' *The Writings of Arthur Hallam* ed T.H. Vail Motter (New York: Modern Language Association 1943) 157

58 Philip Flynn argues that Tennyson 'did not share the Apostles' enthusiasm for the compensating epistemology of the *Aids to Reflection,*' and that his confusion in the decade following Hallam's death may indicate that he was 'engaged in a half-realized debate with the memory of Hallam's late metaphysical position.' 'Hallam and Tennyson: The "Theodicaea Novissima" and *In Memoriam*' *Studies in English Literature* 19 (1979) 705–20. However 'complex and ambiguous' the relation between the two men, their views on love are essentially the same.

59 Charles Richardson *A New Dictionary of the English Language* 2 vols (London: Pickering 1836–7) 1:48–50

60 *Memoir* 259

61 Gordon N. Ray prints James Knowles' notes on *In Memoriam,* 'made by me from Tennyson's dictation as he read the poem to me in August 1870 – & March 1871,' in appendix 1 of *Tennyson Reads 'Maud'* Sedgewick Memorial Lecture (Vancouver: U of British Columbia 1968) 37–42.

62 James H. Stam *Inquiries into the Origin of Language: The Fate of a Question* (New York: Harper 1976); and Hans Aarsleff 'An Outline of Language-Origins Theory since the Renaissance' and 'The Tradition of Condillac: The Problem of the Origin of Language in the Eighteenth Century and the Debate in the Berlin Academy before Herder' both in *From Locke to Saussure: Essays on the Study of Language and Intellectual History* (Minneapolis: U of Minnesota P 1982) 278–92; 146–209. See also Aarsleff's *The Study of Language in England 1780–1860,* passim.

63 Hugh Blair *Lectures on Rhetoric and Belles Lettres* 2nd ed, 3 vols (London: Strahan 1785) 1:127–8

64 Q. Horatii Flacci *Eclogae* ed Guilielmus Baxterus, 2 vols (London: Whittaker 1822) 1:314

65 Kerry McSweeney *Tennyson and Swinburne as Romantic Naturalists* (Toronto: U of Toronto P 1981) 69–97

66 *The Letters of Arthur Henry Hallam* ed Jack Kolb (Columbus: Ohio State UP 1981) 568

67 *Memoir* 91

68 Elizabeth A. Hirsh ' "No Record of Reply": *In Memoriam* and Victorian Language Theory' *ELH* 55 (1988) 233–57

69 Frederic W. Farrar *An Essay on the Origin of Language* (London: Murray 1860) 6

70 John William Donaldson *The New Cratylus* (Cambridge: Deighton 1839) 51

71 Thomas McFarland 'Berkeley's Idealism and Pantheism' *Coleridge and the Pantheist Tradition* (Oxford: Clarendon 1969) 300

72 James Knowles 'A Personal Reminiscence' *Tennyson: Interviews and Recollections* ed Norman Page (London: Macmillan 1983) 92; William Knight 'A Conversation with Tennyson (1870)' *Tennyson: Interviews and Recollections* 184

73 James Burnet, Lord Monboddo *Of the Origin and Progress of Language* 2nd ed, 2 vols (1774; New York: Garland 1970) 1:31

74 Arthur Hallam 'Essay on the Philosophical Writings of Cicero' *The Writings of Arthur Hallam* ed T.H. Vail Motter (New York: Modern Language Association 1943) 169–70

75 Alan Sinfield *The Language of Tennyson's 'In Memoriam'* (Oxford: Blackwell 1971) 55

76 *Memoir* 91

77 *Memoir* 37

78 *Memoir* 272

79 Tennyson's words were recorded by J.A. Symonds 'An Evening at Thomas Woolner's' *Tennyson: Interviews and Recollections* ed Norman Page (London: Macmillan 1983) 83.

80 *Memoir* 272

81 Kenneth M. McKay *Many Glancing Colours: An Essay in Reading Tennyson, 1809–1850* (Toronto: U of Toronto P 1988) 194, 203

CHAPTER SIX

1 For an account of 'the rapid absorption of Continental scholarship by English philologists and their intensive study after 1830 of early English language and literature' (165), see Hans Aarsleff's chapter, 'The New Philology in England to 1842,' in *The Study of Language in England, 1780–1860* (Princeton: Princeton UP 1967) 162–210.

2 John William Donaldson *The New Cratylus* (Cambridge: Deighton 1839) v

3 *Memoir* 528

4 *Memoir* 494–5

5 T. Kington Oliphant *The Sources of Standard English* (London: Macmillan 1873) 319

6  Richard Chenevix Trench *English, Past and Present* 2nd ed (London: Parker 1855) 126–7

7  *Memoir* 589

8  Oliphant *The Sources of Standard English* 319

9  [Augustus William Hare and Julius Charles Hare] *Guesses at Truth* by Two Brothers, 2 vols (London: Taylor 1827) 1:134; 2:203

10  Richard Garnett *The Philological Essays of the late Rev. Richard Garnett of the British Museum* ed [Richard Garnett] (London: Williams 1859) 2

11  Richard Chenevix Trench *On Some Deficiencies in our English Dictionaries* (London: Parker 1857) 34

12  Trench *On the Study of Words* 18th ed (London: Macmillan 1882) 28

13  Trench *On the Study of Words* 109, 28

14  Frederick Denison Maurice *Social Morality* (London: Macmillan 1869) 163

15  *Works* (The Eversley Edition, annotated by Alfred, Lord Tennyson, ed Hallam, Lord Tennyson) (1907–8; New York: AMS 1970) 9:423

16  Linda Dowling 'Victorian Oxford and the Science of Language' *Publications of the Modern Language Association* 97 (1982) 166

17  *The Letters of Alfred Lord Tennyson* ed Cecil Y. Lang and Edgar F. Shannon Jr (Cambridge: Belknap Press of Harvard UP 1981– ) 2:197

18  J.W. Burrow 'The Uses of Philology in Victorian England' *Ideas and Institutions of Victorian Britain: Essays in Honour of George Kitson Clark* ed Robert Robson (London: Bell 1967) 184

19  Max Müller *Lectures on the Science of Language* (1861; Delhi: Munshi Ram Manohar Lal 1965) 26

20  Trench *On the Study of Words* 43

21  Trench *On the Study of Words* 312, 308

22  Trench *On the Study of Words* 6, 7; *English, Past and Present* 124

23  Müller *Lectures on the Science of Language* 38

24  Trench *English, Past and Present* 98

25  Trench *English, Past and Present* 98–9

26  Trench *On the Study of Words* 15

27  [John Mitchell Kemble] 'German Origin of the Latin Language' rev of *Der Germanische Ursprung der lateinischen Sprache und des römischen Volkes* by Jäkel *Foreign Quarterly Review* 10 (1832) 366, 378–9, 377

28  Robert Chambers *Vestiges of the Natural History of Creation* (1844; New York: Humanities Press 1969) 276

29  *Memoir* 186

30  Dowling 'Victorian Oxford and the Science of Language' 173

31  Müller *Lectures on the Science of Language* 18

32  *Memoir* 525

33 Trench *On the Study of Words* 97

34 *Memoir* 519–21

35 *Memoir* 523

36 Trench *On the Study of Words* 9

37 Trench *On the Study of Words* 73, 98

38 Trench *A Select Glossary of English Words Used Formerly in Senses Different From Their Present* (New York: Widdleton 1860) 39

39 John R. Reed *Perception and Design in Tennyson's 'Idylls of the King'* (Athens: Ohio UP 1969) 183

40 *Memoir* 524

41 *Memoir* 554

42 *Memoir* 292

43 Qtd by Charles Richard Sanders 'Carlyle and Tennyson' *Carlyle's Friend-ships and Other Studies* (Durham: Duke UP 1977) 193

44 Trench *On the Study of Words* 110

45 Müller *Lectures on the Science of Language* 38

46 John Stuart Mill 'Nature' *Essays on Ethics, Religion and Society* ed J.M. Robson (vol 10 of *Collected Works of John Stuart Mill* Toronto: U of Toronto P 1969) 379

47 John Horne Tooke *The Diversions of Purley* 2 vols (1805; Menston: Scolar 1968) 2:401–4

48 Trench *English, Past and Present* 98

49 Trench *On the Study of Words* 142–3

50 *Collected Letters of Samuel Taylor Coleridge* ed Earl Leslie Griggs (Oxford: Clarendon 1956–71) 2:697

51 James McKusick *Coleridge's Philosophy of Language* (New Haven: Yale UP 1986) 66

52 *The Letters of Arthur Henry Hallam* ed Jack Kolb (Columbus: Ohio State UP 1981) 261

53 Maurice *The Kingdom of Christ* 2nd ed (New York: Appleton 1843) 288. A useful book on this topic and others is W. Merlin Davies' *An Introduction to F.D. Maurice's Theology* (London: SPCK 1964).

54 John Stuart Mill 'Coleridge' *Essays on Ethics, Religion and Society* ed J.M. Robson (vol 10 of *Collected Works of John Stuart Mill*. Toronto: U of Toronto P 1969) 125

55 Samuel Taylor Coleridge *Aids to Reflection* (Bohn's Standard Library; London: Bell 1913) 272–3

CONCLUSION

1 H.M. Butler 'Recollections of Tennyson' *Tennyson: Interviews and Recollections* ed Norman Page (London: Macmillan 1983) 50

# Index